Unmarked

Unmarked

The Politics of Performance

Peggy Phelan

London and New York

First published 1993
by Routledge
11 New Fetter Lane, London EC4P 4EE

Simultaneously published in the USA and Canada
by Routledge
a division of Routledge, Chapman and Hall, Inc.
29 West 35th Street, New York, NY 10001

Typeset in 10 on 12 point Palatino by
Florencetype Ltd, Kewstoke, Avon
Printed in Great Britain by
Butter & Tanner Ltd, Frome

British Library Cataloguing in Publication Data

A catalogue record for this book is available from the
British Library.

Library of Congress Cataloging in Publication Data
Phelan, Peggy.
  Unmarked: the politics of performance/ Peggy Phelan.
    p.   cm.
  Includes bibliographical references and index.
  1. Arts—Political aspects.   2. Politics in art.   3.
Feminism and the arts.   4. Performance art.   5. Arts,
Modern—20th century.   I. Title.
NX650.P6P47   1993
700'.1'03—dc20   92–7895
ISBN 0–415–06821–5   ISBN 0–415–06822–3 (pbk)

Against Being Right

and for the ones who have shattered

shattered blind

blind alice's looking glass

Contents

List of figures   viii
Acknowledgements   ix

1 Broken symmetries: memory, sight, love   1

2 Developing the negative: Mapplethorpe, Schor,
  and Sherman   34

3 Spatial envy: Yvonne Rainer's *The Man Who Envied Women*   71

4 The golden apple: Jennie Livingston's *Paris Is Burning*   93

5 Theatre and its mother: Tom Stoppard's *Hapgood*   112

6 White men and pregnancy: discovering the body
  to be rescued   130

7 The ontology of performance: representation without
  reproduction   146

8 Afterword: notes on hope   167

  Notes   181
  Bibliography   195
  Index   203

Figures

1 Adrian Piper, *Cornered* (1989)   9
2 Louise Bourgeois, *Nature Study, Velvet Eyes* (1984)   22
3 Robert Mapplethorpe, *Derrick Cross* (1983)   39
4 Robert Mapplethorpe, *Self-Portrait* (1988)   41
5 Robert Mapplethorpe, *Alice Neel* (1984)   43
6 Robert Mapplethorpe, *Brian Ridley and Lyle Heeter* (1979)   44
7 Robert Mapplethorpe, *Leland Richard* (1980)   46
8 Robert Mapplethorpe, *Ajitto* (1981)   48
9 Robert Mapplethorpe, *Ken and Tyler* (1985)   50
10 Mira Schor, *Caul of Self* and *Tracings of Caul of Self* (1987)   53
11 Mira Schor, *The Impregnation of M.* (1987)   54
12 Mira Schor, *small ear* (1989)   56
13 Mira Schor, *Don't Forget Me* (1989)   57
14 Mira Schor, *Audition* (1988)   57
15 Mira Schor, *Imperfect Transmission* (1989)   59
16 Cindy Sherman, *Untitled (Film Still)*, 35 (1979)   61
17 Cindy Sherman, *Untitled*, 93 (1981)   63
18 Cindy Sherman, *Untitled*, 175 (1987)   65
19 Cindy Sherman, *Untitled*, 216 (1989)   67
20 Film still of William Raymond from *The Man Who
   Envied Women* (1985)   78
21 Film still of Yvonne Rainer and William Raymond from
   The Man Who Envied Women (1985)   85
22 Film still of Angie Xtravaganza, Dorian Corey, and
   Willi Ninja from *Paris Is Burning* (1991)   100
23 Film still of Venus Xtravaganza from *Paris Is Burning* (1991)   110
24 Angelika Festa, *You Are Obsessive, Eat Something* (1984)   154
25 Angelika Festa, *Untitled Dance (with fish and others)* (1987)   155
26 Angelika Festa, *Untitled Dance (with fish and others)* (1987)   157
27 Lorna Simpson, *Guarded Conditions* (1989)   159

Acknowledgements

I am extraordinarily grateful to Celeste Goodridge for her patience, her intelligence, and her acute readings of many drafts of this book. Lynda Hart is an ideal colleague: witty, smart, and just a shade on the generous side of honest. Even though she thinks I am wrong about some (?) of what I write here, she helped me believe I should keep trying to write it. I will always be indebted to both of them for their work on mine.

My students in the Department of Performance Studies, Tisch School of the Arts, New York University, have heard and helped me work through many of the arguments recorded here. They allowed me to indulge the illusion I was teaching while I wondered out loud about Lacan, Operation Rescue, and the quantum. They overlooked my many dead ends and asked the next, tougher, question. And they continue to teach me something new about Hope all the time.

The personal and professional support of my colleagues in the Department of Performance Studies, Brooks McNamara, Richard Schechner, Barbara Kirshenblatt-Gimblett, Michael Taussig and Marcia Siegel, has been an invaluable help. Their work has been an inspiration and a challenge to me. Barbara, with her special touch for institutional magic, made it possible for me to take a semester off and write. Richard's contagious curiosity and frank joy in debate have enriched my intellectual, cultural, and political horizons. I am grateful to these five people for all they have done, individually and collectively, for my work.

Some of the artists I discuss in this book are alive and well and living in Manhattan. Mira Schor, Yvonne Rainer, and Angelika Festa have generously provided me with photos and detailed commentaries on my work about them. Adrian Piper talked in a truly inspiring way about her work last Spring at NYU. The Robert Mapplethorpe Foundation has been exceptionally generous with permissions and fees in a climate when they have every reason to be suspicious of reprint queries. Metro Pictures, Josh Baer, Robert Miller, John Weber, and Miramax have all been extremely helpful with my requests for photos; my thanks to them and to the artists they represent for their generosity.

I am especially grateful to Janice Price of Routledge for agreeing to take me on after Helena Reckitt left. Her trips to New York were perfectly timed shots-in-the-arm. I would also like to thank Jill Rawnsley, Jenny Overton, and Nick Thomas for their patience, their many saves, their good will, and their forgiveness.

The people who are closest to me have aided in the completion of this book in many ways. My deepest gratitude to Sluggo who hardly ever gets to go to the beach and almost always gets to see me struggle and for being home that day when I thought I'd break a part and for reminding me again where the poems come from; to the Termite who read pages and pages and met me in diners across downtown to tell me in perfect detail what I got wrong and right; to E. Angel who carried the manuscript up a mountain to read; to Did for making Easter right and for letting me overnight everything and reading all the next day; to Helena who said yes to the book before I understood it and who came from Chicago and London to tell me twice she wanted to read it so I had better write it; and to the boy who still knows what it is to come and go.

Thanks too to my brother Jimmy who got me into this in the first place and to Geoffrey Hartman for keeping me in when I said no more I've had enough; to George Spaeth who keeps the pressure down and to Mark Speaker who stopped the staph; to Elaine Showalter, E. Ann Kaplan, Alicia Ostriker, and Kate Stimpson for teaching me how to be a "feminist critic"; to Jill Dolan, Susan Bennett, and Lynda Hart for making me think most of the time this is still a good thing to be; to Dell Lemmon who tracked down all the photos and talked to all the galleries; to Amy Elliot who did most of the bibliography and more or less FAXED me to London; to Mary Ellen for buying me lunches and giving me the right clothes even though we both know I'll wear the wrong ones; to my Mother for listening to me and telling me to write a novel and for almost always making me laugh; to Gerard for reading everything since Kozloff and talking to me about it all; and to Joe, Terry, and Betsy for always asking how it was going.

Thanks too to Wanna for once wanting to know, especially in Paris and on the back steps of Dolores; to PT for talking to me about Venus' death walking up a green hill to the yellow chariot; to the Big K for always reminding me of the other audience; to Sha who taught me about the "pressure and bruise" of critical prose; to MH who taught me about psychic bruises and for coming to hear "Sea Change"; to TCG for letting me read out loud and for printing maps of different covers; to Matra for translating the guides across the continents; to ARCT for MOMA's sculpture garden, the New York bank, and walking the Hudson; to Pat Hearn for trying with Sophie; to Clara who took care of both of us at

IHOP; to the waiters at the Village Inn who keep pouring me decaf; and to the people at Narrative Poetics who let me read so much of Paris.

My gratitude too to the ghosts who are everywhere in these pages – and in loving memory of the ones who left with proper names intact: Julia Reynolds Cameron, David Kalstone, Rena Grant, David Wojnarowicz, my sister, and my father.

1

Broken symmetries:
memory, sight, love

[B]elief is in itself the image: both arise out of the same procedures and through the same terms: *memory*, *sight*, and *love*.

(Julia Kristeva[1])

The question of belief always enters critical writing and perhaps never more urgently than when one's subject resists vision and may not be "really there" at all. Like the fantasy of erotic desire which frames love, the distortions of forgetting which infect memories, and the blind spots laced through the visual field, a believable image is the product of a negotiation with an unverifiable real. As a representation of the real the image is always, partially, phantasmatic. In doubting the authenticity of the image, one questions as well the veracity of she who makes and describes it. To doubt the subject seized by the eye is to doubt the subjectivity of the seeing "I." These words work both to overcome and to deepen the provocation of that doubt.

As Jacques Lacan repeatedly argued, doubt is a defense against the real.[2] And as basketball players know, sometimes the most effective offense is a good defense. Doubt can be temporarily overcome by belief, that old and slightly arthritic leap of faith. Like Jacob's struggle with the Angel who will not give him a proper name, *Unmarked* attempts to find a theory of value for that which is not "really" there, that which cannot be surveyed within the boundaries of the putative real.

By locating a subject in what cannot be reproduced within the ideology of the visible, I am attempting to revalue a belief in subjectivity and identity which is not visibly representable. This is not the same thing as calling for greater visibility of the hitherto unseen. *Unmarked* examines the implicit assumptions about the connections between representational visibility and political power which have been a dominant force in cultural theory in the last ten years. Among the challenges this poses is how to retain the power of the unmarked by surveying it within a theoretical frame. By exposing the blind spot within the theoretical frame itself, it may be possible to construct a way of knowing which does not take surveillance of the object, visible or otherwise, as its chief aim.

Employing psychoanalysis and feminist theories of representation, I am concerned with marking the limit of the image in the political field of the sexual and racial other. I take as axiomatic the link between the image and the word, that what one can see is in every way related to what one can say. In framing more and more images of the hitherto under-represented other, contemporary culture finds a way to name, and thus to arrest and fix, the image of that other. Representation follows two laws: it always conveys more than it intends; and it is never totalizing. The "excess" meaning conveyed by representation creates a supplement that makes multiple and resistant readings possible. Despite this excess, representation produces ruptures and gaps; it fails to reproduce the real exactly. Precisely because of representation's supplemental excess and its failure to be totalizing, close readings of the logic of representation can produce psychic resistance and, possibly, political change. (Although rarely in the linear cause-effect way cultural critics on the Left and Right often assume.)

Currently, however, there is a dismaying similarity in the beliefs generated about the political efficacy of visible representation. The dangerous complicity between progressives dedicated to visibility politics and conservatives patroling the borders of museums, movie houses, and mainstream broadcasting is based on their mutual belief that representations can be treated as "real truths" and guarded or championed accordingly. Both sides believe that greater visibility of the hitherto under-represented leads to enhanced political power. The progressives want to share this power with "others"; conservatives want to reserve this power for themselves. Insufficient understanding of the relationship between visibility, power, identity, and liberation has led both groups to mistake the relation between the real and the representational.

As Judith Butler points out, the confusion between the real and the representational occurs because "the real is positioned both before and after its representation; and representation becomes a moment of the reproduction and consolidation of the real" ("Force of Fantasy": 106). The real is read through representation, and representation is read through the real.

Each representation relies on and reproduces a specific logic of the real; this logical real promotes its own representation. The real partakes of and generates different imagistic and discursive paradigms. There is, for example, a legal real in which concepts such as "the image" and "the claimant" are defended and decided through recourse to pre-established legal concepts such as copyright, trademark, property, the contract, and individual rights.[3] Within the physical universe, the real of the quantum is established through a negotiation with the limitations of the representational possibilities of measuring time and space. To measure motion that is not predictable requires that one consider the uncertainty of both the means of measurement and the energy that one wants to measure. Within the history of theatre the real is what theatre defines itself against, even while reduplicating its effects.[4] Within Lacanian psychoanalyis the Real is full Being itself. Freud's mapping of the unconscious, as Lacan consistently insisted, makes the Real forever impossible to realize (to make real) within the frame of the Symbolic.[5] Within the diverse genre of autobiography the real is considered the motivation for self-representation.[6] Each of these concepts of the real contains within it a meta-text of exclusionary power. Each real believes itself to be the Real-real. The discourse of Western science, law, theatrical realism, autobiography, and psychoanalysis are alike in believing their own terms to be the most comprehensive, the most basic, the most fundamental route to establishing or unsettling the stability of the real. By employing each of them in *Unmarked* I hope to demonstrate that the very proliferation of discourses can only disable the possibility of a Real-real.

I know this sounds oh-so-familiar to the ears of weary poststructuralists. But what is less familiar is the way in which the visible itself is woven into each of these discourses as an unmarked conspirator in the maintenance of each discursive real. I want to expose the ways in which the visible real is employed as a truth-effect for the establishment of these discursive and representational notions of the real. Moreover, I want to suggest that by seeing the blind spot within the visible real we might see a way to redesign the representational real. If the visible real is itself unable to constitute a reliable representational real its use-value must lie elsewhere.

The pleasure of resemblance and repetition produces both psychic assurance and political fetishization. Representation reproduces the Other as the Same. Performance, insofar as it can be defined as representation without reproduction, can be seen as a model for another representational economy, one in which the reproduction of the Other *as* the Same is not assured.[7]

The relationship between the real and the representational, between the looker and the given to be seen, is a version of the relation between self and other. Cultural theory has thus far left unexamined the connection between the psychic theory of the relationship between self and other and the political and epistemological contours of that encounter. This relationship between self and other is a marked one, which is to say it is unequal. It is alluring and violent because it touches the paradoxical nature of psychic desire; the always already unequal encounter nonetheless summons the hope of reciprocity and equality; the failure of this hope then produces violence, aggressivity, dissent. The combination of psychic hope and political-historical inequality makes the contemporary encounter between self and other a meeting of profound romance and deep violence. While cultural theorists of the colonial subject and revisionary meta-anthropologists have thrown welcome light on the historical pattern of the violence of this encounter, we still have relatively little knowledge of the romance nestled within it.

Unmarked concerns the relationship between the self and the other as it is represented in photographs, paintings, films, theatre, political protests, and performance art. While the notion of the potential reciprocal gaze has been considered part of the "unique" province of live performance, the desire to be seen is also activated by looking at inanimate art. Examining the politics of the exchange of gaze across these diverse representational mediums leads to an extended definition of the field of performance. The "politics" of the imagined and actual exchange of gaze are most clearly exposed in relation to sexual difference. At once an attempt to stabilize "difference" and an attempt to repress the "sexual" itself, cultural representation seeks both to conceal and reveal a real that will "prove" that sexual difference is a real difference.

I

Psychoanalysis imagines a primal scene that is profoundly formative for the subject. The fundamental power of this primal scene is not mitigated by the difference between actually witnessing the scene or "only" imagining it. An imagined history and a history of a real ocular experience have similarly weighted consequences for the psychic subject. Given this concept of psychic history, the familiar argument that psychoanalysis is ahistorical can be seen as a mis-taking of the notion of history which psychoanalysis employs. A noncontinuous psychic subject *cannot* be adequately reflected in a continuous historiography. In refusing to believe that the empirical real is more impressive than the imagined or fantasized (a belief fundamental to Western historiography), psychoanalysis is incompatible with histories that seek to demonstrate the "weight of empirical evidence," if that which is labeled empirical excludes that which is immaterial and phantasmatic.[8]

The primal scene is remembered and (re)visited through the dream and the symptom – through the imaginative attempt of the unconscious to replay the (past) scene on the stage of the present. Self-identity needs to be continually reproduced and reassured precisely because it fails to secure belief. It fails because it cannot rely on a verifiably continuous history. One's own origin is both real and imagined. The formation of the "I" cannot be witnessed by the "eye." The primal scene itself is (probably) a screen memory for the always-lost moment of one's own conception. Moreover, within the logic of psychic displacement, the memory of the primal scene also functions as a rehearsal for one's own death. The primal scene is a psychic revisiting and anticipation of the world without oneself. This vision is devastating and liberating; but it cannot be endured very long. One prefers instead to see oneself more or less securely situated. The process of self-identity is a leap into a narrative that employs seeing as a way of knowing. Mimetic correspondence has a psychic appeal because one seeks a self-image within the representational frame. Mimetic representation requires that the writer/ speaker employs pronouns, invents characters, records conversations, examines the words and images of others, so that the spectator can secure a coherent belief in self-authority, assurance, presence.[9] Memory. Sight. Love. All require a witness, imagined or real.

But what would it take to value the immaterial within a culture structured around the equation "material equals value?" As critical theories of cultural reproduction become increasingly dedicated to a consideration of the "material conditions" that influence, if not completely determine, social, racial, sexual, and psychic identities, questions about the immaterial construction of identities – those processes of belief which summon memory, sight, and love – fade from the eye/I.[10] Pitched against this fading, the words I have lined up here attempt to (re)develop the negative, not in order to produce a clearer print, but rather to see what it would mean to use the negative itself as a way of securing belief in one's self-image.

II

As Lacanian psychoanalysis and Derridean deconstruction have demonstrated, the epistemological, psychic, and political binaries of Western metaphysics create distinctions and evaluations across two terms. One term of the binary is marked with value, the other is unmarked. The male is marked with value; the female is unmarked, lacking measured value and meaning. Within this psycho-philosophical frame, cultural reproduction takes she who is unmarked and re-marks her, rhetorically and imagistically, while he who is marked with value is left unremarked, in discursive paradigms and visual fields. He is the norm and therefore unremarkable; as the Other, it is she whom he marks.

The reproduction of the cultural unconscious proceeds, as Lacan has argued, by taking two terms and forming one: the one they become is gendered male. Sexual difference in this way remains hidden and cultural (re)production remains *hommo-sexual*.[11] Unable to bear (sexual) difference, the psychic subject transforms this difference into the Same, and converts the Other into the familiar grammar of the linguistic, visual, and physical body of the Same. This process of conversion is what Freud called fetishization. Lacan calls it the function of metaphor.

For Lacan: "The sexual relation cannot be written. Everything that is written is based on the fact that it will be forever impossible to write the sexual relation as such. This gives way to a certain effect of discourse called *écriture*" (in Reynaud: 31). Writing re-marks the hole in the signifier, the inability of words to convey meaning exactly. The intimacy of the language of speech and the language of vision extends to their mutual impossibilities. The failure to represent sexual difference within visual representation gives way to a certain effect of the positive/ negative, the seen and the unseen, which frames the visual perception of the Woman, and leads to her conversion into, more often than not, a fetish – a phallic substitute. This fetishization of the image is the risk of representational visibility for women. It secures the gap between the real and the representational and marks her as Other.[12]

Within the realm of the visible, that is both the realm of the signifier and the image, women are seen always as Other; thus, *The Woman* cannot be seen. Yet, like a ubiquitous ghost, she continues to haunt the images we believe in, the ones we remember seeing and loving. *Unmarked* is part of this ghost story – the story of the woman as immaterial ghost. It takes place within the haunted house of the cultural unconscious and it shakes the graves of the restless spirits of psychoanalysis, Freud and Lacan, and follows their feminist familiars – Luce Irigaray, Jacqueline Rose, Juliet MacCannell, and Joan Copjec. Attentive to the political field in which the real and the representational are the reproductive couple *par excellence*, I want to see which of their offspring are draped and which are raped by the psychic and discursive terms of "the visible."

The current contradiction between "identity politics" with its accent on visibility, and the psychoanalytic/deconstructionist mistrust of visibility as the source of unity or wholeness needs to be refigured, if not resolved.[13] As the Left dedicates ever more energy to visibility politics, I am increasingly troubled by the forgetting of the problems of visibility so successfully articulated by feminist film theorists in the 1970s and 1980s. I am not suggesting that continued invisibility is the "proper" political agenda for the disenfranchised, but rather that the binary between the power of visibility and the impotency of invisibility is falsifying. There is real power in remaining unmarked; and there are serious limitations to visual representation as a political goal.

Visibility is a trap ("In this matter of the visible, everything is a trap": Lacan, *Four Fundamental Concepts*: 93); it summons surveillance and the law; it provokes voyeurism, fetishism, the colonialist/imperial appetite for possession. Yet it retains a certain political appeal. Visibility politics have practical consequences; a line can be drawn between a practice (getting someone seen or read) and a theory (if you are seen it is harder for "them" to ignore you, to construct a punitive canon); the two can be reproductive. While there is a deeply ethical appeal in the desire for a more inclusive representational landscape and certainly under-represented communities can be empowered by an enhanced visibility, the terms of this visibility often enervate the putative power of these identities. A much more nuanced relationship to the power of visibility needs to be pursued than the Left currently engages.[14]

Arguing that communities of the hitherto under-represented will be made stronger if representational economies reflect and see them, pro-gressive cultural activists have staked a huge amount on increasing and expanding the visibility of racial, ethnic, and sexual "others." It is assumed that disenfranchised communities who see their members within the representational field will feel greater pride in being part of such a community *and* those who are not in such a community will increase their understanding of the diversity and strength of such com-munities. Implicit within this argument are several presumptions which bear further scrutiny:

1 Identities are visibly marked so the resemblance between the African-American on the television and the African-American on the street helps the observer see they are members of the same community. Reading physical resemblance is a way of identifying community.
2 The relationship between representation and identity is linear and smoothly mimetic. What one sees is who one is.
3 If one's mimetic likeness is not represented, one is not addressed.
4 Increased visibility equals increased power.

Each presumption reflects the ideology of the visible, an ideology which erases the power of the unmarked, unspoken, and unseen.

Adrian Piper, the visual artist and philosopher, has demonstrated that part of the meaning of race resides in the perpetual choice to acknowl-edge or ignore its often invisible markings. In the United States the history of slavery, and its relation to reproduction and rape, has meant that a "pure" match between race and skin color is relatively rare. In her potent video *Cornered* (Figure 1), Piper addresses the "white" spectator and through a slow but increasingly pointed set of questions and propositions gradually overturns the binary of "black" and "white" so fundamental to the performance of racist ideology in the United States.[15] Since race is thought to be "carried" by blood and the history of slavery for African-American women is also the history of rape, the belief that one is "purely" white or black is difficult to sustain. Piper, dressed in blue and draped in pearls, calmly constructs a decision tree for her "white" spectator. First she demonstrates that the statistical probability that the spectator is actually black is extremely high. Then she asks how that knowledge will change, or not change, one's identifications. (Will you tell some of your friends? Will you tell your boss? Will you keep it a secret?) Gradually, as the trellis gets more and more intricate, the logic it is upholding begins to slip. What is the distinction between "blackness" and "whiteness" based on? If "racial identification" is a choice, what motivates it? Who gets to make that choice? In unhooking racial identity from the realm of the visible and making it a matter of "choice," Piper exposes the enormous consequences of racial difference while exposing the utter insignificance of the ground which legislates these differences – gene arrangement, the odd biology of blood.

Installed in "The Windows on Broadway," at The New Museum in New York, Piper's video spilled out onto the street and captivated a whole range of "non-traditional" museum-goers. The video monitor was installed against the rear wall of the window; in the foreground of the window was a large, upended and overturned brown table. On the side wall, birth certificates with the word "race" highlighted were displayed. Within the video frame, Piper herself sat behind a table very much like the one overturned in the window. A series then of mimetic frames opens up as one tries to "locate" the event. The window replicates the video screen: on video, Piper sits at a table; in the window, the video monitor (placed on another similar table) represents her image from behind an overturned table, calmly speaking. The double framing, the marked reproduction of the real production via the return of the tables, make the notion of apprehending the elusive, invisible properties of "race-blood" seem absurd. Piper's representational frame-up corners the spectator and disables the habitual notion that race is visibly marked on skin.

The decision to "identify" as an African-American or to "pass" as white – a question Piper poses for her "white" spectator in *Cornered* – is part of an ongoing performance of identity. The same physical features of a person's body may be read as "black" in England, "white" in Haiti, "colored" in South Africa, and "mulatto" in Brazil. More than indicating that racial markings are read differently cross-culturally, these variations underline the psychic, political, and philosophical impoverishment of linking the color of the physical body with the ideology of race. Race-identity involves recognizing something other than skin and physical inscriptions. One cannot simply "read" race as skin-color. The tendency to do so leads to the corollary proposition that all people with the same skin color believe the same thing, and that there is, for example, such a thing as a coherent African-American community. The fiery debate in 1991 over Clarence Thomas, President George Bush's nominee to the Supreme Court, makes plain the diversity of the African-American

Figure 1 Adrian Piper, *Cornered* (1989), installation shot. (Photo: Fred Scruton. Courtesy: John Weber Gallery, New York)

community in the United States. The "visibility" of black skin is not, and cannot be, an accurate barometer for identifying a community of diverse political, economic, sexual, and artistic interests.

The focus on skin as the visible marker of race is itself a form of feminizing those races which are not white. Reading the body as the sign of identity is the way men regulate the bodies of women. Lorene Cary tells a West Indian folk tale in *Black Ice*. A woman drapes her skin across a chair in the bedroom she shares with her husband and slips out a window to enjoy the night. Night after night she leaves their bed. (Indigenous dream interpreters, as against Freudian ones, would say she is walking with The Invisible.) She is always careful to return before her husband wakes. She slips back into her skin and then back into their bed. But one night her husband wakes and sees her skin across the chair. He is distraught. He seeks the advice of "an old woman in the village." She tells him to take some salt and rub the inside of the empty skin with it. A few nights later, the woman leaves again and the husband applies the salt to her skin. When she returns to her skin it will not yield: "Skin, skin, ya na know me?" she screams (Cary, *Black Ice*: 131). Caught between her body and her spirit, her insides keep her out. The husband who believes he has the right to the entrances and exits of her body can coat the inside of her skin with salt but he cannot keep her home. His failure to hold her in their bed prompts him to make her skin unable to house her spirit. Both exiled, her question hangs in the air: "Skin, skin, ya na know me?" The woman's voice cannot reanimate her skin. And she remains lost to her own body because of his desire to mark it as his.

In conflating identity politics with visibility, cultural activists and some theorists have also assumed that "selves" can be adequately represented within the visual or linguistic field. The "hole in the signifier," "the Real-impossible" which is unsayable, unseeable, and therefore resistant to representation, is ignored in the full fling forward into representation.[16] The danger in staking all on representation is that one gains only re-presentation. *Pace* Baudrillard, the real continues to exert its allure and provoke our frustration despite the pervasiveness of "the precession of simulacra," despite our inability to recover it independent of its representation.[17]

If representational visibility equals power, then almost-naked young white women should be running Western culture. The ubiquity of their image, however, has hardly brought them political or economic power. Recognizing this, those who advance the cause of visibility politics also usually call for "a change" in representational strategies. But so far these proposals are rather vague. What is required in order to advance a more ethical and psychically rewarding representational field, one that sidesteps the usual traps of visibility: surveillance, fetishism, voyeurism, and sometimes, death? How are these traps more or less damning than benign neglect and utter ignorance? There is an important difference between willfully failing to appear and never being summoned.

Given capitalism's continual degradation of women's reproductive value – from the crude ideology of the familiar feminization of poverty which matter-of-factly turns up as a 59 to 63 cent wage differential in the U.S., to the failure to recognize human reproduction itself as labor, except in the case of surrogacy – that is, through the agency of the biological other and under the hood of capitalism's fellow, the contract – it is imperative that those interested in women as subjects find other ways of thinking about the relation between representation and reproduction. This requires attention to that which eludes both reproduction and representation. It is not enough to dismiss "the negative status of what cannot be seen" (Sue-Ellen Case, "Introduction," *Performing Feminisms*: 13) without considering what that negative negates.

Visibility politics are additive rather than transformational (to say nothing of revolutionary). They lead to the stultifying "me-ism" to which realist representation is always vulnerable. Unable to see oneself reflected in a corresponding image of the Same, the spectator can reject the representation as "not about me." Or worse, the spectator can valorize the representation which fails to reflect her likeness, as one with "universal appeal" or "transcendent power."

Visibility politics are compatible with capitalism's relentless appetite for new markets and with the most self-satisfying ideologies of the United States: you are welcome here as long as you are productive. The production and reproduction of visibility are part of the labor of the reproduction of capitalism. I am trying here to remember the traps of the visible and to outline, however speculatively, a different way of thinking about the political and psychic relationship between self and other, subject and object, in cultural reproduction. The psychoanalytic dimensions of the encounter between who one is and who one sees, an encounter most comprehensively explained by Lacan's reading of Freud, can be employed as a departure point for a more emphatic accenting of the political dimensions of the encounter between self and other.

III

Oscar Wilde [. . .] gave us the added insight that criticism was the only civilized form of autobiography.[18]

For many years of my childhood in the heat of the summer my six brothers and sisters, two parents, the ghost of my dead sister and I drove from Long Island, New York to Carmel, Massachusetts in a green station wagon with brown sideboards. We'd all be crammed in the car, perched on the green vinyl seats, sweating to Massachusetts. On the roof of the car, like a precariously large hat, were three suitcases stacked from bottom to top. We divided ourselves into three sets of three, arranged left to right. My father drove and my mother sat in the front with my eldest brother. My next oldest brother and my two older sisters sat in the middle, while my next oldest sister, myself, and my younger brother sat in the "way back" and faced the opposite direction of the rest of them and the way we were going.

When my mother couldn't stand us any longer she'd say, "Let's have a keep quiet contest." Whoever could keep quiet the longest won a prize. I can't remember what the prize was, but I remember trying very hard to listen to the sound of the tires on the asphalt, the sound of my sister's breath, the sound of the wind turning over as the car went through it. These contests had a strange tension for me, not so much because I was burning to speak, but because I thought my mother's weary sadness might infect us and render us all permanently mute. Eventually of course someone of us would break the silence. Sometimes one of my brothers would start tickling one of my sisters. Or my mother herself would speak to my father and we'd all yell with delight to see her undone by her own game. Sometimes she'd laugh at herself; sometimes she'd say it didn't count since she was the mother and the referee of the game, not a participant.

After years of this I realized that the games were meant to be lost at least as much as they were meant to be won. No one really expected nine people to drive six hours in silence. Part of "losing" the game meant winning a certain kind of relief. A relief from the potential grief we all knew waited at my mother's elbow ready to carry her far away from us. And knowing when to lose the game – how to break the silence in such a way that we would not break our mother's temper – required a very specific intelligence, one schooled in the subtle calibrations of a substantive and mobile silence. An intelligence whose very expression, utterance itself, was hedged in on all sides by doubt.

In the years since I've spent a lot of time trying to understand what a captivating presence my sister's ghost was and is. There were nine of us in that car, but it was the one who was not with us that we worried about, thought about, remembered. In the clarity of her absence, we redefined ourselves. The real was the absence of her; we were representations of that loss. The incorporeal presence of my sister mattered to us I think because we were so bounded by the strange body we were – not octagonal and no longer pentagonal we were a nine-headed creature with a distressing sameness to our features. We were living maps of one another's physical history and future. The younger ones recorded the older ones' past; the older ones showed the younger ones their future.

The girls showed the boys themselves as girls and the boys showed the girls themselves as boys. And no one, including our mother, got our names right. (My father evaded the whole thing by renaming us altogether.) The absolute break between the sign and the referent was a joke in our house, and the failure of the proper name to render an identity was an accepted fact. We recognized that distinct identities would not emerge from names which were so often misapplied, nor did we believe that within the tight resemblance of our physical bodies a singular image would tell us who we were. The similarity of our bodies, our uneasy sense of physical redundancy, made us especially conscious of my sister's swift escape from skin. And because we were so consciously caught up in the substitutional economy of the family (the string of wrong names that preceded your own address) she functioned as "a ghost that is the phantom of no flesh" (Derrida, "The Double Session": 206). For while we were each reproducing one another's bodies across the unstable and always redoubled divide of time and gender, her non-corporeality reproduced our bodies as fleshless.

Even as we named my mother's sadness "grief" and silently attributed it to the death of my sister, we also recognized, however dimly, the possibility that her silence had nothing at all to do with the loss of her child, but rather had to do with the enormous weight of her living children – or more distressing still, had nothing to do with any of us at all. Such thoughts could not be borne by us, so we did not try them out. Like our missing sister, they rested somewhere we could not often visit.

Identity cannot, then, reside in the name you can say or the body you can see – your own or your mother's. Identity emerges in the failure of the body to express being fully and the failure of the signifier to convey meaning exactly. Identity is perceptible only through a relation to an other – which is to say, it is a form of both resisting and claiming the other, declaring the boundary where the self diverges from and merges with the other. In that declaration of identity and identification, there is always loss, the loss of not-being the other and yet remaining dependent on that other for self-seeing, self-being.

IV

Taking the visual world in is a process of loss: learning to see is training careful blindness. To apprehend and recognize the visible is to eliminate as well as absorb visual data. Just as surely as representational technologies – the camera, the canvas, the theatrical frame, language itself – order visual apprehension to accord with a (constructed) notion of the real so too do human eyes. As Lacan puts it:

When you see a rainbow, you are seeing something purely subjective. [. . .] It is not there. It is a subjective phenomenon. And yet, thanks to a photographic apparatus, you will be able to record it quite objectively.[19] Is it not true to say that the photographic apparatus is a subjective apparatus constructed entirely through the assistance of x and y which inhabit the domain in which the subject lives, that is the domain of language?[20]

(Lacan, *Les Ecrits*: 91)

The camera, modeled on the human eye, reproduces the (faulty) sight of the eye. Together, the eye and the camera, in mimetic correspondence, naturalize the visible real by turning it into something "seen."

The desire for the real is impossible to realize, Lacan believed, but that impossibility maintains rather than cancels the desire for it. The physiological understanding of vision, like both the psychoanalytic conception of the gaze and the technologies of aesthetics, is also a theory of loss and distortion.

Concentrating on the history of optics and technologies of observation in the nineteenth century, Jonathan Crary charts the Western epistemological shift from a belief in a transparent optical system in which perceiving subjects apprehended the pure light of the visible to a notion of seeing in which "the subjective contents of vision are dissociated from an objective world, in which the body itself produces phenomena that have no external correlate" ("Techniques of the Observer": 6). When Newton discovered the prismatic properties of light the human eye became a poor creature, an organ whose limitations define its properties more precisely than its powers. (Aristotelian philosophy is undone by Newton. Vision cannot be the guarantee of knowing once one knows that vision is never complete.) Unable to perceive the full range of color inherent in light, the human eye is physiologically falsifying.

This notion of the eye's inability to see fully may well have prompted the subsequent description of consciousness' inability to absorb fully psychic data. Just as physiologists posited the idea of an "after-image" – a shadow of an image which remains on the retina for a brief second after the image has actually vanished from the visual field (a memory that makes the perception of cinematic continuity possible) – so too did psychoanalysts posit that a "trace" of a psychic event remains in the unconscious, Freud's mystic writing pad. In other words, the after-image participates in a kind of "optical unconscious" (the phrase is Walter Benjamin's) – a realm in which what is not visibly available to the eye constitutes and defines what is – in the same way as the unconscious frames ongoing conscious events. Just as we understand that things in the past determine how we experience the present, so too can it be said that the visible is defined by the invisible.[21] Or, as Marianne Moore put it, "The power of the visible/is the invisible."[22]

This power threatens to expose one's lack-in-being. In order to counter the physiological and psychic impoverishment of the eye/I, visual representation makes ever more elaborate promises to deliver a satisfying and substantial real. Representation appeases a deep psychic impulse to employ the image seen as a mirror for the seeing eye/I and to forget that it is also a screen which erases the subject's own blankness and blindness.

The position of the looker within Lacan's psychic economy is known in relation to the position of the image seen and vice versa. It is not accurate, therefore, to speak of "the gaze(r)" exclusively: the looker is always also regarded by the image seen and through this regard discovers and continually reaffirms that s/he is the one who looks. The positions which define the distinction between the subject and the object in the visual field are psycho-linguistic. Just as the sign within Saussure's linguistic field acquires meaning by its difference from its surrounding signs, so too does the image gain its status as object by its difference (and distance) from other objects in space and from the perceiving subject.[23]

Sight then is both imagistic and discursive. Language expresses the position of the I as it sees the image. The image seen is a product of and a position within language; in apprehending the image the subject suffers the same mark of all Symbolic exchanges, castration. (One speaks and is spoken; one sees and is seen. This is the double drama of the Mirror Stage.) The eyes look out; one needs always the eye of the other to recognize (and name) oneself. In other words, the gaze guarantees the *failure* of self-seeing. ("I am unable to see myself from the place where the Other is looking at me": Lacan, *Scilicet*: 120.) It is precisely the failure of the subject, as Copjec puts it, to "ever becom[e] a fully observable being" that propels the desire to see the other – the external gaze is a compensatory way of returning a failed inward gaze ("Orthopsychic": 70). The supplement offered by words also compensates for the failure of self-seeing. (And the image compensates for what can't be said – eloquent "body" language supplementing "poor" speech.) But these compensations are inadequate. The given to be seen is always a deferral, a substitute, for what it is one wants to see. The history of Western painting faces and falls away from this failure.

Derrida notices that self-portraits are usually recognized by viewers through their titles, rather than through the content of the visual image:

> It is not enough to *simply see* the work to decide what the subject is [. . .] at the edge of the work, neither inside nor outside, readable rather than visible, the title is our only recourse. As for deciding the subject, the initiative is always left to words.[24]

Without words, the self-portrait, the subject's "own" image, the one the subject always fails to possess and must forever re-enact and re-present, cannot be recognized or named.

All seeing is hooded with loss – the loss of self-seeing. In looking at the other (animate or inanimate) the subject seeks to see itself. Seeing is an *exchange* of gazes between a mirror (the image seen which reflects the looker looking) and a screen (the laws of the Symbolic which define subject and object positions within language).[25] Looking, then, both obscures and reveals the looker. For Lacan, seeing is fundamentally social because it relies on an exchange of gazes: one looks and one is seen. The potential for a responding eye, like the hunger for a responsive voice, informs the desire to see the self *through* the image of the other which all Western representation exploits.

While Lacan theorized a potential reciprocal gaze he also recognized that such an exchange took place within an unequal political, linguistic, and psychic field. In this field the signifier of sexual difference "sends forth its light into the shadow of incomplete significations" (*Ecrits*: 152). Positioned within the "incomplete signification" of a binary sexuality the subject's relation to the signifier of sexual difference is never secure. Illustrating the signifier's attempt to (over)compensate for this insecurity, Lacan's rhetorical flourishes reveal the psychic hollowness of "sexual difference" which sociality and language always (re)cover and dress up. A young boy and girl, seated on a train, look out the window as the train pulls into the station. "Look," says the boy, "we're at Ladies!" To which the sister replies, "Idiot! Can't you see we're at Gentlemen." Lacan's gloss is worth quoting at length:

> [O]nly someone who didn't have his eyes in front of the holes (it's the appropriate image here) could possibly confuse the place of the signifier and the signified in this story, or not see from what radiating centre the signifier sends forth its light into the shadow of incomplete significations.
>
> (*Ecrits*: 152)

But of course our eyes are never allowed to rest "in front of the holes" and we do always fail to see the "radiating centre" precisely because, as Lacan himself demonstrated, such a centre cannot be seen or "possessed." The arbitrariness of the signifier does not reproduce random referents – and that's only the beginning of the problem. In his mock-epic style, Lacan continues to outline other consequences:

> For this signifier will now carry a purely animal Dissension, destined for the usual oblivion of natural mists, to the unbridled power of ideological warfare, relentless for families, a torment to the Gods. For these children Ladies and Gentlemen will be henceforth two

countries towards which each of their souls will strive on divergent wings, and between which a truce will be the more impossible since they are actually the same country and neither can compromise on its own superiority without detracting from the glory of the other.

(Ecrits: 152)

Since one sees oneself in the image of the other *and* sees the other in one's image, the degradation of one necessitates the degradation of the other. But not all degradation is equal. Operating within the tight equations of heterosexuality, Lacan's theory of sexual difference negates the female in order to create a theory of the psychic subject, one who (regardless of "sex") can only "*be*" in the economy of the negative. To put it somewhat differently, the square root of nine can be satisfied by either positive three or negative three. But suppose only "positive" numbers represent and reproduce *integers* and negative numbers reproduce *fractions*. The split-subject of Lacan's theory can only "be" (figured) within the economy of the negative.

The proposition that one sees oneself in terms of the other and the other in terms of oneself, is itself differently marked according for men and women. When the unmarked woman looks at the marked man she sees a man; but she sees herself as other, as negative-man. Within the frame of the phallic mark, she sees that which she is not. "It is through the phallic function that man takes up his inscription as all" ("A Love Letter," in Mitchell and Rose, *Feminine Sexuality*: 150). She then can only be the not-all. "There is no such thing as *The* woman since of her essence [. . .] she is not all" ("God and the Jouissance of The Woman," in ibid.: 144).[26] But these unequal terms reproduce another series of material and psychic consequences. As "not all" her representation lends itself to "this *belong to me* aspect of representations, so reminiscent of property" (Lacan, *Four Fundamental Concepts*: 81). The image of the woman is made to submit to the phallic function and is re-marked and revised as that which belongs to him.

Perhaps the best performative example of the phallic function is the theatre of drag. A man imitates an image of a woman in order to confirm that she belongs to him. It is necessary and desirable to perform her image externally and hyperbolically, however, because he wants to see himself in possession of her. Performing the image of what he is not allows him to dramatize himself as "all." But the performance of drag does not and cannot reproduce "the woman." It re-enacts instead the performance of the phallic function – marking her as his.

But for Lacan, because the phallus is the transcendental signifier which has no referent, the phallic function also re-marks castration and loss for all speaking subjects. If the phallus were secure, the phallic function would be redundant. If one already possesses the desired object, it is unnecessary to spend one's life reclaiming it. But the phallus cannot be had, so one does endlessly try to represent it.[27]

"[W]hen any speaking subject whatever [that is, male, female, or "whatever"] lines up under the banner of women it is by being constituted as not all that they are placed within the phallic function" (Lacan, "God": 144). In other words, the position of "woman" within language is open to "any speaking subject whatever" precisely because it is "not all." This incompleteness is fundamental to speech, to psychic identity, and to the gaze itself. *The* psychic subject for Lacan, then, is the castrated subject – the subject Freud defined as female. Lacan's revision of Freud's project reorders sexual difference itself. In using Oedipus to plot the narrative of heterosexual desire, Freud committed himself to the development of a theory of the male psychic subject. In using language and the gaze as the fundamental Symbolic rules which govern desire, Lacan invented a theory of the castrated subject – "male, female or whatever." But because men and women have a different relation to the phallus, Lacan also believed sexual difference entailed a different relation to these Symbolic expressions.[28]

These accents on castration and loss may sound a bit pessimistic, but it is exactly because the gaze is "not all" that empathy and Symbolic identification are possible. Opening up the "not all" of vision requires patience with blanks, with blindness, and with the nonreproductive. To take the humility and blindness inscribed within the gaze seriously, one must accept the radical impotency of the gaze. This impotency underscores the broken and incomplete symmetry between the self and the image of the other.

Joan Copjec and Jacqueline Rose have suggested that the fertility of Lacanian psychoanalysis resides in this psychic paradox: one always locates one's own image in an image of the other *and*, one always locates the other in one's own image.[29] While Lacan was most interested in the implications of the latter on the development of the subject, I am concerned here with the political and aesthetic consequences of the different access certain people have to "the image of the other." While there has been much written about the gaze, particularly by feminist film theorists and art historians, insufficient attention has been paid to the desire for a reciprocal gaze. The desire to see is a manifestation of the desire to be seen, in live performance as well as in the spectator's relation to inanimate representation.[30]

All vision doubts and hopes for a response. (William James: "[D]oubt and hope are sisters.") To see is nothing if it is not replied to, confirmed by recourse to another image, and/or another's eye. This confirmation is negotiated through representation – which is to say through distortion, and principally for this discussion, through the distortions produced by the desire for the real. "Saying the whole truth is materially impossible:

words fail. Yet it's through this very impossibility that truth holds onto the real" (Lacan, "Television": 7). Relatively comfortable with this notion of the failing signifier, we can begin to extend this proposition to the visible itself. Inverting Lacan's theorem about the signifier to the eye, one can say: "Seeing the real is materially impossible: eyes fail. Yet it's through this very impossibility that the given to be seen holds onto the real." Possibly, through the impossibility of saying a wholly material truth, we might see what the possibility of the immaterial is (which is perhaps to see how to say it). Lacan and Freud called this immateriality the unconscious; it speaks through the symptom. I am calling this immateriality the unmarked; it shows itself through the negative and through disappearance.

I am speaking here of an *active* vanishing, a deliberate and conscious refusal to take the payoff of visibility. For the moment, active disappearance usually requires at least some recognition of what and who is not there to be effective. (In short, this has largely been a possibility for white middle- and upper-class women.)

A group of women artists and feminist theorists in New York call themselves the Guerrilla Girls. They make posters and signs underlining the everyday racist and sexist practices which constitute business as usual in the mainstream art market. They take the real facts of exhibition space, art market prices, and the sexist and racist policies which have influenced the collections of most galleries and museums, as the ground of their representational strategies. Much of this work is witty and wry. In their poster straightforwardly listing the ten advantages of being a woman artist, for example, one benefit is the relief of never having to worry about being labeled a genius. While their work has become increasingly lauded by both establishment and anti-establishment critics and art world commentators, the Guerrilla Girls continue to remain anonymous. When they do make appearances, they wear gorilla masks and mini-skirts. By refusing to participate in the visibility-is-currency economy which determines value in "the art world," the members of the group resist the fetishization of their argument that many are, at the moment, quite ready to undertake. By resisting visible identities, the Guerrilla Girls mark the failure of the gaze to possess, and arrest, their work. Their posters go up with glue on temporary construction sites, on the sides of buildings, on the doors of closed galleries. They remain there until other messages, often advertisements, overtake them. Underneath the new representations, the racist and sexist "facts" of the Guerrilla Girls' real continue to "exist," while remaining obscured. Always failing to keep the real in view, representation papers it over and reproduces other representations.

It is in the light of the generative failure of the gaze that Lacan's famous sardine-can allegory needs to be seen. Lacan is boating with some fishermen; observing a can floating on the water, one of the sailors says to him: "Do you see that can? Do you see it? Well, it doesn't see you!" (Lacan, *Four Fundamental Concepts*: 95.) While the can does not "see" La/can, insofar as it focuses his vision it places him in a particular position (the angle by which the light of the can converges into an object on the water) and therefore *returns* his I/eye, precisely by orientating that I/eye in relation to the can.[31] In this returning regard, however, the subject sees where he is and recognizes himself as other-than the can.

Thus it is not enough to speak of the gaze in terms of the laws of optics and the result of the rules of spatial perspective. For spatial orientation provides a position from which to see the subject, but it cannot fully reflect or fully screen the subject. "I am not simply that punctiform being located at the geometral point from which perspective is grasped" (Lacan, *Four Fundamental Concepts*: 96). In other words, the subject *exceeds* the can and fails to appear "within" the image of it. At the same time, however, the subject, precisely by looking at the visual field through the agency of the gaze, interrupts its unity. "[I]f I am anything in the picture, it is always in the form of the screen, which I earlier called the stain, the spot" (ibid.: 97). This "stain" is the gaze's screen. This seeing cannot be fully explained by geometry and the rules of spatial perspective.

But nor can it be explained and tamed, as quantum theorists and anthropologists have suggested, through an explicit account of the weight or location of the observer's gaze. Quantum physicists have attempted to measure the altering "energy" of the observer – and to transfer the desire for an epistemology of secure scientific facts to a more insecure epistemology of probabilities and uncertainties. And yet the particle continues to turn into a wave and a wave keeps becoming a particle. Anthropologists and ethnologists have attempted to use "re-flexivity" as a new model for observing the other, but such attempts have done little to unsettle the fundamentally unequal relation which prevails in this mode of scholarship. The project is not to *locate* the observer but rather to see that the given to be seen – from the quantum to the "native" – is apprehended (and of interest) because of the failure of the perceiver to be seen.

"Light may travel in a straight line, but it is refracted, diffused, it floods, it fills – the eye is a sort of bowl – it flows over, too, it necessitates, around the ocular bowl, a whole series of organs, mechanisms, defenses" (Lacan, *Four Fundamental Concepts*: 94). Desire itself activates this "whole series"; and desire shows itself through failure. Desire is recognizable because we are not in the image we see/k. The failure to secure self-seeing leads again to the imagination of annihilation and castration. The scopic drive returns us to the failure of representation, the inability of the gaze to secure symmetry or reciprocity. Seeing secures only the fact that "you never look at me from the place I see you" (ibid.: 91); and the (failed) desire for a reciprocal gaze keeps the looker looking.

Louise Bourgeois' marble sculpture, *Nature Study, Velvet Eyes* (1984) can be seen profitably in relation to Lacan's allegory of the sardine-can (Figure 2). Installed within the museum honoring the mobile eyes of the viewer, Bourgeois' sculpture looks like a rather large and ordinary rock. Surprised by its apparent ordinariness, the viewer saunters over to it to get a better look and peering down, (s/he) sees nestled within the cavity of the rock a pair of all too human looking eyes staring back up. Startled by the hidden eyes, one sees how thoroughly blind one is to the eyes of images. But the feeling of shock soon fades and one feels oddly reassured. By giving the potential gaze (back) to the art object, Bourgeois makes visible the symmetrical *drive* of spectatorship: the desire to see always touches the desire to be seen.[32] It is necessary then to speak of both the object of the gaze and the gaze of the object.

Seeing the other is a social form of self-reproduction. For in looking at/for the other, we seek to re-present ourselves to ourselves. As a social relation the exchange of gazes marks the failure of the subject to maintain the illusionary plenitude of the Imaginary.[33] In the Imaginary there is no exchange of gaze precisely because there is no distinction between what one sees and who one is, and thus the economy of exchange so fundamental to speech and sight, is completely unnecessary. If the infant Mary watches Jane fall down, Mary thinking she is continuous with Jane, cries. Discovering oneself to be a singular bounded body within a physical frame marks the end of the Imaginary continuity between what one sees and who one is. Mary sees she is not connected to Jane and tries to re-establish their connection by speaking to her. If she is answered, the cut is deepened for Jane too recognizes and confirms their distance. If Mary is not answered, she is also cut because she has no other means of re-establishing that connection. (Sexual desire, *as* a speech act, relies on subject positions, and therefore disconnections and separations. The energy to overcome such separation is libidinal. It relies on the subject's ability to remain blind to the impossibility of (re)joining.)

The exchange of gaze marks the split *within* the subject (the loss of the Specular I of the Imaginary) and *between* subjects (the entry into the Social I of the Symbolic). The "here/there" articulated with Lacan's story of the sardine-can, and also elaborated in his commentary on Freud's *fort/da* game, reflects the linguistic distinction between the positions of "I" and "it."[34] Just as that distinction casts speech as an inscription of suffering, so too does visual distance measure the eye's rupture from the Imaginary. The impossibility of fulfilling the desire of the Specular I for

Figure 2 Louise Bourgeois, *Nature Study, Velvet Eyes* (1984). (Photo: Allan Finkelman. Courtesy: Robert Miller Gallery, New York)

unity which inaugurates and maintains the Social I makes the desiring gaze and its return the guarantee of lack and loss.[35]

Unable to reverse her own gaze (the eyes obstinately look only *outside* the self), the subject is forced to detour through the other to see herself. In order to get the other to reflect her, she has to look for/at the other. (She sees herself *through* looking at the other.) And that other is forever looking for/at himself through looking at her. (Trying to hold that gaze, each looker makes herself into the image she believes the other wants to see.) "The subject presents itself as other than what it is, and what it is given to see is not what it wants to see" (Lacan, *Four Fundamental Concepts*: 104). Operating within the realm of the substitute, the "original" exchange of gaze that marks the entry into the Symbolic is continually repeated and disguised.

One of the functions of the Symbolic is to turn back, to speak of "original moments." Lacan's Mirror Stage explains the Symbolic, but within the terms established by the Symbolic. (Insofar as the Imaginary is the Symbolic's Other, this framing is inevitable.) The story of origin that Lacan tells must be understood not so much as an empirical moment in the subject's "continuous" history, but more like the series of frames in Piper's *Cornered*. The window which frames the video monitor, for example, doubles it so that the spectator can "forget" it and maintain the illusion that Piper is (or once was) there. *Fort. Da.* The Imaginary doubles the fantasy of the Symbolic and keeps the subject desiring its return. The substitutive economy of the Symbolic is itself a substitute for the relations which prevailed in the Imaginary.

Lacan's story of origin begins with the primary identification the subject feels with the Symbolic Mother. To be valued by the Mother the child must offer that which the Mother desires: the phallus. Lacking it, the child decides the Mother must already contain it and cedes to her the authority of the phallus, transforming her into the subject supposed to know. Imputing to the Mother a unitary wholeness (bodily and psychically), the subject then implores her to return this unity so that the subject may feel as satisfied and complete as s/he imagines the Mother to be. But the Mother, who lacks the phallus, cannot return this wholeness. (No one can for the phallus cannot be had.) In other words, to the subject's appeal for wholeness, an appeal that arises out of a recognition of lack, the Mother returns her own lack. Zero meets zero and what is confirmed is the endless substitution of deferred desire – which in the Symbolic is signaled by metaphor.

Everyone knows that if zero appears in the denominator the value of the fraction no longer has meaning, but assumes [. . .] infinite value. [. . .] In so far as the primary signifier [the phallus] is pure non-sense, it becomes the bearer of the infinitisation of the value of the subject, not open to all meanings, but abolishing them all, which is different.

(Lacan, *Four Fundamental Concepts*: 252)

Different too is the distinction between the abolishment of meaning and the abolishment of value. For while metaphor can be understood as the erosion and loss of "original" or "singular" meaning it does not follow that this erosion negates value. On the contrary, metaphor makes value.[36] And perhaps nowhere more meaningfully than in the metaphoric values of sexual difference. Again, this economy works both discursively and imagistically.

Just as language exists anterior to the subject's relation to it, so too does the marked visual field exist anterior to the subject. (And just as different languages employ different grammars, so too do visual fields, cross-culturally and across genres.) Lacan used the rules of linguistics to illuminate the unconscious – particularly as it became imaged in the transference – and the rules of perspective can illuminate the Western frame of vision – and particularly as it is enacted in its political register.

In the familiar story of the history of Western painting the rules of perspective rely on a symmetrical relationship between the viewing point and the vanishing point. As Norman Bryson argues, this neat relationship establishes and maintains the centrality of a single perception and a coherent unified looker.[37] Perspective is essentially a theory of relationships, an illustration of visual exchanges, from which Lacan elucidated psychic consequences.

In this elucidation, however, Lacan repeatedly asserted that perspective itself was an insufficient explanation for vision. In her essay "The Orthopsychic Subject," Copjec clarifies Lacan's impatience with the laws of optics:

Because it alone is capable of lending things sense, the signifier alone makes vision possible. There is and can be no brute vision, no vision totally devoid of sense. Painting, drawing, all forms of picture-making, then, are fundamentally graphic arts. And because signifiers are material, that is, because they are opaque rather than translucent, because they refer to other signifiers rather than directly to the signified, the field of vision is neither clear nor easily traversable. It is instead ambiguous and treacherous, full of traps.

("Orthopsychic": 68)

The trap of the visual field is that it seems to promise to show all, even while it fails to show the subject who looks, *and* thus fails to show what the looker most wants to see. The looker is the "not all" which is left out of the promise of visual plenitude. Seeing is a (false) assertion that the world can be mastered by the gaze *and* a recognition of the world without one self.

In Western art history the centrality of the single perception (the "perfect" viewpoint) is fortified *through* the experience of its loss, just as the endless process of establishing psychic identity is punctuated by its loss. The symmetrical relation between the viewpoint and the vanishing point means that the viewpoint *will be reflected* in the vanishing point; the looking eye sees itself as a vanishing emptiness, as a blank. The language of "the [singular] eye" re-marks the violence of this vanishing.

The history of optics, aesthetics, Freudian and Lacanian psychoanalysis, and that curious hybrid Bataille's *Story of the Eye*, each speaks of the singular "eye." The other-eye is always already lanced in language. In the symmetry between the vanishing point and the viewpoint Western painting registers the loss of that other-eye. As Bryson argues in "The Gaze in the Expanded Field":

> The viewpoint and the vanishing point are inseparable: there is no viewpoint without vanishing point, and no vanishing point without viewing point. The self-possession of the viewing subject has built into it, therefore, the principle of its own abolition: annihilation of the subject as center is a condition of the very moment of the look.
>
> (Bryson, *Vision and Visuality*: 91)

The symmetry between the vanishing point and the viewing point reflects the other side of the promise of the plenitude of visual fulfillment – the imagination of annihilation and disappearance. In this sense the historical force of perspective in discussions of Western art history acquires something of an Oedipal character. For the installation of the symmetry between the vanishing point and the viewing point (a symmetry accented more strongly in the theory and history of painting than in the act of painting itself), reflects the notion that art is a mirror for the looker – and in fact, that all looking is an attempt to find a mirror. Such a notion of looking leads to the potential annihilation of the looker. Bryson calls this aspect of Lacan's argument a "paranoid" account of a "negative and terrorizing gaze" (*Vision and Visuality*: 104–5). But I think Bryson understates the productive power of facing the inevitability of annihilation, castration, misrecognition. For if one could face these features of psychic life, a different order of sociality might be possible.

As Copjec points out, the not-all of visual representation creates in the looker a sense that there is something "beyond" the picture (and the signifying system itself) that is not shown – that is, the subject her or himself. This belief maintains desire. But for Lacan, there is nothing there at all. It is that (internal/ized) absence that visual representation continually tries to re-cover.

Representation is almost always on the side of the one who looks and almost never on the side of the one who is seen. As feminist film theorists have demonstrated, the fetishized image of the female star serves as a deeply revealing *screen* for the construction of men's desire. The image of the woman displays not the subjectivity of the woman who is seen, but rather the constituent forces of desire of the man who wants to see her.[38]

Visibility and invisibility are crucially bound; invisibility polices visibility and in this specific sense functions as the ascendant term in the binary. Gaining visibility for the politically under-represented without scrutinizing the power of who is required to display what to whom is an impoverished political agenda.

Within the psychic and aesthetic economy of the Western gaze, the visible image of the other necessarily becomes a cipher for the looking self. To overturn these economies the failure of the inward gaze to produce self-seeing needs to be acknowledged. If one could confront the internal/external other as always already lost one would not have to rely so heavily on the image of the external other to produce what the looker lacks. This suggestion is not a refusal of multicultural diversity or of a more inclusive representational landscape. It is rather a way to isolate the impotency of the inward gaze as a fundamental aspect of representational economies.

Breaks in the reciprocity of visual exchange offer opportunities to disrupt the neat substitutions of the psychic economy of seeing. Until the image of the other can be other-than a cipher for a looking self, calling for greater visibility of the under-represented will do nothing to improve the quality of our political or psychic imaginations.

How to enrich them? Seeing the hollow blindness of our own eyes is dangerous because it risks both self-absorption (one sees nothing other than the self) and self-annihilation (one sees only the nothing of the self). But until one can accept one's internal other as lost, invisible, an unmarked blank to oneself and within the world, the external other will always bear the marks and scars of the looker's deadening gaze.

What is needed to challenge the pessimism of Lacan's belief that there is nothing beyond the gaze on the one hand, and the bleak poverty of our access to identity on the other, is a different relation between the looking subject and the image of the other.[39] Arguing for ever more specific identity-quotients within *the content* of the image of the other will not upset representational economies. This new relation between the looker and the image of the other requires more attention to communicating nonvisible, rhetorically unmarked aspects of identity, and a greater willingness to accept the impotency of the inward gaze. If we could accept that impotency and loss, we would not have to press quite so hard on the visible configurations of the other. We might be able to give up – or at least to lessen our enthrallment with – the particular configurations of power and desire which inform and infect our external gaze.

V

Unmarked concentrates on the broken symmetry between the self and the other, and the possibilities this break affords for rehearsing the political consequences of an acknowledgment of a failed inward gaze. Precisely because the gaze is "not-all," representation cannot be totalizing. Representation always shows more than it means: in the supplement one can see ways to intervene in its meaning.

In writing the unmarked I mark it, inevitably. In seeing it I am marked by it. But because what I do not see and do not write is so much more vast than what I do it is impossible to "ruin" the unmarked. The unmarked is not the newest landscape vulnerable to tourists. The unmarked is not spatial; nor is it temporal; it is not metaphorical; nor is it literal. It is a configuration of subjectivity which exceeds, even while informing, both the gaze and language. In the riots of sound language produces, the unmarked can be heard as silence. In the plenitude of pleasure produced by photographic vision, the unmarked can be seen as a negative. In the analysis of the means of production, the unmarked signals the un(re)productive.

Having no particular home, no boundaries dictated by genre, the unmarked can be mapped across a wide terrain. The following chapters are concerned with the performative politics operative in photographs, paintings, films, theatre, political protest, and performance art. By suggesting that all these forms of representation participate in a performative exchange I hope to broaden current disciplinary boundaries which define the field of the gaze, the animate and the inanimate, and the seen and the unseen. Performance is the art form which most fully understands the generative possibilities of disappearance. Poised forever at the threshold of the present, performance enacts the productive appeal of the nonreproductive. Trying to suggest that the disappearance of the external other is the means by which self-assurance is achieved requires that one analyze the potential payoffs in such disappearance: performance exposes some of them.

The broad range of material considered here begins to hint at what "cultural reproduction" actually means, and suggests something of what it might take to interfere with its labor. Under the ever-growing shadow of the politically powerful New Right in the United States, I am writing against the perpetual fracturing of disciplines, specializations, and identities progressive political and critical theory has wrought. These fractures make us easy targets for a relatively unified Right. These chapters seek to establish a different idea of mutuality, sociality, and the real than those currently offered by the false monotheism of the Right and the fractured identity politics of the Left. Resisting both the moral ideological assurance of the Right and their notion of social unity and coherence, and the concentrated effort to secure visibility for the under-represented which galvanizes the Left, I hope to excavate the ruptures within visibility as deep, if always unmarked, graves – not graves to sleep a long sleep in, but graves that everywhere mine the representational field.

Chapter 2, "Developing the negative: Mapplethorpe, Schor, and Sherman," analyzes the work of Robert Mapplethorpe, Mira Schor, and Cindy Sherman. Portrait photography posits the photographer's subjectivity through recourse to the model of the other. Having access to the model of the visible other for (white) men allows contemplation of an other's body; for (white) women, access to the visible other is negotiated through the image of her own body. Mapplethorpe discovered his most revealing mirror/screen in the model of the African-American male nude. Sherman found her most potent mirror/screen in her own image, but this self-image is always already an image of the other. At once a plea for self-possession and a stark declaration of self-alienation, Sherman's photography focuses on the destructive force of visibility for white women in this culture. At first, this leads her to create images of annihilation, emptiness, and waste within the cultural landscape (films, advertisements, pornography). Eventually, however, it leads her to critique that great cemetery of female images, Western high art portrait painting. Mira Schor's work as a painter and theorist implicitly (and sometimes explicitly) critiques the projects of Mapplethorpe and Sherman. Focusing on the different reproductive claims of painting and photography, I consider the gender and sexual politics of representing the human body within these forms of representation. Exposing the negative has more than a technological application for photography.

Independent cinema has taken as one of its main projects the critique of the image articulated by Hollywood cinema; feminist independent cinema has been particularly astute at reimagining another way to represent the image of the woman. At the end of her 1985 film *The Man Who Envied Women*, Yvonne Rainer suggests that one direction for feminist representation might lie in "a-womanliness." Chapter 3, "Spatial envy: Yvonne Rainer's *The Man Who Envied Women*," considers what is often called "the negativity of feminist theory": the idea that since women in representation are always misrepresented it might be better to withhold the image of the woman altogether. In Rainer's film, Trisha, the female protagonist, is never imaged. The positive possibilities of registering filmic presence with no visible image are remarked at length. What Rainer's film provokes is a consideration of the usefulness of the term "woman" as a category for visible being.

While Rainer suggests the positive values of "what cannot be seen," Jennie Livingston's film *Paris Is Burning* documents the "appropriation" of the image of the woman by those who remain politically unseen. African-American and Latino gay men and transsexuals perform in balls in which they imitate the "other woman." Frequently she is the white woman celebrated throughout the history of Hollywood film and often disdained by progressive feminist theorists, many of whom are white. The political and sexual appropriation operative in the balls reveals a deep sympathy with "the image of the [usually white] woman," and a recognition that in relation to the image of a Latino transsexual, her image is "valued." The complex questions of symbolic identification, capitalist appetite, and the hierarchy of race raised by Livingston's film are amplified, if not resolved, by considering the film in relation to the codes of the genre of the ethnographic documentary. Chapter 4, "The golden apple: Jennie Livingston's *Paris Is Burning*," examines the paradox of staging costume balls and exhibiting one's appearance as a rehearsal for going unnoticed and looking unremarkable on the larger stage of "everyday life."

The last three chapters of the book, "Theatre and its mother: Tom Stoppard's *Hapgood*," "White men and pregnancy: discovering the body to be rescued," and "The ontology of performance: representation without reproduction," consider frames of "live" bodies in relation to a political and aesthetic field. I consider Tom Stoppard's play *Hapgood* in terms of the phantom which haunts the theatrical past, the previous performance. Investigating the claims of quantum physics as a metaphor for understanding theatrical spectatorship, Chapter 5 outlines the relationship between metatheatre and metaphysics proposed by Stoppard. Grounded in the character of "Mother," Stoppard's play suggests that the "double" haunts all our observations. The chapter concludes with a brief speculation on the possible sympathy between the Belgian physicist Ilya Prigogine's "dissipative structures" and the asymmetrical relations which adhere in the psycho-political concept of the Mother as enacted by Stoppard's titular character.

Uncomfortable with the asymmetrical legal, biological, and psychical relations between men and women around pregnancy, Operation Rescue, the anti-abortion group, has staged a series of demonstrations in which the image of the pregnant woman is erased and the independent image of the fetus becomes the focus for political action. Chapter 6, "White men and pregnancy: discovering the body to be rescued," argues that in making a visual displacement from the pregnant woman to the fetus, Operation Rescue unwittingly makes visible the consequences of the psychic and legal shift from the invisibility of paternity to its visibility. The political and legal ramifications of that shift are unsettling for both the Left and the Right, for those who are "pro-choice" and those who are "pro-life." The demonstrations and counter-demonstrations may be read as performative exchanges which formulate a new relation to paternal visibility for both groups.

The (Symbolic) Mother will never be the "proper" subject of psychoanalysis and will always be a problematic subject for Western art because as an image who potentially contains the other within one continuous body, she wreaks havoc with the notion of symmetry and reciprocity fundamental to understanding the exchange of gaze operative in both. As an image which contains simultaneously the I and the not-I, the visibly pregnant woman's body contains two sets of eyes/I. In place of the split subject and the drama of lack, the Mother raises the spectacle of a double-subject and the drama of overwhelming presence. The pregnant woman, in other words, enacts and makes Real the Imaginary unity between subject and other. As a continuous double-body, the pregnant woman extends the Imaginary into the Symbolic and overwhelms it. Lest this sound overly romantic or "essentialist," I should stress that the visibility of pregnancy is never absolute. Due to this non-absolute visibility, almost all women are seen as potential mothers.

Classical psychoanalysis cannot adequately "see" the woman-mother because she threatens to make visible the real repression of psychoanalytic theory, the limit of the reciprocal gaze. The Symbolic Mother does internalize the eyes of the other; men cannot repeat or imitate that internalization; nor can they bear its return. Operation Rescue attempts to remove the skin of the pregnant woman to reveal the eyes of her internal other, the "independent" fetus. By displaying the fetus as the single image within the triangulation of reproduction, Operation Rescue attempts to ignore the dilemma of the pregnant woman entirely and to leave unmarked the freedom of (invisible) paternity. As paternity moves more clearly into the domain of the visible, the drama around abortion and reproductive control intensifies.

While the members of Operation Rescue are extreme in their methods, they merely make manifest a persistent and pervasive desire to employ visibility to control women's bodies. Increasingly, such control extends to both the inside and the outside image of our bodies. This fascination motivates Cary's retelling of the West Indian folk tale in which the husband rubs salt on the inside of his wife's skin, and also provokes the brilliant collapse of the cinematic and gynecological gaze in David Cronenberg's *Dead Ringers*. In excessively marking the boundaries of the woman's *body*, in order to make it thoroughly visible, patriarchal culture subjects it to legal, artistic, and psychic surveillance.[40] This, in turn, reinforces the idea that she *is* her body.

Just as law cannot conceive of a pregnant body as a continuous body and searches endlessly for the exact moment in which a fetus is "independent," neither can Freudian psychoanalysis – and the (male) psychic subject constructed there – tolerate a gaze which does not include him.[41] Insofar as women's bodies contain the symbolic potential of reproducing another set of eyes, eyes that look only at the inside of their bodies and not at him, he will long to tear their bodies open, to spread their legs wider, to make their "insides" visible to his eyes.

In my final chapter, "The ontology of performance: representation without reproduction," I consider the ontological claims of live performance art as a means of resisting the reproductive ideology of visible representations. Defined by its ephemeral nature, performance art cannot be documented (when it is, it turns into that document – a photograph, a stage design, a video tape – and ceases to be performance art). In this sense, performance art is the least marked of all the texts I consider here. In the work of Angelika Festa, a so-called "ordeal artist," staging disappearance becomes a signature expression of women's subjectivity within phallocentric representation. The price of that disappearance is difficult to calculate. However, part of its summarizing force comes from the enactment of a nonreproductive performing female body. Feminist theorists concerned with reconceiving the associative links between women and reproduction would do well to take seriously what this art work suggests about the possibilities and limits of that project.

This particular cultural moment exerts an urgent pressure to account for what cannot be reproduced. As those artists who have dedicated themselves to performance continually disappear and leave "not a rack behind" it becomes increasingly imperative to find a way to remember the undocumentable, unreproducible art they made. The paradox is that in writing a testimony to the power of the undocumentable and nonreproductive I engage the document of the written reproducible text itself.

This is the paradox of Lacan's Real, the Real-impossible toward which we aspire and whose failure to realize is utterly assured. In the fulsome guarantee of this failure, writing records the memory of the image of the future that will not be – the one I will never see. (They are dying and they have taken that future with them.) I am writing in that blank about that disappearance.

The impossible tense and tension of this time are always already written. A fragment then from Rilke, who saw the generative power of nostalgia for a future that will never become past.

On nights like this my little sister rises.
She was born and died before me. Very small.

On nights like this she combs her hair. They watch

the moon afraid to move. I watch her choose
her dress, her shoes.

There have been other nights. Mostly long ago.
She is so beautiful now. Tomorrow, the hopeful will call.[42]

(After Rilke's "A Stormy Night," Part VIII)

VI

The work of theory, under current economic conditions can only be, for most of us, a labor of love. Insofar as love is a labor, a trying, an essay, it, like theory, cannot *be* anything but an offering, a giving of what one does not have, a description and transcription of what one cannot see or prove with visible evidence. Shoshana Felman has suggested that in this giving of what one does not have the speaking body perpetuates a "scandal":

> The scandal [of the speech act] is always in a certain way the scandal of the promise of love, the scandal of the *untenable*, that is, still and always, the scandal [. . .] of the promising animal, incapable of keeping his promise, incapable of not making it, powerless both to fulfill the commitment and to avoid *committing* himself.
>
> (original emphases; The Literary Speech Act: 150)

But if this scandal "is always," "that is, still and always" present, what makes us (mis)recognize it as scandalous? Perhaps the failure of the promise, like the failure of erotic love, is not so much scandalous as the constituent force of the banal and normative theatre of the everyday. In the deep hope of that promise and the repeated enactment of its failure, the looker, like the lover, desires an/other revision of memory, sight, and love.

The scenario of the erotic is framed between the promise and the failure of this revision. The repetition of failure is the ground from which memory, sight, love, and their theories are re-experienced. "Failure, to be sure, pervades every performance, including that of theory, which in turn becomes erotic for *being nothing* but a failed act, or an act of failing" (my emphases; Felman, *The Literary Speech Act*: 111). The eroticism of the failure of writing, like the eroticism of love's failing, is the energy necessary to maintain the belief in a blind eye.

With every mark, the unmarked summons the other eye to see what the mark is blind to – what the given to be seen fails to show, what the other cannot offer. The dramas of concealment, disguise, secrets, lies, are endemic to visual representation, exactly because visual representation is "not all." The myth of Oedipus is a central psychoanalytic myth because it makes knowledge itself productive of blindness. Oedipus' self-blinding is less a symptom of his regretful desire, and more a marking of the impossible desire to see oneself. By declaring our eyes blind and impotent we may be able to resist the smooth reproduction of the self-same. We may begin to be able to inhabit the blank without forcing the other to fill it.

At the limit of the physical body, at the limit of the blind eye, at the limit of the signifier, one sees both the knowledge of failure and the performance of belief propped up on all sides by serious and comic doubt. Certain of failure, I inscribe, again, my hope for blind (and forgiving) eyes.

2

Developing the negative: Mapplethorpe, Schor, and Sherman

[C]onfronted with the photograph, as in the dream, it is the same effort, the same Sisyphean labor: to reascend, straining toward the essence, to climb back down without having seen it, and to begin all over again.

(Roland Barthes, *Camera Lucida*: 66)

[T]he relation between the gaze and what one wishes to see involves a lure. The subject is presented as other than he is, and what one shows him is not what he wants to see. It is in this way that the eye may function as *objet a*, that is to say, at the level of the lack.

(Lacan, *Four Fundamental Concepts*: 104)

Barthes' *Camera Lucida* is a lamentation for his mother. An anatomy of the grief of the surviving singular I/eye, *Camera Lucida* details the search for the perfect image, the *punctum* of the photograph which will return her to him. Employing public and "private" photographs, Barthes educates his eye to see that he has not seen what he wants to see *and* to look again. This double action, the recognition of not-seeing and the will to look again, is the lure of the image repertoire. The double action confirms the distinction between the gaze and the eye: the eye, ever hungry, ever restless, temporarily submits to the law of the gaze, the ocular perspective which frames the image, sees what is shown and discovers it to be "lacking." Not quite the thing one wants/needs/ desires/to see. And what is that thing? An image of self-seeing that is complete. An impossible image precisely because the law of the gaze prohibits self-seeing.

Always compensatory, however, the law of the gaze is invested with a lure, an image to distract one from that failure. The lure is the erotic kernel of the gaze. Desire is enflamed by the lure, by the gaping space between the gaze and the eye. In the opening created by the distinction between the eye and the gaze, the seeing I is split (again). The burden of portrait photography is both to reveal and conceal this gap.

In *Camera Lucida* Barthes attempts to find an image which captures some "essence" by which he might recognize and thus retain his dead mother. Restlessly, he rummages through a private and public collection of portrait photographs. Unsatisfied, Barthes keeps looking for the *punctum*, the partial image (the *objet a*) which might return her to him. *Fort. Da.* His partial gaze must see her partial image. In writing of his ongoing search for her return, he plots the perfect image – the glimpse of "essence" that will distill who she was for him. (We are, despite our best intentions, stuck with essences, and essentialisms. And perhaps never more fully than when the body of the beloved has vanished. For in that disappearance we are made to feel again the grief of our own essential absence from our deepest selves, our failure to answer our most central questions: "Margaret, are you grieving?")

At last Barthes secures the image he believes will return her to him. He calls it the Winter Garden photograph and withholds it from us. (To display her "perfect" image to us would be to reveal both too much and too little. The paucity of the image would not withstand our hungry all-consuming eyes.) Barthes turns the image over, shows us the blank back, and locates her in his imagination of her childhood. Grieving because she will not be a witness to the rest of his life, Barthes consoles himself with an image of her life before he was a witness to it. In turning back to an image of her before his birth, he is able to imagine himself without her.

I

All portrait photography is fundamentally performative. Richard Avedon argues that portrait photographers learned about acting from the great painters of self-portraits, and especially from Rembrandt. Avedon encounters a carpenter in his home who is the spitting image of Rembrandt. After Avedon shows the carpenter Rembrandt's self-portraits (and the carpenter agrees the portraits are him – "This one, of course, was when I was younger"), Avedon sets up his camera and asks the carpenter to imitate the images he has just seen.

> Rembrandt the carpenter acted Rembrandt the painter exactly. It seemed undeniable to me that Rembrandt must have been acting when he made his own self-portraits. [. . .] Not just making faces, but always, throughout his life, working in the full tradition of performance. Elaborate costumes, a turban, a beret, a cloak, the rags of a beggar, the golden cloth of a sultan, and someone's dog – really performing in a very self-conscious way.
>
> ("Borrowed Dogs": 16)

Like Barthes who called photography "a kind of primitive theatre"

(*Camera Lucida*: 32), Avedon accents the artificiality (the art-fiction) of photographic portraiture. Portrait photography tries to make an inner form, a (negative) shadow, expressive: a developed image which renders the corporeal, a body-real, as a real body. Uncertain about what this body looks like or how substantial it is, we perform an image of it by imitating what we think we look like. We imagine what people might see when they look at us, and then we try to perform (and conform to) those images.[1] These ideas are based on what we think we see when we look at people we believe we resemble – beggars, sultans, dog owners. Costume and fashion function to perfect the image stereotype. Wanting to look like someone else, we quote and imitate the look of the visible model. And even trend-setting models like Madonna try to look like someone else – Marilyn Monroe, for the moment.

To recognize oneself in a portrait (and in a mirror) one imitates the image one imagines the other sees. "To imitate is no doubt to reproduce an image" (Lacan, *Four Fundamental Concepts*: 100). The imitative reproduction of the self-image always involves a detour through the eye of the other. "The gaze I encounter [. . .] is not a seen gaze, but a gaze imagined by me in the field of the Other" (ibid.: 84). Like Virginia Woolf's conception of letter-writing as an attempt "to give back a reflection of the other person," portrait photography reflects the transference of image between the photographer and the model.[2] Like a good correspondence, the model's reply to the inquiry of the photographer is based on the quality of the photographer's question. Portrait photography is the record of the model's self-inquiry, an inquiry framed and directed by the photographer's attempt to discover what he sees. Models imitate the image they believe photographers see through the camera lens. Photographers develop the image as they touch the shutter; models perform what they believe that image looks like. And spectators see again what they do and do not look like.

The performative nature of portrait photography complicates the traditional claims of the camera to reproduce an authentic "real." Champions of photography at the turn of the century praised the camera for capturing nature so adequately that photography made art the "same" as nature.[3] To see a mountain and to see a photograph of a mountain communicated the same feeling of awe, or so the argument went. But as Heidegger succinctly pointed out, "for something to be the same, one is always enough. Two are not needed" (*Identity and Difference*: 23–4). In the photographic field, however, one is never enough.

Reproduction within portrait photography is always a double copy: an imitation of the gaze of the other *and* a copy of the negative. As Rosalind Krauss has argued in her rereading of Walter Benjamin, the very concept of artistic "originality" is made impossible by the ontology of the photograph itself.[4] Without a stable "original," the status of the real also comes under scrutiny. The model's body is "real," but the image of that body is, like all images, an account of the gaze's relation to the lure.

The art of the photographer resides in the staged confrontation with the surface of the print, and the art of modeling resides in the confrontation with one's body, the surface image upon which subjectivity is visible to the camera's eye.[5] For Avedon the performative emerges in the dual manipulation of the surface of the photographic image and the surface of the model's body.

> Portraiture is performance, and like any performance, in the balance of its effects it is good or bad, not natural or unnatural. I can understand being troubled by this idea – that all portraits are performances – because it seems to imply some kind of artifice that conceals the truth about the sitter. But that's not it at all.
>
> The point is that you can't get at the thing itself, the real nature of the sitter, by stripping away the surface. The surface is all you've got. You can only get beyond the surface by working with the surface. All that you can do is to manipulate that surface – gesture, costume, expression – radically and correctly.
>
> ("Borrowed Dogs": 17)

Perhaps no contemporary photographers are better known for their manipulation of the image of the body, the surface of subjectivity, than Robert Mapplethorpe and Cindy Sherman. In contemporary culture that subjectivity is related to a discourse of sex and sexuality. The aesthetic motivations and ideological impulses behind their manipulations are different and yet the fundamental desire to toy with the surface of the image and to expose the erotic theatricality of the sexual body, is common to each. Mira Schor, a contemporary painter and feminist art theorist, offers an important corrective to Mapplethorpe's assumptions about the connection between male subjectivity and sexuality; her work anticipates some of the issues raised by Sherman's most recent performative self-portraits which are inquiries into the history of fine art's portrait paintings.

II

Mapplethorpe often declared his antipathy toward photography. Trained as a sculptor, much of Mapplethorpe's work aspires toward three-dimensionality. Borrowing the canvas of painting and printing his photographs on linen soaked in platinum, he created a geometrical alphabet of shapes draped in silk and velvet which he hung above or behind the "printed" canvas. Lush, large, and lyrical, Mapplethorpe's photographs are images angling to be objects.[6] In a 1987 interview, Mapplethorpe remarked: "I never liked photography. [. . .] I like the object. I like photographs when you hold them in your hand" (*Robert Mapplethorpe*: n.p.). Like the desire to transform the phallus into the penis, changing the image into an object seems to hold a promising payoff – "you [can then] hold them in your hand."

Much of Mapplethorpe's photography depicts the male nude, and a significant part of that *oeuvre* is devoted to black men. His photography is shot through with a heady classicism, a reverential attitude toward the statuesque poses of the Greeks, and a rigorous formalism (Figure 3). What distinguishes his work from painting is the way in which photography's mechanical ontology transforms the attitude of his compositions. Like other artists working in the epoch presaged by Walter Benjamin's "art in the age of mechanical reproduction," Mapplethorpe's work uses the camera eye to investigate subjectivity. His wager is that for men the sexual is the most deeply subjective, that in fact, the two are synonymous. For him, men's – and especially gay men's – most dramatic confrontations involve the battle between the mechanical "objective" and the sexual-subjective. The gaze ravages the print, the eye accosts the model: the lure for the looker is to touch him – to hold him in your hand. Mapplethorpe's cool camera serves the model up untouched; the image's impression on the paper invites the spectator to fantasize the pressure of that touch. Erotic photography solicits the touch and defers it: instead of skin, paper. Instead of sex, the devouring gaze.[7]

Now that Mapplethorpe is known as "the photographer who died of AIDS" we are prompted to reconsider the ontological relation between the reproduction of the photographic body and the reproduction of the sexual body – and especially in nonreproductive "safe" sex. What David Cook and Arthur Kroker call "sex without secretions" is sex as only secret.[8] Secret sex. The sex of secrets. Safe sex as the end of shared secrets? The fluid body converted into a solid, impervious to porousness: safe sex reverses the orderly chemistry of sexual exchange – from solid to fluid – and remains solid. Mapplethorpe's late work can perhaps be seen as a complicated reply to the terror of the reproductive, proliferating virus in relation to the reproductive possibilities of photography. (I want to accent that this is extremely speculative – and I'm offering it with some trepidation. Such readings are especially vulnerable to charges of naïve formalism (at the least): I'm offering it here only as a terrain that might be followed more carefully by others.) Mapplethorpe's desire to turn his images into objects might be an attempt to erase the porous moment in the negative pan which can be repeated indefinitely with the same negative. Mapplethorpe's "images-as-objects" cannot proliferate with the same abandon as the (simple)

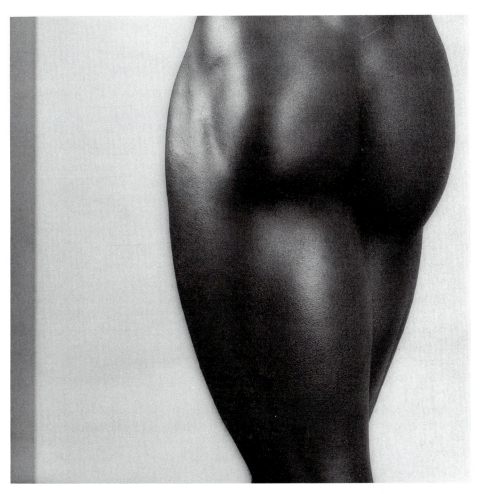

Figure 3 Robert Mapplethorpe, *Derrick Cross* (1983). (Courtesy: The Estate of Robert Mapplethorpe, New York)

print. The secrets of the replicating virus will not be secreted in an infinitely expanding circle of correspondence.[9]

The satisfaction promised (if always deferred) by looking is the possibility of the reciprocal gaze – if one looks one might possibly be seen. These satisfactions we now see may also be censored if "they" win. (If one never sees oneself reflected, perhaps one does not, cannot, exist.) The same pressure that leads the press to formulate and repeat the apposition "Mapplethorpe, the photographer who died of AIDS," hopes to create a "safe sex" mantra for the gaze itself – a pre-sterilizing gaze legislating and screening less "safe" looking. But I hope their non-subtle secret has soaked through their smoke screen. The stain is the screen of the gaze.

> Ope then, mine eyes, your double sluice,
> And practice so your noblest use;
> For others too can see, or sleep,
> But only human eyes can weep.[10]

Mapplethorpe's self-portrait of 1988 portends his death and also makes clear the aim of his earlier self-portraits. In this, Mapplethorpe's fascination with Catholicism is made manifest: the "last" self-image redefines the earlier ones in much the way the moment of death defines (all too clearly) the narrative of the life lived. In the 1988 portrait his face floats in a sea of black (Figure 4). Wearing a black sweater, his torso is already "swallowed up" by the negative pan. On the left side of the frame, his fist clutches a walking stick. At the top of the stick, above his white hand, an eyeless skull greets the viewer's gaze, threatening to "reflect" that gaze as itself on the brink of vanishing. The image of the self, Mapplethorpe suggests, can only be glimpsed in its disappearance. To greet it, one risks blindness, vanishing. The "disguise" of his earlier self-portraits becomes more pointed in relation to this one. Disappearing behind the lipstick and eye shadow of a woman (1980), behind the leather jacket and machine gun of a terrorist (1983), edging over to the far right of the frame and leaving his left arm flung out across the space of the frame (1975) – Mapplethorpe's previous self-portraits arrest the self-image as it slides into becoming an image of an "other." The image captured by the camera is an image which is performed in order to define the central absence of the self-image.

The perfect circle of the skull at the top of the cane of the 1988 portrait recalls another perfect circle captured by Mapplethorpe's lens. His portrait of the painter Alice Neel (1984), shortly before her death, focuses on her open mouth (Figure 5). Cropped just below her neck, the photograph closely focuses on her shut eyes, a few hairs beneath her chin, the texture of her facial skin. The vanishing point of the photograph is the painter's hollow open mouth. The cavernous chasm of the painter's

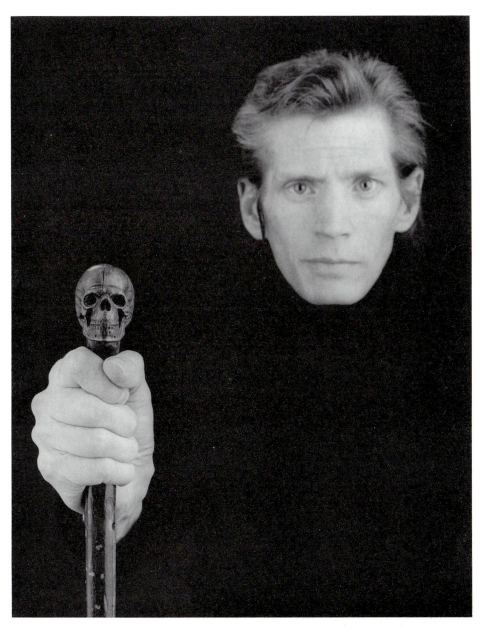

Figure 4 Robert Mapplethorpe, *Self-Portrait* (1988). (Courtesy: The Estate of Robert Mapplethorpe, New York)

body, her open mouth, is "stolen" and then copied by the photographer's open eye. Perfectly mirroring the circle of the camera's lens – aperture open to receive the vanishing light of Neel's image – her mouth *is* his eye. Neel's open mouth makes viewers shudder when they see the moment when Mapplethorpe's shutter shut.

When then did it open?

In the beginning of his career Mapplethorpe sought a visual equivalent for the relationship between the "real" penis, and the phallic structures it symbolized.[11] *Man in Polyester Suit* (1980) is perhaps the best-known example of this tendency, but it appears in an earlier and more complicated image as well. In *Brian Ridley and Lyle Heeter* (1979), two men in leather and chains posed amid a bizarrely equipped living room (Figure 6). Mapplethorpe, following Genet, suggests the affinity between sado-masochistic erotic pleasure and the police – and uncannily foreshadows the controversy his work has incited: the House and Senate locked together hovering nervously over their complicity in supporting the "documentation" of s/m.[12]

The comparison with Genet is not superficial. Genet's notion of the theatrical is deeply enfolded within his notion of the sexual. The theatrical promise of the double and the reversal appeals to Genet because this is the same promise as the sexually perverse – a promise which is logically and emotionally pure. (This is in part because perversity solicits the *reversal* of purity – an inversion Genet loved to touch as much as Bataille.) Mapplethorpe's formalism was his version of Genet's purity. Genet, who was illegitimate and wore only the name of his mother, loved flowers because they said his name (*genêt*: broom-flower, ginestra).[13] Like his fascination with crosses, Mapplethorpe's steady concentration on flowers can be seen as an *hom(m)age* to Genet. Man to man. To return then to this early image of those other two men, *Brian Ridley and Lyle Heeter*.

The perfect shadow in profile against the curtain suggests the silhouette of "the police officer" powerfully mythologized in Hollywood film and television. The hand cuffs, the "prisoner" in chains on the chair, the wary gaze of the standing man, all connote the iconography of the police state. While seemingly examining what links these two visible men, the photograph also records the bond between the man in chains and the one in shadow who wants to put him there. "Normal" desire cannot be conceived without the possibility of transgressive desire – both s/m couples and the police rely on one another's shadows. Photography, Mapplethorpe suggests, is complicitous in maintaining these negatives. At once the instrument of surveillance and fodder for "the pornographic imagination," photography polices even while maintaining the "sexually perverse." These categories of "pornography" and "perversity" depend on the curious fascination of the spectator's

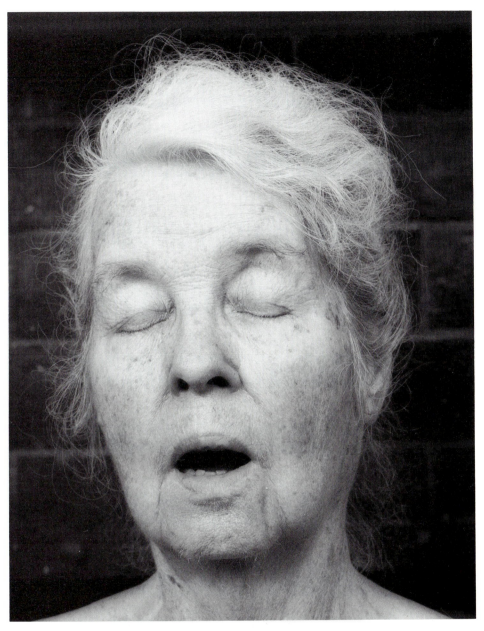

Figure 5 Robert Mapplethorpe, *Alice Neel* (1984). (Courtesy: The Estate of Robert Mapplethorpe, New York)

Figure 6 Robert Mapplethorpe, *Brian Ridley and Lyle Heeter* (1979). (Courtesy: The Estate of Robert Mapplethorpe, New York)

voyeuristic pleasure, a pleasure that pivots on the axis of purity/ perversity.

Structured within Mapplethorpe's photograph is an acknowledgment of its creation and reception. The shadow behind the men mirrors the spectator in front of them. The first such spectator is Mapplethorpe himself, the man behind the box surveying his subjects. In this, Mapplethorpe is the "mother" of the image in the way that Irigaray speaks of the mother as the "origin" of the shadow and the copy in Plato's cave.[14] The negative and the print in Mapplethorpe's work (re)produce an image which reflects Mapplethorpe himself – one that "resembles" him and also allows him to recognize himself as "different."

Mimesis seeks always an aesthetic of resemblance. What Mapplethorpe's work insists on, however, is how deeply such resemblance requires a detour through "the other," if only as a way of affirming a basic resemblance. Mapplethorpe's aesthetization of and love for black men is complex. His work makes use of a racist mythos which exploits the tropes of black male virility and appropriates the history of slavery.[15] Mapplethorpe is alert to these implications, if not always suspicious enough about them to make him completely "innocent" as an artist-spectator. In his photographs of black men, Mapplethorpe tries to suggest a symmetrical relationship between the visible image of the black man *in* the frame and the invisible image of the white man behind the camera. In *Leland Richard* (1980), he suggests the possibility that the pose performed by his model, fists behind his back, is also an imitation of Mapplethorpe's own pose as the photographer behind his lens holding a time release shutter (Figure 7). What he risks in establishing this symmetry is that the image of "a black man" turns out to be a portrait of a white man. Such an effort can only reveal "the blind spot of an old dream of Symmetry" (Irigaray, *Speculum*: 11). Broken by the history and practice of racism, such symmetry can only be established by its negative.

The Other then is transformed into the image of the Same, an image projected by he who looks at the other in order to see himself. The economy of representation, like the economy of reproduction, takes two and reproduces One. In Mapplethorpe's photography the black man functions in much the way the woman functions in Freudian and Lacanian psychoanalysis. "It is not enough for women to lack the penis, they must be envious, driven by the desire to have it, thereby confirming to men that they still possess it" (Diamond, "Mimesis": 63). In Mapplethorpe's portraits, the virility of the black model is emphasized in order to assure the white male spectator of his own. The assurance is performed by allowing the viewer to "possess" the image which remains immobile within the frame of Mapplethorpe's photograph and within the frame of the spectator's gaze.

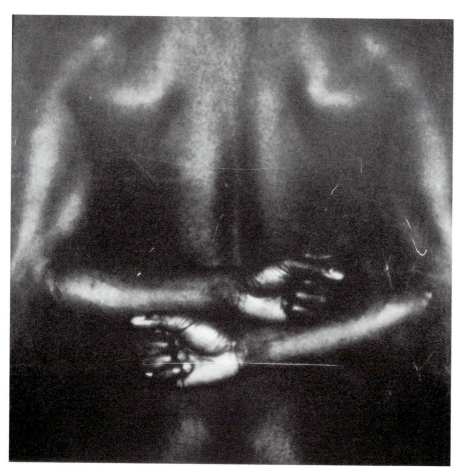

Figure 7 Robert Mapplethorpe, *Leland Richard* (1980). (Courtesy: The Estate of Robert Mapplethorpe, New York)

While white heterosexual culture accuses the white gay man of effeminacy – and relies on a pervasive misogyny for the accusation's powerful
sting – Mapplethorpe's work repudiates that accusation by employing
the black "stud" as an assurance of gay virility – and relies on pervasive
racism to sharpen the sting. The performance required of the black
model is the imitative pose of white culture's stereotypical images of the
black man – the soldier, the dancer, the playboy, the slave.

Mapplethorpe's treatment of the racially marked body replicates the
operative power of whiteness, politically and psychically. The photographs confirm and reproduce the dominant ideology of a normative
whiteness, an ideology which employs blackness as a commodity to be
purchased and/or appropriated. (Whiteness is "confirmed" by the
hyper-accessibility of the image of blackness – the assumption of entitle-
ment operative in the "close up" look links – however unconsciously
and dimly – the surveyors of these photographs with slave owners.)

And yet the images are undeniably beautiful, alluring, captivating.
Within the economy of the aesthetics of Western art history,
Mapplethorpe finds the "new" Greek white statue in his black model,
Ajitto (four portraits from 1981). Like the cropping of the face of his model
in *Man in Polyester Suit*, Mapplethorpe averts the face of Ajitto (Figure 8),
rendering him as "pure" body in perfect form, lacking the "subjectivity"
usually registered by a returning gaze. In 1987, Mapplethorpe refigures
Leonardo's *Vetruvian Man* as *Thomas in a Circle* (1987): the value of
symmetry so central to Western art history is upheld, while the model's
face is again averted.[16] I shall return to this aversion later, but for now I
want to emphasize that Mapplethorpe's replication of Western art history's formalist values securely established him as a serious aesthetician –
albeit working in a "low" art with degraded models.[17]

Mapplethorpe's "radical" pursuit of the question of homoerotic desire
can be seen, then, to be purchased by the conservative replication of
racist and formalist ideology. This in no way upsets the market economy
of the art world. The market, as Victor Burgin rightly insists, "is 'behind'
nothing, it is *in* everything" (*End of Art Theory*: 174). The question is
then: can there be a resistant artistic practice when the commodification
of that practice is always already at work? Abigail Solomon-Godeau
argues that such resistant work "must be predicated on its ability to
sustain critique from within the heart of the system it seeks to put in
question" ("Living with Contradictions": 207). The "heart of the system"
Mapplethorpe questions is neither the commodification of art, nor the
formal values of art history. The system Mapplethorpe "puts in question" is heterosexism. His failure to see the relationship between heterosexism and racism is significant, but so too is the critique of
heterosexism that his work manages to sustain.

Mapplethorpe's celebratory erotics of the image of the male body

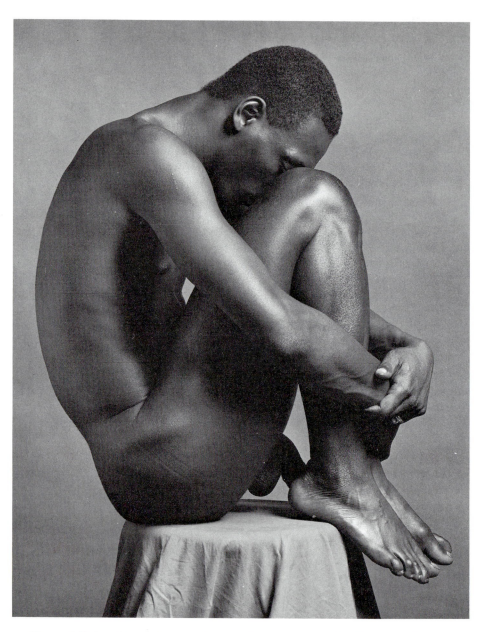

Figure 8 Robert Mapplethorpe, *Ajitto* (1981). (Courtesy: The Estate of Robert Mapplethorpe, New York)

opens up a slightly different psychoanalytic terrain than usual accounts of visual pleasure. Hunger for the same – including the sexual same – *demands* a difference, if only to elicit the pleasure of resemblance. If there is no perceived effort to "convert" or "transform" the apparently different into the Same then there is no "production" at work. And in looking there is always (re)production. The conversion of the abject other (the racially marked, the sexually unmarked) into the Same is an integral part of artistic production. Artistic reproduction transforms the always-abject other into the Same by making that other its object. As Freud reminds us, "the finding of an object is in fact a refinding of it" (*Three Essays*: 81).

In focusing on the physical resemblance between the bodies of Mapplethorpe and his male models (taking the Same as his beginning point rather than his ending point), a surplus of desire for the-other-to-be-converted is created and is "answered" in part by the image of racial difference. In *Ken Moody and Robert Sherman* (1984) posing in almost exactly matching profiles, the models' skin color carries the charge of difference. Even more pointedly, in the beautifully echoic pose of *Ken and Tyler* (1985), the physically "same" and the racially "different" dance (Figure 9). Mapplethorpe is concerned with the difference of al/chemical color which produces and reproduces images in black and white. The desire to read difference, so as to convert it back into the Same, is accented by Mapplethorpe precisely because he creates almost exact model-copies *within* the image of the photograph.

This doubling of the image within the frame points to the doubling crucial to the ontology, in its visual and temporal spheres, of photography. Rosalind Krauss, elaborates some of the consequences of this doubling:

> [D]oubling [. . .] produces the formal rhythm of spacing – the two-step that banishes the unitary condition of the moment, that creates *within* the moment an experience of fission. For it is doubling that elicits the notion that to an original has been added its copy. The double is the simulacrum, the second, the representative of the original. [. . .] But in being seen in conjunction with the original, the double destroys the pure singularity of the first. Through duplication, it opens the original to the effect of difference, of deferral, of one-thing-after-another, or within another: of multiples burgeoning within the same.
>
> (original emphasis; *Originality*: 109)

In other words, the "original" moment in which Ken and Tyler posed is "preserved" and thus doubled by the photograph itself. In the "recollection" prompted by the image, a return to and repetition of that moment is made possible. Moreover, the double image within *Ken and Tyler*

Figure 9 Robert Mapplethorpe, *Ken and Tyler* (1985). (Courtesy: The Estate of Robert Mapplethorpe, New York)

illustrates the way in which all seeing is relational and dependent upon a negation. The space between the models defines their bodies – and their bodies are differentiated by the distinction between their skin colors.

Kobena Mercer observes that "the way in which the glossy allure of [Mapplethorpe's] high-quality monochrome print becomes consubstantial with the shiny texture of black skin" transforms his model into a fetish. "Such fetishism," Mercer continues, "only eroticizes the most visible aspect of racial difference – skin color" ("Looking for Trouble": 187). Mapplethorpe's prints make the black nudes look as if they are soaking up all the light in the print itself. The model's body becomes like a pool drawing the viewer's eye in to the "vanishing point" of blackness itself. Resisting this pool the spectator's eye seizes the skin of the nude and hangs on it.

Mapplethorpe's photography does "objectify" men, but what is astonishing about his work is how much room there is for dignity despite this objectification. His photography demonstrates that love and understanding of a body, while always involving objectification, precisely because it is made over in the mind and eye of the other, do not have to violate or eliminate the private grace and power of the model. It should be stressed, however, that it very much matters that this is accomplished primarily with male models. Sexual objectification of men allows for an ascendancy toward "power" while sexual objectification of women almost always implies a degradation. This is absolutely and crucially connected to how men and women are seen within a patriarchical ideology of heterosexuality and sexual difference. The men in Mapplethorpe's photography avoid becoming objects precisely because they carry the charge of the sexual, while women who carry the same charge within representation are almost always degradingly objectified.[18] Despite the fact that the homoerotic aspect of Mapplethorpe's photographs would seem to prompt a "degraded" valuation of his work, in fact the heterosexual valuation of maleness *per se* lends his work value.

III

For several years Mira Schor's painting has employed a kind of disguised allusion to photography and film. She paints on a series of small canvases, usually 16 by 20 inches, and stacks them vertically. A cross between a very complicated jigsaw puzzle, an homage to Polaroid artists like David Hockney, and a precisely edited film, Schor's painting works by accretion – the carefully elaborate arrangement of a narrative and visual image. Two images from 1987, *Caul of Self* and *Tracings of Caul of Self*, for example, are complexly related to one another and express the main themes of the work I will discuss here (Figure 10). *Caul of Self* is composed of five canvases stacked vertically, while *Tracings of Caul of Self* mirrors that image by tracing the painting on rice paper and covering the image over with another layer of rice paper. The covering paper is arranged in exactly the same proportions as the painting. Intended to be exhibited side by side, the canvas and the paper mirror one another in a kind of extended pun on the artist's first name (the mira/mirror which amplifies "the call of self"). The rice paper which covers over the image has the artist's handwriting printed on the interior side. The words attempt, unsuccessfully, to paper over the image. Like the membrane which sometimes covers the head of the fetus at the birth of a caul baby, *Tracings* doubly veils the self represented. When seen next to each other, the two images create a two-eyed figure with a double embryo – suggesting that the force of reproduction which is highlighted as so essential to photography also informs the work of the painter, and especially informs the work of women artists.

Inspired in part by Leo Steinberg's study *The Sexuality of Christ* (1983), Schor has made a series of paintings examining sexuality and repro-duction which can be seen as an important counterpoint to Mapplethorpe's work. *The Impregnation of M.* (1987) depicts the body of the Virgin Mary (Figure 11). In the middle of the Virgin's body where one expects to see the navel/uterus Schor paints an immensely erotic ear. The word of God, in all its potency, penetrated Mary's singular ear and Christ was conceived, or so the story goes. The "ear" functions as a displaced uterus and positions women as auditors; they are both those who hear and those who keep the accounts. Additionally, the link between the mother-woman is also clarified. Since the "Virgin" is impregnated via the word, all women who hear phallogocentric language are potential "mothers" waiting for a potent and generative word. The fecundity of the ear becomes the key to reproduction as Schor's work depicts in exhaustive detail the strange twinning of ears and penises.[19]

Schor's 1989 painting *small ear* seems like a direct response to Mapplethorpe. Taking his claim that the penis can be the source of subjectivity, Schor paints the penis as the face and wittily adds a tiny ear to it (Figure 12). If potency is the soul of this character, he won't hear much and he won't see much – he'll just fire off missiles and missals of words.[20] The painting works as a displacement of a previous displace-ment. The displacement from the genitals to the face which Freud described as a regular feature of the unconscious in *The Interpretation of Dreams* (p. 422) is here reversed by Schor. Instead of transforming the penis into a face, she transforms the face into a penis. Rather than the usual "effacement" of women by their sexuality – the artistic send-up of which can perhaps best be seen in Judy Chicago's *Dinner Party* – Schor

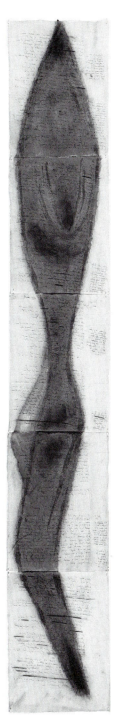

Figure 10 Mira Schor, *Caul of Self* and *Tracings of Caul of Self* (1987), one image of two paintings. (Photo: Sarah Wells. Courtesy: Mira Schor)

Figure 11 Mira Schor, *The Impregnation of M.* (1987). (Photo: Sarah Wells. Courtesy: Mira Schor)

implicitly assents to Mapplethorpe's idea that men are coequal with their genitals.[21]

In *Don't Forget Me* (1989), Schor infantilizes the penis (Figure 13). Terribly small and plaintive, the penis crawls on the bottom of the canvas toward two large female ears, to whom it seems connected, drawn. The ears seem to represent the mother and the lover, the two women to whom the eternally young boy-man seems forever bound. The double-eared woman is truly doubled: double hearing is necessary for a woman in a world which constructs her genitals as lack and effaces her face; she must listen as hard for that which is not and cannot be uttered as for that which is. In *Audition* (1988), the thrust of power between the ear and the penis is overwhelming: at 40 by 112 inches, the scale of the painting is imposing (Figure 14). A commentary on the politics of hearing and speaking, writing and reading, the painting seems to suggest that all "try outs," all hearings, are inextricably sexual, and that even when the man seems most ear/nestly listening, he is most earnestly ready to penetrate. Geoffrey Hartman has called our dangerous susceptibility to words "ear fear," and argues that the tease of the literary text "provokes an erection of the ear" (*Saving the Text*: 143). Hartman argues that "this ear fear is fundamental," and citing Nietzsche, suggests that it can only be allayed by rhyme "and other forms of a repeated and compulsive tonality" (ibid.: 157). The constant doubling in Schor's work stresses this repetition compulsion. It also suggests the mimetic *imitatio* of all painting – the repeated tracing of the brush, the repetition of color, the shape of the image. A kind of visual rhyme, complete with assonance, alliteration, and iambs, is integral to painting; like photography it too must consider its own relation to reproduction.[22]

Even as I write this, though, Schor's painting refuses my argument, and resists its status as a kind of literary text by reversing the left-to-right order of my reading. *Audition* suggests that even when the "ear" is "speaking," (an unusual condition) her auditor is thrusting forward – the energetic Turnerian yellow on the right side makes "his" ear seem even larger. The detailed ear canal recalls the birth canal, suggesting the reproduction and mimicry associated with hearing and birthing. "Ear fear" is here cataloged as a warning against the susceptibility of the ear to penetration, an homage to the power and fear of mis-hearing. It also suggests that painting's repeated resistance to being only "read/red" might be related to women's resistance to being seen as only receptacles for reproduction.

Schor's best painting in this series, *Imperfect Transmission* (1989), tries to conceive of an equality between the sexes, between hearing and speaking. The "transmitting voice," the generative text, is outside the main line of the painting (Figure 15). The mini canvas of a small red

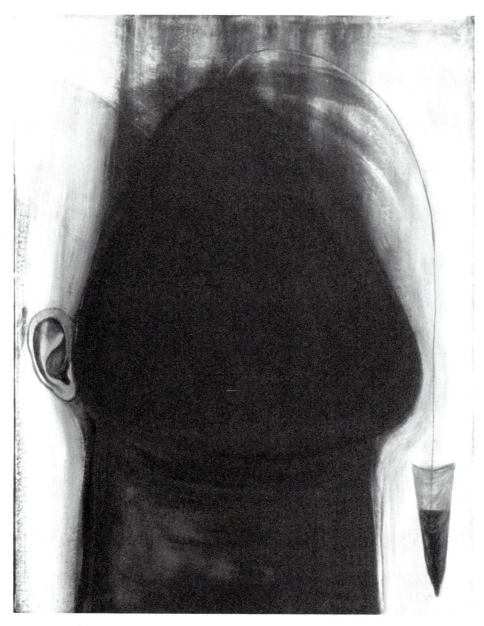

Figure 12 Mira Schor, *small ear* (1989). (Photo: Pelka/Noble. Courtesy: Mira Schor)

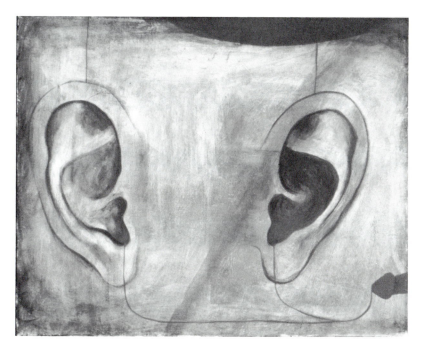

Figure 13 Mira Schor, *Don't Forget Me* (1989). (Photo: Pelka/Noble. Courtesy: Mira Schor)

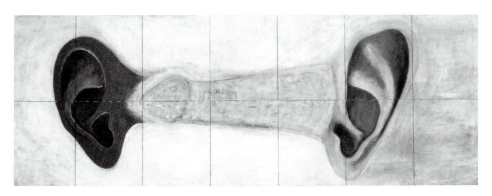

Figure 14 Mira Schor, *Audition* (1988). (Photo: Pelka/Noble. Courtesy: Mira Schor)

penis is attached to the main field of the painting with a short strip of "correct-o" typewriter ribbon; the ribbon of the word runs through the exchange between the ears, generating the colorful and powerful energy between them, and comes out the other side as a single thread which leads to another canvas covered with the artist's handwriting, again in a reverse image, making it impossible to decipher. *Imperfect Transmission* is "about" the spread of disease, and the near-impossibility of generative exchange – sexual, visual, aural. The image, Schor suggests, is equally open to the generative "misreadings" of literary and philosophical texts which have fueled critical theory for the past decade.[23] The "correct-o" type points to the "imperfect transmission" between the image and the word, and protests the neglect of the image in favor of the word. (Perhaps the most pernicious effects of this over-valuation of the word can be seen in the reception of Andres Serrano's "notorious" photograph. The title, *Piss Christ*, foreclosed readings which resisted the conservative insistence that the beautifully haunting image "meant" Christ equals urine.)[24]

Trapped within the pervasive meditation on the phallic, it may well be that Schor's own obsessive refiguring of the penis merely upholds and reinscribes the power of the phallus. Finally, the lure of painting, like that of Mapplethorpe's photography, is the incitement to touch. Painting is a record of the painter's hand touching pigment, paint, canvas. The "matter" of painting – whether figurative, abstract, or expressionistic – reflects the repetitious gesture of the artist's hand stroking the image. In the case of a woman repainting the penis this is perhaps less than revolutionary. Not surprisingly, in 1990 Schor temporarily suspended her renderings of the penis and began painting breasts. They look a bit like wine goblets and many of them flow with milk. The "ooze" of paint drips from the nipples; they are erect figures in the ground of paint's (wet) body.[25] However, when the Persian Gulf war began in 1990, Schor went back to missiles and warheads and found herself again repeatedly returning to the penis. Her *War Frieze* (1991) frames the United States flag, the penis, and the "ground" of Kuwait as an "arena" in which the ear receives the punch of phallic and militaristic power.

It is important that Schor's work is in painting and not photography – if only because in its very medium, her work insists that the costs of sexual difference will be paid individually, one at a time. Repetitious inequalities and the reproduction of patriarchy remain laboriously, rather than instantly, copied, which also seems to suggest, albeit quietly, that each of us can still do something to block its "imperfect transmission."

Schor's work, like all work which frames individual body parts, risks the charge of essentialism. But I think such a charge is misapplied. Schor

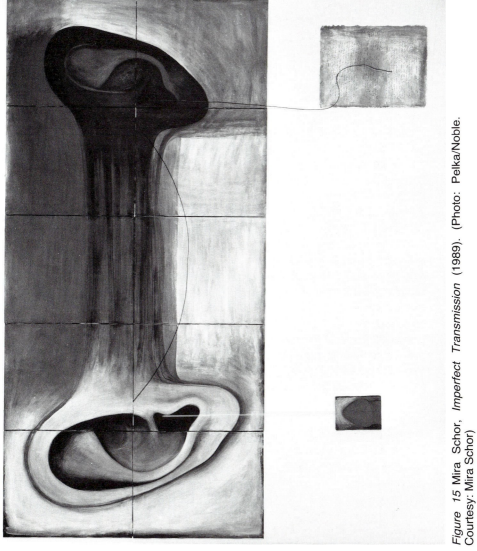

Figure 15 Mira Schor, *Imperfect Transmission* (1989). (Photo: Pelka/Noble.
Courtesy: Mira Schor)

is suggesting how impossible it now is to unhook the link between the penis and the phallus. Even with wit and a generous ear the unseen and effaced woman will bear unequally the burden of that imagistic, psychic, militaristic, and political connection.

Schor's work argues that female subjectivities, in fact and in representation, always confront what it costs to live with and without men, and with and without their representations of us. The contrary labor of living with and without women is blissfully absent from Mapplethorpe's work, and that to me is finally what is so shocking about his photography. The critique of culture undertaken by Schor is much more subversive of sexual "normality" than the explicitly "perverse" poses of Mapplethorpe's naked men.

IV

Like Mapplethorpe and Schor, Cindy Sherman is also uneasy about the limitations of photography. In fact, she dislikes the label photographer, preferring to call her work performance art. As Avedon remarks of Rembrandt's self-portraits, Sherman's work must be seen in the "full tradition of performance." Sherman knows that if Mapplethorpe is right to suggest that male subjectivity resides in the image and/or the object of his body, for women it is not quite so simple. The image of the other cannot be so easily distinguished for women as it seems to be for men. Nor can the image of the other be so easily appropriated by women – not because they are ethically superior to men or more intrinsically noble, but rather because – as we shall see with *Paris Is Burning* – appropriation requires a firm distinction between here and there, us and them, him and her, black and white. But exactly because the "thereness" of women is perpetually in doubt and because women's image is employed as a fill-in for the fantasy of the other, it is difficult for women to appropriate the image of the other for their own fantasy. As Lacan bluntly puts it, "There is no Other of the Other" (*Television*: 40).

Sherman's work suggests that female subjectivity resides in disguise and displacement. She uses the self-portrait to investigate the foundational otherness of women within contemporary Western representation. Taking the contradictory notion of white woman's representability very much to heart – that she is unrepresentable and yet everywhere imaged – Sherman made a series of photographs of herself disguised as film stars, housewives, young starlets, lost teenagers (Figures 16–19). Recognition and resemblance were derived from the imitation of cultural models: at first glance one "recognizes" Sherman as a Hitchcock heroine, just as Avedon's carpenter recognized himself within Rembrandt's self-portraits. In her early *Film Stills*, done between 1977 and 1980, Sherman's "real" was an endlessly varied performance of her

Figure 16 Cindy Sherman, *Untitled (Film Still)*, 35 (1979). (Courtesy: Metro Pictures, New York)

own disguises. The sheer number of disguises, however, pointed to the instability of female subjectivity; as one kept recognizing Sherman in a Hitchcock film, in a Godard film, in a Peckinpah film, one began to recognize as well that the force of culture's energetic image-making betrays the difficulty of "fixing" that image. Each of Sherman's images refers to another image. The "real" which photography reproduces seems in Sherman's work curiously evacuated. Adding to the anonymity and ubiquitousness of her images, Sherman left them all "untitled."

Perhaps the most surprising thing about these photographs is their condensation of narrative within the single frame (see Figure 16). Each "film still" conveys an overwhelming sense of narrative. Sherman's performances – the assembly of clothes, the constructed set, the lighting, the precise gesture – compress and express the life story of someone we recognize, or think we recognize, in a single image. Sherman's early work suggests, then, that the "image of woman" seems to be diverse, multiple, rich – and yet we "know" everything about her – she is a familiar, predictable "type." In the variety of Sherman's poses there is a claustrophobic sameness. The image of the woman is always white and, in this early work, attractive.

Sherman was disturbed to discover that the narrative situations she was condensing were repeatedly read as sexual narratives. In *Untitled* (Film Still 93), a woman lies on a bed staring at the light coming from the left rear of the frame (Figure 17). For Sherman, the intended narrative is of a woman waking from a hangover, but most people read this image as a woman who has just had sex, or is just about to.[26] A bed, mysterious light, a half-dressed woman: these totems provoke, Sherman soon recognized, a sexual narrative. Feeling restricted by these interpretations, Sherman began to protest what she believed to be overly sexual readings of her photographs. Judith Williamson, for example, remarked in *Screen*: "So strongly is femininity evoked [in Sherman's narrative] situations that they have to be *sexual* – is there any definition of femininity that isn't?" ("Images of Women": 104). Sherman attempted to find it.

Abandoning the image of "pretty femininity," Sherman created images of rage and horror between 1987 and 1988. While she continued to use herself as a model, her photographs became much more confrontational, aggressive, and ugly than the film stills. Disappearing into the framed space of the violent props, Sherman's self-image is much harder to find. In *Untitled*, 175, Sherman's face is visible only in the reflection on the sunglasses, and she is surrounded by human waste (Figure 18). But the abject image of woman is (only) the other side of her "beauty." Displaying the feminine as a landscape of horror did not "protect" it from being read as sexual. (The economy of the self-same always makes

Figure 17 Cindy Sherman, *Untitled*, 93 (1981). (Courtesy: Metro Pictures, New York)

femininity erotic, in the same way the "person of color" is always seen as a representative of "the racial other." This is the trap of contemporary "visibility politics.") Just as Schor realized that painting the penis did not show the phallus to be a mere man hiding behind a curtain like the Wizard of Oz, Sherman discovered that showing the lopsided and imbalanced equation between horror and women did not lessen its summarizing force.

In Mapplethorpe's work with male bodies, the evocation of "the sexual" was a means to approach the sublime. In Sherman's work with her own body, the evocation of "the sexual" pushed the images into a psychologically more treacherous and physically more appalling context. For Mapplethorpe the sexual sublime was expressed through the body of the other, and most powerfully through the image of the body of the black male nude. That distance allows for both adoration and horror. In overcoming initial horror, one adores *oneself* for possessing the (moral/aesthetic/political) strength to overcome this initial aversion. To the degree to which the other is identified with this overcoming, the other is also (temporarily) adored. But, obviously, such a tenuous and displaced association also invites a reversal.

Sherman's work, however, refuses to use the other as the mirror. Almost cannibalistic in her appetite, Sherman purposefully distorts her self-image in order to see the sociality of that image's construction and the way in which it is smoothly reproduced. Attempting to disrupt that smoothness, Sherman replaced the image of her own body with gruesome life-size dummies, but these too were seen as stand-ins for Sherman, or "a woman." Since the porn industry uses life-size dummies for the commodification of sexual desire, Sherman did not get very far in her attempt to avoid the (hetero)sexual narrative.

In these two phases of Sherman's work, she intended to comment ironically on the surface construction of femininity. But her critique could only be launched by her own mimetic re-posing. (Re-posing as the only form of responding. For women, all correspondence is a reply, including the initial letter.) In order to critique the imitative pose she enacted that pose and thereby reproduced it. As Craig Owens observes, Sherman's work participates "in the very activity that is being denounced *precisely in order to denounce it*" ("The Allegorical Impulse": 235). The imitative pose, Sherman found, was almost too easy to frame with her camera. Her work suggests that the camera itself *demands* the imitative pose because it only can read, speak, and reflect the surface.

Wedded forever to surface, the photograph gestures toward an interior image it cannot see. The visible photograph is the developed image of a negative. The "unconscious" image behind what is displayed gives the photograph the illusion of an interior. Thus to return then to the distinction between the gaze, the eye, and the lure: the "given to be

Figure 18 Cindy Sherman, *Untitled*, 175 (1987). (Courtesy: Metro Pictures, New York)

seen" of the image is seized by the gaze but the eye remembers the negative underneath it (the eye's own self-portrait cannot be seen). The lure is the possibility of joining the two together, a lure encouraged by the ontological joining of the negative and the developed image. The reproduction of the photograph, like the reproduction of sexual differ- ence, takes two and makes one. That one is the impression left on the photographic surface; the one left unmarked/undeveloped is the nega- tive image.

To read the photographic surface then recalls the effort to see "the/a woman" within the representational and reproductive economy. As Williamson points out: "For what we construct from the surface of each picture is an interior, a mixture of emotions. Each setting, pose and facial expression seems literally to express an almost immeasurable interior which is at once mysteriously deep, and totally impenetrable: a feminine identity" ("Images of Women": 103). For Sherman feminine identity is expressed by its disguise, by its retreat from the gaze of the other. That retreat, however, guarantees the lure of looking in general and the erotic allure which is an integral aspect of visual desire. Was there a way, Sherman wondered, to look under the surface of the photographic print? To reposition the negative, ontologically and psy- chically? If so, perhaps "feminine identity" might be seen as something- other-than a surface pose, an endlessly reproductive imitation of nothing but surface. She wanted her own work to do something-other- than reproduce the thing she wanted to denounce.

Sherman's most recent work (1989–90) investigates painting as pho- tography's negative (Figure 19). Moving from referencing another photographic image, as in the film stills which quote directors like Hitchcock, Sherman now quotes fine art portrait painters such as Holbein, Goya and Ingres. In shifting her model from a photographic image to a painted image, Sherman refigures both the classic and the postmodern debates concerning the distinction between painting and photography.

At the turn of the century champions of photography described the camera as superior to the art of painting because it could copy nature exactly. Photography, Marius De Zayas wrote in an essay for *Camera Work* in 1913, "is the means by which the man of instinct, reason and experience approaches nature in order to attain the evidence of reality."[27] As a realistic document the photograph was allied with "the truth" (as against the art/ificial). But by the time the Surrealists began their experiments with the camera, and as Melies' camera tricks began to be absorbed and copied by other filmmakers, the photograph began to be seen as a perversion of truth, as a trick and a lie. And by the time Sherman picked up a camera, the "precession of simulacra" had led the photograph to a state where it – perforce – reproduced only other

Figure 19 Cindy Sherman, *Untitled*, 216 (1989). (Courtesy: Metro Pictures, New York)

photographs, and rarely captured the Real at all.[28] Now, the "retouched" photograph is the hallmark and expectation of mainstream photographic representation.

In the meantime, as painting moved from Impressionism to its "death" in Pop, it was revived/revised by deconstruction. By the 1980s painting began to be seen as an art form which had a truer relation to the real than photography because the human body impresses itself (and rehearses for the "truth" of its eventual absence) through the effort to paint the image. Photography, on the other hand, with its mechanical shutter, its processing labs, its Cibachrome technology, its "retouching" capabilities, seems to record the evacuation of the human in the making of an image. The history of the photographic model in high art and in fashion advertising is a steady fleeing from a "human" look; as Sherman's work makes clear, each image looks progressively more like an image of another image.

In her search for (feminine) subjectivity then, Sherman abandons the photographic tradition and returns to the putative subjectivity encoded in fine art painting. Now working exclusively with color, Sherman's photographs make visible the relationship between the "stylization" of painting and its consequences for the stylization of the human body itself. The Renaissance convention of the Madonna Lactens, for example, distorts the "real" breast of women, and the distortion is reproduced and accented in fashion, posture, and sexual taste. Sherman registers the reproductive capability of distortion (and thus of human mutation) by making visible the prosthesis of the "single" painted breast across historical styles and conventions of the Madonna Lactens. The "real" breast, as ever, remains impossible to see. Sherman makes the conventional image so thoroughly strange one both laughs and is horri-fied. After looking at a series of these photographs, in which she re-enacts the postures, poses, and *mise-en-scènes* of portraits of both men and women, the human body itself seems like a handy holder for a thousand prostheses. But, crucially, the body in and of itself – the body-without-disguise – becomes a vacant, unmarked canvas. The attempt to see and paint the body, to make it visible, requires that the artist "add" a prop to that stage. The body-proper disappears into the interior of that prop – the false nose, the breastplate, the gloved hand – which marks the body *as* appearance. The performative record of the disappearance of Sherman's body is the lure which keeps the spectator looking for Sherman. Additionally, the inability to secure the body-proper without the body prop accents the failure of the proper name to reproduce Sherman herself. Canceling the Being promised by her middle and communal "r" ('are'), Sherman wryly notes that within the alphabet of phallocentric representation she can only appear as She-man.

If the Being promised by the human body is "disappeared" in both portrait painting and photography how do these arts imagine humanity is linked to the world? How is the self linked to the other? I am trying to suggest that perhaps through the ethical acceptance of our failure to be rendered within the terms of the visible, we may find another way to understand the basis of our link to the other within and without our selves. The conversion of the image into the mirror, the transformation of the different into the Same, leaves us clutching thousands of negatives under a glaring light. The ethical/psychic disappearance of the Other *as* Other-to-be-converted into the Self-Same, might be rehearsed by coming to terms with the psychic and ethical meaning of Sherman's photography. As we observe Sherman develop the human body's disappearance into the prop, the prosthesis, we observe as well the *mise-en-abyme* of self-production and reproduction.

The visible body, then, like the word, conceals rather than reveals the real of its Being. To turn away from the "precession of simulacra" is to blind oneself to the images of body parts displayed like weather all around us. In that blindness, the ungloved hand gropes again for the shape of that disappearing and reappearing face, the one which we project behind our lidded eyes. *Fort. Da.* The screen memory of that Other, phallocentric culture calls the mother.

While much of this argument sounds like the familiar "femininity is masquerade" argument I think the inflection is slightly, but importantly, different. In Joan Riviere's blunt declaration, "[G]enuine womanliness and the masquerade [of womanliness] are the same thing," there is no room for the affective power of mimicry, either for the performer or the observer.[29] Mary Ann Doane and Sue-Ellen Case in their respective reformulations of Riviere's thesis have emphasized the surplus political effect of a performed and excessive hyper-femininity, and Irigaray and Diamond have isolated the philosophical and psychoanalytic relation to the copy engendered by femininity and mimicry.[30] This latter work returns us to the maternal, not in the spirit of an unreconstructed essentialism, but rather with a new awareness of the limits of psycho-analytic theory to see the mother.

Irigaray thinks that the maternal is a confrontation with the always failing desire to find the origin. This origin is a blind image – what one is never permitted to see.[31] So the woman-mother becomes the screen which allows the (other) image to be seen. As a limit the mother is a screen upon which Plato's shadows dance. But whose shadow-image is it then? The one who pre-forms it (the photographer/the viewer) or the one who per-forms it (the model/the print itself)? That this is unde-cidable is the degree to which photography subverts the goal of Western philosophy (of which aesthetics is a vital chapter); for photography is unable to champion the figure and stability of the one. As such, photo-graphy is – quintessentially – feminine.

Irigaray has argued that woman is the sex which is not one: that is, the sex which is always already a double – or a triple or a quadruple. The double lips of the genitals copy the double lips of the mouth. The woman's reproductive body reproduces copies of her own reproductive organs. Like the photograph whose development and visibility depend on filling in and embodying the negative, the woman is made visible through her embodiment of the not-male. It is the energy needed to fill in the negative other/wise that sutures both the photograph and the woman to the ontology of the copy. Always already linked to a reproductive body, the ontologies of women and photographs are profoundly matched. Neither will admit the singular: it is only accurate to put a slash through "the woman" and "the photograph." Founded upon the terrain of the negative, both reproduce the visible. To expose this reproduction is, perhaps, to ruin the security of the single subject endlessly seeking the perfect image s/he can (call her or his) own.

3

Spatial envy: Yvonne Rainer's
The Man Who Envied Women

Yvonne Rainer's engagement with feminist film theory in her 1985 film *The Man Who Envied Women* illuminates several possibilities and limitations within that body of work. Rainer takes the critical work of Laura Mulvey and Ann Kaplan to its logical conclusion: if the male gaze is an integral structure of cinematic desire, so integral that it is inscribed by everything from camera position to narrative structure, what happens when the usual object of that gaze, the heroine, is denied a visual presence within the film? By creating a two-hour film in which the female protagonist is not imaged, Rainer's film sets up the possibility of a different kind of relation between filmic protagonist and filmic spectator.[1]

Trisha, the central female character of *The Man*, is never imaged. Rainer seems to have taken Teresa de Lauretis' appeal to feminist filmmakers very much to heart; in *Alice Doesn't* de Lauretis asks feminist filmmakers to create "another (object of) vision and the conditions of visibility for a new social subject" (*Alice Doesn't*: 68). Rainer does just this when she withholds Trisha's visual image. By denying Trisha's visual image, Rainer implicitly challenges the nature of filmic presence.

If presence is registered not through a visible body but through a voice, an invisible but audible consciousness, how are the models of identification between spectators and their screen surrogates challenged? Rainer's film suggests that the terms of analysis which have helped explain these models of identification must themselves be revised. Some of the privileged terms of feminist film criticism derived from psychoanalysis – the male gaze, voyeurism, scopophilia, and fetishism – come under scrutiny in the course of Rainer's film.

Trisha's absence challenges the forms of identification between spectators and cinematic characters. Her invisibility tends to make her a spectator of her own film. Rainer thus reverses the traditional conventions of filmic identification; instead of assuming that audiences exist in order to identify with characters, Rainer creates a character who assumes that she might identify with the audience. As a spectator to her own life, Trisha recognizes that she is in the middle of a very old script. Both her past and her future are always already "imaged" within that script – the script of the heterosexual narrative – and thus only her voice contains the possibility of Trisha being present – and in the present. When Trisha interrupts one of Jack Deller's long speeches about how thoroughly he knows women and supplies her own predictive commentary, "This is where he says, 'A man is nothing without a woman,' " Trisha is like a savvy spectator who has seen it all before. Given what we know about Jack and Trisha's relationship (who speaks, who listens), we can assume that Trisha probably *has* heard it all before from Jack. As *his* perpetual audience, she learns to see herself – and what she sees is that she is not there. Re-marking her spectatorship within the plot and outside it underlines for the audience the familiarity of Jack's claims even while the act of remarking it suggests a different, more overtly conscious, relation to that old script. The assumption of passive spectatorship is immediately called into question – and Trisha challenges both herself and her filmic audience to discover a new "condition of visibility" within *his* plot.

Rainer's project in *The Man* is not, however, motivated exclusively by feminist concerns. In fact, Rainer's meditation on *filmic space* in *The Man Who Envied Women*, which incorporates her feminist and narrative concerns, is the most radical and innovative aspect of the film. Rainer employs a wide variety of spatial arrangements as an integral aspect of her narrative method. As a meditation on what I call "spatial envy," *The Man Who Envied Women* advances and challenges feminist film criticism and filmic narrative.

I

Near the end of *The Man Who Envied Women*, the frame is filled for the second time with Donald Judd's large grey concrete sculptures luxuriating in an open Texas field.[2] The camera walks across these sculptures like fingers over a piano: they seem to hold a kind of tune half hidden, half audible. The sculptures are concrete outlines of squares the color of tombstones. The heaviness of their frame accentuates the hollowness of the air they embrace. Like a Wittgensteinian word game, or better still, like Mark Strand's witty poem "Keeping Things Whole," Judd's sculptures suggest that "space" is that which negotiates between airy fields (infinite possibilities) and concrete architecture (finite facts), while not residing entirely in either the one or the other. As Strand puts it anthropomorphically: "When I walk/I part the air/and always the air moves in/to fill the spaces/where my body's been." Filling in the spaces created by departing persons, places, and things is the central concern of *The Man Who Envied Women*. Judd's sculptures, with their refusal to locate or define a spatial point of origin or termination, are the objective correlative for the difficult idea of space that Rainer's film alternately vigilantly argues for, and whimsically hopes for.

Judd's "empty" frames echo the central visible "lack" in Rainer's film. In displacing Trisha from the visual field, Rainer forces the spectator to concentrate on the way the filmic frame both fills and limits the space of the film. She is attempting to elucidate how the given to be seen requires a strict prohibition on what and who remains unseen.

In breaking the symmetrical relationship between the spectator and the female protagonist, Rainer interrogates the cinematic frame that keeps the character inside the frame, and the spectator outside. In leaving Trisha outside the visible content of the frame, Rainer displaces her from filmic space into the spectator's psychic space. Berenice Reynaud suggests that it is the sound of the invisible woman's voice which allies her with the mother "whose voice engulfs, scolds and consoles the helpless child" ("Impossible Projections": 27). As a mother who has somehow "lost" her daughter (Alicia goes off to Antioch in the opening moments of Trisha's monologue) Trisha seems very "available" to the spectator. She has no home; her dead father haunts her; she has left her husband and her art work; and her mother appears only in a dream. Rupturing the psychic frame of Trisha's family parallels Rainer's investment in rupturing the cinematic frame in which we want to place her.

Using video transfers as kind of windows (frames-within-frames), grainy Super-8 as an interruption of the smoother surface of the film, and fragments from classic Hollywood and avant-garde films as Jack's interior mental landscapes, Rainer disallows the pleasurable illusion of a visually polished art piece and forces in its stead a reconfiguration of the traditional architecture of the frame. Rainer describes her attempt to break down the frame as a

> disruption of the glossy, unified surface of professional cinematography by means of optically degenerated shots within an otherwise seamlessly edited narrative sequence [. . .] I'm talking about films where in every scene you have to decide anew the priorities of looking and listening.
>
> ("Some Ruminations": 25)

By refusing to maintain a unified visual surface, Rainer interrogates the frame's relation to the expected symmetries dividing filmic characters and spectators.

The Man Who Envied Women's subject is not so much "a week in the life of Trisha," although it is partially that; the film primarily chronicles the manifestations and consequences of the pervasive malaise of spatial envy. This subject makes issues as apparently diverse as the politics of

Central America, the Manhattan real estate crunch, the vicissitudes of sexual and social relations, the virility and impotence of poststructuralism, and the medicalization of women's bodies, seem deeply intertwined. Imperialism in Central America and New York love affairs are similar, for example, in that they are each motivated, in part, by the desire to gain space. In Rainer's film the latter is wryly represented by the only half-funny one-liner: "When are we getting married so I can have your apartment when we get divorced?" The Central American situation, as we shall see, is treated more somberly. Using a collage of "moving pictures" as a kind of collective interpretative Rorschach, Rainer is able to swing a wide and fluid net over these seemingly unrelated topics. These moving pictures and the commentaries they elicit function as a kind of classical Chorus marking the drama Rainer's film does not quite show. Initially assembled by the visually absent but-very-present Trisha, the pictures are rearranged no fewer than six times in the film; their spatial rearrangements parallel the shifting spaces and stories of spatial envy which animate *The Man Who Envied Women*.

Rather than beginning with a "feeling for form," Rainer's film begins with underlining the incoherence of form. Postulating that form always involves the possession (imaginative or actual) of space, Rainer begins her narrative proper with Trisha's double loss of space. After moving out of the apartment she shares with Jack, she is evicted from her studio. Trisha, the mysteriously elusive artist, begins between "spaces"; she is dis-possessed. She can create only in fragmented images, in cut-outs that she must – perforce – leave behind. This is the parable of loss, of always fragmented and interrupted formal concentration that the film slowly unfolds. Rainer's consistent disruption of the frame's space technically mirrors Trisha's cut-up "home" and her cut-out art.

Trisha's opening monologue is just the first layer of Rainer's associative meditation on the implications of losing and gaining space:

> It was a hard week. I split up with my husband of four years and moved into my studio. The hot water heater broke and flooded the textile merchant downstairs; I bloodied up my white linen pants; the Senate voted for nerve gas; and my gynecologist went down in Korean Airlines flight #007. The worst of it was the gynecologist. He used to put booties on the stirrups and his speculum was always warm.[3]

Although these events are linked in time, they are linked in other more subtle ways as well. To put it simply: splitting up with Jack sets off a series of dismissals and departures. Trisha's flooding menstrual blood and her studio's flooding water heater are alike in their fits of unruliness against their spatial confines. This private and individual unruliness, moreover, finds its public and political image in the dark drama of

Korean Airlines flight #007. Overstepping, overflowing, or overflying the boundaries of space, no matter how visible or invisible such boundaries might appear, can have tragic consequences.

Trisha's overflowing menstrual blood is crucial; Rainer's title plays on the Freudian notion that women are beset with penis envy. Part of Rainer's aim is to turn the tables: she wants to suggest that men envy women in part because of their internal biological space. (Women, as it were, carry their "air space" inside them. To employ this metaphor psychoanalytically (and from the woman's point of view), violations of "air space" are assertions of power: the physiological and social arrangements of heterosexuality combine to maintain women in a subordinate position to men. Insofar as male sexual desire is motivated by spatial envy, rape becomes not only a logical, but an inevitable consequence of the psychological-physiological architecture of heterosexuality.) Rainer uses the woman's body and the functions of its still mysterious spaces as a kind of lens through which contemporary "problems" can be evaluated. She tries to link the mind that thinks and the body that feels in a specifically womanly way; one might say she attempts to reinvestigate the traditional oppositions of Western metaphysics, in the wake of Derrida, from a feminist point of view.

Part of her correction to the story poststructuralism tells is stylistic. Metaphysics in Rainer's view cannot go too long without a joke; the film's most serious moments (with the exception of the last ten minutes or so) are continually undercut with jokes. In what J. Hoberman thinks is the best line in the film, Rainer, in a distorted off-center close-up reminiscent of Hitchcock, invites "all menstruating women [to] please leave the theatre" ("Purple": 64). This invitation is symptomatic of Rainer's most congenial habit of mind. Her most consistent impulse, and her most comfortable perspective, is from a distance – almost over her shoulder. This is not a film that asks the spectator to like the characters, to enjoy the scenery, to laugh heartily, or to nod knowingly at all the familiar conversation. The effort at the heart of this film is as engaged in throwing you out as it is in settling you in.

II

Rainer's troubled and troubling male protagonist, Jack Deller, begins the film "on the couch." Deller's doctor is off-screen and voiceless (perhaps the ultimate representation of Rogerian client-centered therapy), and his confessions are actually the ponderously sounding words of Raymond Chandler's letters and diaries. The analyst, the Lacanian subject supposed to know, like Trisha is not seen. But whereas this invisibility assures analytic authority, Trisha's own authority remains insecure. This is because Rainer creates a different form of spectatorial identification with the analyst than she establishes with Trisha. Trisha, by overtly declaring herself on the side of the spectator, pre-empts a certain form of voyeuristic-fetishistic spectatorial identification which the analyst continues to provoke.

Deller sees himself as a man more gifted and blessed than troubled and cursed. He is a university professor – he teaches film theory, sort of – with leftist leanings who uses words to seduce everyone (especially himself) into a cocoon of babel more hypnotic than revealing. During his "sessions" Jack sits in a chair facing the camera. He sits on the left side of the "stage," and continually gazes beyond the left vertical end imposed by the frame. This invisible space is acutely present in his monologues, just as the visually absent Trisha is acutely present in the narrative texture of the film.[4] Jack, more than any other character in the film, is desperately dependent upon an audience – and after Trisha leaves, his desperation increases. That the audience for his intimate meanderings turns out to be "the spectator" who is forced into the position of "the doctor" is just one overt example of Rainer's obsessive tendency to suggest that film's effort to address is, absolutely, dependent upon an erasure. The first word of the film, "doctor," addresses someone who is not there. The standard critical claim that the spectator always identifies with the camera requires that the camera become a surrogate spectator. The camera, in so becoming, literally effaces the spectator. The power of the camera's eye (the potentially ideal I/eye) in addition to showing us objects and lending us its gaze, also shows us up.

The camera's vision is presented but not possessed in much the way that Rainer's characters seem to borrow their language from other people. Rainer's frequent tendency to have characters quote from other texts is part of her larger argument with narrative, and specifically with her sense that narrative constructs (inevitably) singular characters and singular points of view. In a 1985 article in *Wide Angle*, Rainer comments that her indefatigably quoting characters help "foreground not only the production of narrative but its frustration and cancellation as well [. . .] Words are uttered but not possessed by my performers as they operate within the filmic frame but do not propel a filmic plot" ("More Kicking": 8). The lack of connection between the words of the characters and the bodies of the actors uttering them, works to destabilize the authority of the visual field as well.

The illusion of cinema's visual realism is continually undercut by Rainer's meandering and deliberately disunified visual frames. Her most sustained investigation of the ontology of the filmic image occurs, suitably, in Jack's struggle to separate and make coherent his parceled past: that is, in Jack's sessions with the invisible doctor.

At one point, Jack sits in his chair facing the doctor/spectator to the left, and the camera moves back to reveal an audience completely absorbed in watching the film clips playing next to his head (Figure 20). Jack's interior landscape is made up of film history. (For Rainer, the psyche of any film character is always derived from a filmic past.) The scene is unsettling because the film clip is from *The Night of the Living Dead* and the spectators begin to attack each other as the film images grow more chaotic and the sound track more discursive. In a three-way phone conversation Trisha summarizes Nancy Chodorow's and Dorothy Dinnerstein's arguments about the reproduction of mothering and ruminates on the associations between the name "Jack Deller" and fairy tales. Despite all the aural and visual ornamentation, this sequence of images forces the spectator to re-experience the acute psychic discomfort that comes from the recognition of the profound connection between voyeurism and cinema. There is nothing original about this connection of course, but what is striking (and awful) is the disturbing connections this particular sequence demands. The mayhem produced by the images of *The Night of the Living Dead* literally incites the spectators to perform their own aggressive mayhem. Given that these clips are in the same spatial frame as Jack's "confessions," the underlying connection implicitly suggests that psychoanalysis, like cinema, in relying on "projection" as its paradigmatic principle, is inherently voyeuristic. To discover that the only position one can take in this "long shot" is the role of the doctor, is to discover as well that one's interest in Jack (cinematically and psychoanalytically) stems from a desire to "treat" him; and much more uncomfortably, that one's interest in the similarities between the "cinematic apparatus" and the psychoanalytic paradigm stems from one's own desire to be "treated."

Jack's central concern in these sessions is his relationship to women, a relationship that undergoes a radical change after the death of his first wife. Trisha, his second wife, has left him after four years, in part because of his inability to be sexually faithful. His well-designed explanations for his lack of fidelity essentially consist of his belief that after his beautifully idealized first wife died, he became incapable of seeing women as anything other than sacred gifts. To turn down such a gift verges on the sacrilegious – and Jack is no heretic. One gift he has inherited from Trisha, a gift he did not ask for, is her "art work." Jack asks Trisha to take it with her when she moves out. She says she'll return for it. Insofar as *The Man Who Envied Women* has a narrative "plot," it is this early promise of return that the film uses as its departing point. Like everything else, the meeting is interrupted, even superseded, by the promise of another meeting between Jack and Jack-ie Raynal, who are also ex-lovers; this meeting actually does occur and it is from the unsettling perspective of their relationship that almost all of the varied threads the film unwinds come together. But as we wait for the party, the "meaning" of the art that is left behind, the hieroglyphics of

Figure 20 Film still of William Raymond in front of a clip from Nicholas Ray's *In A Lonely Place* (at his therapy session) from Yvonne Rainer's *The Man Who Envied Women* (1985). (Courtesy: Yvonne Rainer)

an unreachable woman – visually and romantically – consume more and more of our attention.

This art work is a collage of magazine clippings; three come from *The Sunday New York Times* and two come from *Mother Jones*. They include: an "About Men" column written by a priest; an advertisement for a Central American cigar which features a rich man and his dog as the Barthesian "sign" of success; an advertisement for a drug – conjugated estrogen – which promises to treat the "real problem" of menopausal depression; a cover from the Sunday *Times* which profiles a Soviet dissident; and a gruesome photograph of decapitated bodies with a caption which seems to identify one of the victims as a 6-month-old Guatemalan child. The spatial arrangement of these images is continually revised. Off-screen voices create narratives of coherence about them. The connection between the cigar ad and the mutilated bodies is described allegorically: the successful cigar-selling man profits, both directly and indirectly, from the mutilation and death of Salvadorean peasants. The United States' interest in Central America is read as an imperial lust for the control of geographic space.

The plea for the "emotional" space of men represented by the "About Men" column is seen both economically and socially. That the space for this column occupies the Sunday paper, while the "Hers" column is put in the "Home" section of Thursday's *Times* ("among the latest sofas") is seen as an ideological and economic manifestation of the privilege of space.[5] (As the woman narrates her objection to the partitioning of column space in a slightly whining voice, the column becomes another source of spatial envy as well.)

The advertisement for the menopausal drug is seen as part of the larger treatment of "women's problems" historically. It is linked to the theme of sexual difference in poststructural discourse. The precise relationship of the by now axiomatic connection between the textual body and the sexual body is explored with a twist that would make Roland Barthes cringe.[6] Rather than seeing this connection as the source of Barthes' *jouissance*, a kind of perpetual foreplay which teases one to contemplate a mental and spiritual communion so intense it holds the potential for an absolutely infinite ecstasy, Rainer suggests that the link between the mind that thinks and the body that feels is one of loss – a kind of permanent grief. The difference between these two conceptions of the body is fundamentally related to the gender of those bodies. Early on, Trisha makes a provocative connection between the ovaries and the brain: "The ovaries of a 7-month-old fetus contain almost 1,000,000 egg cells. From then on, the ova constantly decrease in number without replenishment. The only other cells to do this are those of the brain." The mutual process of dropping eggs and losing brain cells, neither of which are regenerative, revises the traditional (masculine) "mind/body" split into a more radical affinity. The body that feels and the mind that thinks are unified in their similar physiological movement from abundance to loss. The brain and the ovary then are the physiological kernels which sow, or so it would seem, a metaphysics not of acquisition, but of inevitable depletion. To speak 'essentially': the dispersal and loss integral to identity are sown into the woman's body while men's bodies, perhaps, seek to enact such loss and dispersal on other physical bodies – those in Latin America, those under the real estate construction company's boulder, those under the pharmacological lens of science.

The horrific image of the decapitated bodies (the literal split between the mind and the body makes Western metaphysics' concern with it seem like a faint echo of a terrible fear), is the image which elicits the deepest meditation. In one of the only moments of unification between the sound track and the image track, the voice of one of the off-screen commentators (Martha Rosler's) breaks off as Deller's hand trails away from the wall after shifting the images around in an effort to bury the gruesome image (and the naked bodies) under all the other clippings. It is a moving sequence, not only because Deller at last seems "in sync" with the world of the film, but also because one of the questions of "owning space" hinges – apparently absolutely – on someone else losing it.

This relationship is explored with a poignant befuddlement as Rainer follows the sequence of public hearings called to consider the city of Manhattan's proposal to allocate housing funds to artists moving into the Lower East Side. The idea behind this plan was to keep New York City as a congenial "space" for art and artists – a cynical observer might say that the idea exposes the city's own imperial lust for cultural supremacy – but leaving that aside: contemplating "moving to Jersey" is viewed with equal horror by all members of the hearings. One of the consequences of this proposal was that it pitted the artists, most of whom are white, against the working class, most of whom are people of color. Rainer implicitly and explicitly calls into question the efficacy of art and the aesthetic impulse to manipulate and re-order space for some artistic good. The immense space of Donald Judd's sculptural field and the huge canvases of Leon Golub which drape the walls of the documentary footage Rainer inserts in her film suddenly seem absurd: do images and representations deserve/need to consume so much space? Do we participate in the construction and maintenance of a world in which representation literally dominates our lives and robs some people of four walls? "Almost overnight we met the enemy," Trisha declares, "and it was us."

III

If the spatial arrangements and rearrangements of Trisha's abandoned art work constitute the melody of the film, part of its rhythmic structure comes from Jack's magic headphones. Like some fantastic state-of-a-future-art Walkman, Jack's oversized mechanical ears make him privy to the conversations of Manhattan street-strollers. It is perhaps the triplicate repetition of these scenes that prompts Hoberman to dub Rainer "the Purple Rose of Soho," and to compare her films to Woody Allen's. Rainer's one-liners are dry and infectious. They are also obsessively concerned with sex. The space between Jack's ears, by implication, seems overloaded with sexual puns: in other words he selectively receives the world from a sexual point of view.

In the first issue of *Motion Picture*, Rainer writes that the purpose of these scenes is to convey the idea that the city, for Jack, is a "place full of sexual anxiety, obsession, and verbal assault, litanies of sexual distress [. . .] [It is] a barrage – a veritable eruption – of ordinarily repressed material" ("Tell 'Er": 8). But the problem is that the conversations are all in one key: if it is a jungle it specializes in one animal. These jokes are all about sexual stereotypes: gay men as housewives, feminism as a badge of admittance for politically correct men to a wider set of women's bedrooms, and so on. If these clichés are supposed to frighten a man who spouts off the subtle seductions of Foucault and who speaks of the cinematic apparatus as an intimate echo of Lacanian subjectivity, then he is in really sorry shape. But I think Rainer's aim and its effect are quite different. Rather than seeming symptomatic of Jack's fear, these jokes function instead as welcome comic relief.

Jack's "character" is a literal embodiment of Bakhtin's "heteroglossia" in that it comes to us only through other texts.[7] Rainer refuses to have him cohere. Played by two actors (Bill Raymond and Larry Loonin) and with little or no laughter, he seems a strange bird indeed. As we've seen, Jack's sessions are framed by Rainer in such a way as to make the notion of a "filmic secret" or "intimate confession" completely oxymoronic. His inaugural speech to the doctor is interrupted by the title "Screen Tests," and he reads much of Chandler's text as if he is auditioning for a film by Godard. His psychic "revelations" are the machismo fantasies of Chandler augmented by Hollywood films playing next to his forehead. In one exceptional exception, instead of seeing one of these clips, we see a slow motion black-and-white clip from Bubette Mangolte's film of Trisha Brown's riveting performance of *Watermotor*. The dance floods the frame within the frame; Brown's movements are enchantingly suggestive of the body as water; her body flows with an eroticism that is seemingly incorporeal.

To see this lyrical moment as part of Jack's world (either his imaginative dream or his hallucination of his first wife) is to reassess his own position therein. One wants to credit him, however marginally, with some dignity: if he can talk in a way which evokes this woman dancing, he might have once moved in circles which once touched her. His incredibly nostalgic descriptions of his first wife, which initially seem like one more layer of defense about the failure of his second marriage to Trisha, are rearranged and reconfigured as Brown dances; his descriptions of her turn into something much less defensive, something verging on an accurate testimony of a real gift. That his response to the evocation of this world also includes masturbating while clutching *Playboy* and seducing students with his many tongues makes our response to his several selves more complicated.

The ambivalence of our response to Jack is most strongly felt in the climactic hallway scene. At last Jack and Jackie meet; at last *The Man Who Envied Women* fulfills one of its narrative promises. They meet, suitably, at the edge of the party – in the hallway facing the elevator (and its promise of exit) and perpendicular to the door leading to the exuberant party (and its promise of social entry). Placed within this claustrophobically narrow hallway, Jack and Jackie's seduction is filmed in the manner of a conventional seduction; *except*, it is impossible to know who "controls" the seduction: Jack or Jack-ie Raynal, his former lover who appears only in this scene. In about a twenty-minute editing *tour de force*, Rainer juxtaposes the visual narrative of seduction – two bodies in various layers of clothing move toward and away from one another, embrace and then disentangle themselves from the embrace – with other narratives which make their seduction alternately comical, bitter, absurd, necessary, delightful, euphoric, and ridiculous. These juxtapositions include: cuts to and from the Manhattan City Council's vote against Artist Housing, film clips from Max Ophuls' *Caught*, and an Oedipal romp of a dream whose main characters are Jack, Trisha, Trisha's mother, and a one-eyed cat. These juxtapositions occur in the midst of a harrowing and hilarious rhetorical contest between Jack and Jackie; he quotes Foucault's *Discipline and Punish* and she responds with Morris' "The Pirate's Fiancée." As Jackie moves in on Jack, she gets to utter questions like this: "What is happening when women must work so hard in distinguishing the penis and the phallus?" Jack's reply is a Foucaldian proposition about power-knowledge which sets up Rainer's elaborate pun on the (lack of) difference between the penis, the phallus, and the penal system. This scene is more than a rhetorical Olympics (first prize: The Other); it is a sort of Joycean epiphanic moment: not for the characters (who are by this time almost completely peripheral to the "coherence" of Rainer's plots) but for the film itself.

Jackie is not speaking *to* Jack: she addresses a different spectator altogether. She seems to be addressing an off-screen Trisha. Or at least, it would seem that Trisha hears Jackie more clearly than Jack does.

Jackie's voice, thick with a French accent, is passionate and sounds half sleepy. She wears a kind of shimmering gown that half reveals her breasts.[8] The camera scrutinizes her with a pleasure it simply cannot find in Jack. Her voice makes the sounds of Morris' words resonant with the confidence of their own originality; they are sure they have never been spoken in quite this way before.

The pleasure of this seduction comes not only from the verbal and political connections Rainer's deeply associative mind keeps turning up, but from the self-reflexive stance she takes toward her own use of film. By cutting back and forth to Ophuls' *Caught* (it turns up three times in the hallway scene), Rainer at once acknowledges the tradition of filmic seduction she is working to undercut and also acknowledges its hold on the spectator's imagination. Most avant-garde films work so hard to thwart narrative structure that the rigidity of the exclusion paradoxically increases the spectator's desire for its presence. Rainer here shows the convention she is actively revising; the clip from *Caught* ends with Mason and Belgeddes dancing.

Despite all the cuts and juxtapositions, there is never any doubt that this is a seduction. Despite Rainer's cuts, neither Foucault's assertive pronouncements nor Morris' dizzying speculations can distract anyone too long from the inevitableness of Jack and Jackie's embrace. The elaborate rhetorical disguise does not completely cover the banality of their desire for each other; nor does it let us escape ours for them. But it does make the whole exchange seem funny and wry. Rainer's embellished and stylized distance from her characters, a distance measured by the elaborate editing and cutting in this sequence, makes the seduction we see almost diametrically opposed to the conventions of seduction operative in Ophuls' *Caught*. By refusing to let either Jack or Jackie be exclusively "the aggressor" or "the pursued," Rainer also robs the spectator of these familiar points of view with which to identify. Jack and Jackie's tangled and shifting rhetoric mirrors the psychological knots Rainer creates for her spectator.

The slow pace of the seduction undercuts Jack's stubborn insistence on repeating Foucault's axiom: "There is no opposition between what is said and what is done." As Jack and Jackie move intellectually further and further apart, their bodies move closer and closer together. As Jack continually repeats Foucault's arguments about the ubiquitous dispersion of power, Jackie categorizes and delimits differences in the power to discriminate power. Jack is content to ignore "what is said" for what might "be done." He seems not to hear a thing she says. Jackie is, in almost a literal sense, speaking a different language:

> Only the naive humanist feminist thinks she can change something
> by changing her consciousness. The rigorous feminist plumbs the

hidden depths of subjectivity, studies its construction in language [. . .] winds through the labyrinth to find not a monster but a new position of the subject. [. . .] One awkward consequence of the freudo-marxist marriage presided over by language, is to open up an inviting space for marxist and feminist laborers which can only be defined by the systematic evacuation of certain questions – political, economic, and above all historical questions. [. . .] Theory as a watch-dog is a poor creature: not because it is nasty or destructive but because for attacking the analysis of confrontations, it simply has no teeth.

As if this is the permission Rainer has been waiting for, the remainder of *The Man Who Envied Women* moves steadily away from the theoretical pronouncement (the world of Jack) to a more personal, and more tentative, meditation. Rainer moves more comfortably and more completely into the world of the imagination. This world, entered only through the portal of the feminine, is formally invoked (evoked?) by Jackie, who again borrows Morris' words:

Passing from the realm of the theory of the subject to the shifty spaces of feminine writing is like emerging from a horror movie to a costume ball. [. . .] Feminine writing lures with an invitation to license, gaiety, laughter, desire and dissolution, a fluid exchange of partners of indefinite identity.

Abandoning Jack's "horror movie" playing *The Night of the Living Dead*, Rainer cuts to Trisha's costume ball, her narration of an Oedipal dream (Figure 21). In this revisionary dream of The Family Romance the spectator can only be relieved to see that Trisha and Trisha's mother not only have the same lover (Jack – of course) but that they also have the same body (Rainer's own). Just as Jack gets to play both father and lover in Trisha's Oedipal trauma, so Trisha (here played by Rainer behind a paper mask) gets to play both mother and lover (played by Rainer half behind a door). Just as Trisha gets adjusted to Jack and her mother as lovers, the point of view switches and now Trisha (ever the spectator) watches her mother watching her make love to Jack. Her response is, of course, to become blindly furious with her mother. (Fittingly, a one-eyed cat slinks across the frame as Trisha sputters with rage.) The narrative doubling of the dream is precisely the kind of psychological doubling Rainer hopes to incite in her spectator. This impulse in Rainer's work comes not so much from an effort to increase "audience participation" or from some liberal sense of aesthetic democracy, but from the more radical hope that a continually shifting point of view might transform the means by which we know and perceive one another. Cut back to the hallway. Jack and Jackie are embracing all the rhetorical possibilities of physically embracing.

Figure 21 Film still of Yvonne Rainer and William Raymond in the 'dream sequence' from Yvonne Rainer's *The Man Who Envied Women* (1985). (Courtesy: Yvonne Rainer)

And then again Trisha's voice: "If a girl takes her eyes off Lacan and Derrida long enough to look she may discover she is the invisible man." That the film's invisible woman, Trisha, says this only heightens the irony; the film abandons the poetics of theory and individual masculinity for a more persuasive look at Trisha's moving pictures.

As it happens when theory is not the loudest voice in the room, what the eye sees when it looks again is a different image altogether. Trisha's concluding ruminations, unlike Jack's initial confessions, are tentative and groping:

> Lately I've been thinking yet again I can't live without men but I can live without a man. I've had this thought before, but this time the idea is not colored by stigma or despair or finality. I know that there will sometimes be excruciating sadness but I also know something is different now, something in the direction of unwomanliness. Not a new woman, not non-woman, or misanthropist, or anti-woman, and not non-practicing lesbian. Maybe un-woman is also the wrong term. A-woman is closer. A-womanly. A-womanliness.

Just what Trisha means by this is not immediately apparent. She seems willing and ready to bury Jack's hold on her. And ready to bury something larger as well. Among the more enigmatically haunting sequences in the film is an early one in which Trisha complains that her father chose this week to "pop out." In Trisha's various retellings of her stories of "life with Jack" there is a feeling that she is telling the story of life with Pop as well. Trisha's exasperation with the way the memory of her father interrupts her recollection of "life with Jack" speaks to the doubleness of the pain of mourning. The father, like Jack, intrudes on Trisha – both as a maddeningly inadequate presence and as a persistently unwelcome absence. In this speech, Trisha seems willing to abandon some of the thinking that gives "the absent father" and the unfaithful man such a hold on her imagination. Within Trisha's announcement of "something different now" is the persistent hope that if a-womanliness means anything at all, it might have some impact on Trisha's Oedipal dreams. With Pop and Jack tucked back in the suitcase, maybe Trisha, her mother, and the one-eyed cat can create a new dream. One that may well be filled with "excruciating sadness," but one that might yet be allowed the representation of a new dream-text, one that might raise the hitherto repressed.

We return again to the art work for one last revision. This time Rainer asks, "If this were an art work how would you critique it?" The answer brilliantly recasts the connections between the images and suggests that spatial arrangements, artistic and rationalistic, are inherently political. I quote just briefly from Rosler's long argument:

I would feel I was being tricked into trying to deal with things that have become incommensurable as though they weren't incommensurable. That I was being told that the myths of civility at home and the problems of daily life are only a veneer over the truth that the state destroys people. It is as though I were being told that when dealing with the ultimate, my worries about how I live my life in America are not important.

She then goes on to elucidate the ways in which the arrangements of the images tell political and visual stories. The uncaring emotional façade of men that the "About Men" column argues against, "determine[s] how we conduct our foreign policy. It isn't only a matter of economic interest, but of how we choose to pursue that interest. If we're willing to grind up other people because we can't be bothered to feel about them then it does matter." What she argues for then is a new notion of spatial privilege – an anti-privilege; or maybe that's the wrong term – privilegelessness is closer. A world in which the space one occupies (publicly and privately) is not subject to or the object of envy; a world that Judd's sculptural embraces create when their spatial beginnings and endings cannot be defined or located. The fact that the sculptures themselves dominate a wide open field in Marfa, Texas underlines the distance we need to traverse before such an ideal spatial arrangement might occur. The placement(s) of Judd's sculptural frames within the filmic frame Rainer continually revises, demand a second look. Rainer's film proposes a democracy of spatial equality so radical that its very proposal requires a continual rearrangement not only of the images within the frame but of what the frame keeps out.

IV

I said earlier that the identification between the camera and the spectator inevitably effaces the power of the spectator and that implied within this effacement there is a failure of address. Jack's sessions, for example, which address an absent doctor and are augmented by films addressed to an audience alert to other texts underscore the difficulty of filmic address. The spectator is the film's invisible hearer, its unseen doctor and deliverer of catharsis. The spectator is also the film's "next" patient, the one waiting just outside the (door) frame.

Teresa de Lauretis argues that Rainer's film "constructs a critical space in which I am addressed, precisely, as a woman and a-woman" ("Strategies of Coherence": 124). Brilliantly analyzing the impossible Real of a-womanliness, de Lauretis nonetheless concludes that the terms of address (and thus of identification) are gendered in Rainer's film. Insofar as the distinction between gender-specific points of view has any validity, it is certainly true that *The Man Who Envied Women* is animated from and for a woman's eye. But I think de Lauretis underplays the more troubling implication of Rainer's film. By upsetting the conventions of filmic point of view (e.g. not showing Trisha at all and thus making it impossible to follow her gaze; the conflicting narrative angles of the plot(s); the lack of differentiation between "quoted" language and "original" language *et al.*), Rainer also challenges the notion of filmic address itself. *The Man Who Envied Women* illustrates that in narrative films, identification is dependent upon a stable point of view. By continually disrupting and complicating the visual and narrative devices which maintain the coherence of point of view, Rainer's film complicates the spectator's ability to "identify" with filmic characters. She suggests that film's deep dependency on point of view (gender specific or otherwise) as the primary means by which the spectator is given intimate access to a kind of knowledge, no matter how relative – as in the elegant equivocations of *Rashomon* – is what needs to be dismantled and understood as a seductive fiction. Insofar as Trisha's concluding remarks about "a-womanliness" can be seen as an abandonment of gender as a shorthand notion of identity, Rainer is trying to abandon the ownership of (and perhaps film's conspiracy in the maintenance of) single identity itself.

The relationships between language, image, and character are individually and collectively rearranged in *The Man Who Envied Women*. Rainer's ambitious film underlines the ways in which narrative coherence demands and creates a spectator alert to a too simple coherence. The project of the film is not to delineate the reasons and motivations for Jack's envy of Trisha or Jackie; nor is it the story of Jack's transformation from bully to lover; I don't even think it's about the way in which film theory informs film practice although that is sort of distractingly interesting. *The Man Who Envied Women* is actually about the appetite for rearranging and reconfiguring the connections between image, language, and character in film, the desire to rearrange and reconfigure sexual relationships in "Life" and economic-political-spatial relationships in "Art" and in "The World," and it is about Rainer's own appetite for a new aesthetic of filmic architecture. (There is a difference between delineating an appetite for something and delineating the thing itself. The film is much more of a proposal and speculative dream than it is a programmatic manifesto; this too is in keeping with Rainer's witty metaphysics and Trisha's wide ruminations.)

"Filmic architecture" borders on the oxymoronic: architecture tends to connote stability and the fixing of and within space. It tends to connote sculptural fields like Judd's and towers like Trump's. Rainer's *filmic* architecture takes flexibility and flow as defining principles, and film's inevitable failure to meet the desire to fix or possess space itself as its philosophic spine. *The Man Who Envied Women* rejuvenates the political/ aesthetic agenda of the avant-garde film in its method, and it challenges contemporary critical theory's thralldom with masculinist modes in its argument. *The Man Who Envied Women* reframes theory's own desire for possession and coherence. Theory's panting after discursive space is perhaps not only a logical but an inevitable consequence of the separation and parceling out of "space" in critical discourse itself. Film studies, feminist or otherwise, exists in a discursive space that encourages (even demands) "possession." The bitter irony, of course, is that film's most radical potential lies in its inability to be possessed or owned.[9] Rainer exploits film's ability to move pictures continuously, to endlessly rearrange the cut-outs by which and through which we come to see and project identity and ownership, and through which we come to desire them both, in order to unsettle our comfort with the conventions of coherence. In film, the particularly comfortable conventions Rainer seeks to upset are sharply delineated points of view (owning stories) and the modes of address typical of narrative and documentary film. From the first ten minutes of Super-8 film through the video documentary of the housing hearings, Rainer constantly manipulates the surface of her film. We, like Jack, are left with cut-outs whose "meaning" lies in its potential to be endlessly rearranged. What makes this film more than a smart leftist manifesto, is the innovative way in which Rainer matches her political vision of privilegelessness with the aesthetic possibilities of interrupted and shared filmic space. Rainer degrades the values of the ownership of ideas, discourse, and Manhattan lofts, by continually rearranging what we expect film to own: the space of its frame.

Rainer suggests that the consequence of feminist film theory's reliance on gender-specific forms of identification, and the implicit valorization of the difference between a male gaze and a female one integral to that identification, implies that female presence in film might be best mediated through her visual absence. Rainer's destabilization of point of view, and her constant questioning of the spectator's position in relation to those images and language-acts which produce a filmic presence, undermines the category of "woman" as she has been figured in and by feminist film theory. For while that theory has been dedicated to the woman who appears, as an arrested projection, it has been blind to the woman who fails to appear. The inability to attend to the woman who cannot appear has been attributed to the unconscious racism and heterosexism which prevail(ed?) in feminist film theory.[10] While there is certainly a significant truth in this explanation, it too assumes a belief in the progressive politics of visibility *per se*. Non-heterosexist and non-white subject positions can certainly be (and have already been) articulated within feminist film theory,[11] *but* several very important, and to date still inadequately recognized aspects of this enterprise, must (again) be stressed:

1 Subject position in most films cannot be established independent of the given to be seen. Subject position in spectatorship is established through a complex relation to what is shown. While some films work with sound as the source of spectatorial identification – the brilliant leaking ear of the John Goodman character in *Barton Fink* for example – visual pleasure still continues to be the ground of most narrative cinema.

2 Since the given to be seen is always exclusionary, subject positions must attend to the affective consequences of the *failure* to be recognized. This failure implies that subject positions are always related to the negative, to that which cannot be or is not developed within the visual field. Therefore, subject positions are always partial.

3 The failure of self-seeing which representation seeks to hide but always affirms implies that the impotency of the inward gaze is a necessary condition for the intensity of the external gaze. To see, again, how the external gaze works to hide the impotency of the inward gaze is to recognize that the failure of self-seeing fuels the desire to see the other. The given to be seen, the Other, is a cipher for the looking self.

4 To reject the sterility of this process, the impotency of the inward gaze must be revalued. As a gaze which cannot be reproduced, precisely because it does not generate the reproduction of metaphor, the conversion of two into one, the inward gaze reveals nothing but itself. (Lacan: "If beyond appearance there is nothing in itself, there is the gaze.") Completely self-referential, the inward gaze is essentially performative and locked in the Present, rather than representational and available for re-play.

5 As something which is not reproductive, the inward gaze is, perhaps, not marked by gender. Therefore, it is not useful to speak of "the male gaze" or "the female gaze." I want to stress that I am not talking about the pervasive internalization of the panoptic ("male") gaze here – but rather I am speaking of the inward gaze's recognition of the subject's inability to appear to itself – a failure experienced by all genders.

In refusing to ally the cinematic gaze with a gendered gaze, Rainer insists that the gaze itself is, and can only be, partial. Film theory's effort to elucidate the "apparatus of the gaze" as a route to critical mastery is, I believe, mistaken. Copjec suggests that film theory took Foucault's notion of the panoptic gaze and applied it to film theory under the rubric of a mistaken psychoanalytic account of identification. She suggests that it is precisely the failure of the gaze to be absolute that makes symbolic identification – which is to say, the misrecognition which all representation exploits – possible.

> [N]o position defines a resolute identity. Nonknowledge or invisibility is not registered as the wavering and negotiations between two

certainties, two meanings or positions, but the undermining of every certainty, the incompleteness of every meaning and position. Incapable of understanding this more radical understanding of non-knowledge, the panoptic argument is ultimately *resistant to resistance,* unable to conceive of a discourse that would refuse rather than refuel power.

(original emphases; "Orthopsychic": 56)

The refusal of a monolithic power, like the refusal of possession and a fixed perspective, leads Rainer to resist the power of a gender-specific theoretical analysis as well.

6 In staging the failure of the Other to appear representationally, Rainer forces the spectator to redesign the reciprocity of the external gaze. The frustration of the external gaze serves to mark the impotency of the inward gaze.

7 Once that failure becomes an accepted necessity of seeing, rather than, as now, something that must be overcome and hidden by the surplus of the given to be seen, it might be possible for the Other to be other-than a cipher for the looking self.

To effect this, however, a representational shift will also have to occur. Rather than living under the ideology of the visible, which is to say the phallocentric regime of a reproductive representational economy in which the Other is converted into the fetishized Same, the possibilities of the unreproductive must be revalued. Performance, the genre of art in which disappearance (the failure of the given to be seen to remain fixed in an arrested projection) is part of the aim of the work, must take a more central place than it currently holds in the landscape of contemporary representation. As more and more artists working in a wide range of visual forms, from sculpture, to photography, to film, to dance, take up the appellation "performance artist," we begin to witness the recognition of the necessity of this shift.

Subjectivity can only be "had," that is to say, experienced and performed (through the performance one has the experience of subjectivity), in the admission and recognition of one's failure to appear to oneself and within the representational field. The discontinuity engendered by the failure to appear sustains our dependence on visual representation as a mirror. But, could we learn to revalue the failure to appear (and thereby also effect a change in our relation to the continuities secured in and through historiography), we could perhaps also begin to develop a different relation to the given to be seen. Rainer's film is one attempt to bring this different relation into being.

If we lose the opportunity to redesign this relation to the given to be seen, we risk changing only the content of visual representation. The Other will continually be converted into the Same and the Same will continually discover new Others (or new aspects of the Same will be discovered until the terrain of the visible is as absolute as the map in Borges' allegory). And gazing at everyone we will see no one.

Note: A version of this chapter was originally published in 1991 in *The Hysterical Male: New Feminist Theory*, ed. Arthur and Marilouise Kroker, New York: St Martin's Press, London: Macmillan, Montreal: New World Perspectives.

4

The golden apple: Jennie Livingston's *Paris Is Burning*

... and they saw the lights going on all over the city, the fireworks, and the great crowds cheering, and plenty to see and plenty to buy everywhere, and amidst all this they felt entitled to walk the streets these two, they felt entitled to stand side by side, to be as remarkable as they were and yet go unremarked.

(Neil Bartlett, *Ready To Catch Him Should He Fall*: 300)

Jennie Livingston's controversial film *Paris Is Burning* (1991) documents one of the most difficult and complex performance texts I've seen. The film chronicles the competitive drag balls staged in Harlem clubs (most of the film was shot at the Imperial Elks Lodge) between 1987 and 1989. The models, who walk and compete for huge trophies during the ball, are Latino and African-American gay men, transvestites, and transsexuals, most of whom are poor. Counter-intuitively, the balls reveal the performers' longing to be made unremarkable – to pass as "normative" (and thus be unnoticed) rather than to be seen as "other" (and constantly surveyed by the upholders of the normative). Excessively marked as "other" outside the arena of the balls, the walkers employ the hyper-visibility of the runway to secure the power and freedom of invisibility outside the hall.

Livingston's film of the balls gives another twist to the already knotted set of reversals and inversions around the politics of visibility generated by the performances themselves. In other words, the film itself inflects and transforms the politics and meanings of the balls. The temptation to read Livingston's film *as* a transparent record of the performances is much like the temptation to read skin color as racial identity, and gender categories as the consequence of sexual difference. The balls themselves, however, argue against this kind of singular transcription. Attempting to make her subjects visible to a mainstream audience, Livingston presents them within the strict genre codings of ethnographic documentary. That the walkers themselves remain somewhat impervious to the law of the ethnographic documentary allows them to retain some of their subversive power, the power of the unsurveyable. The degree to which the spectator is made conscious of what the film cannot and/or will not show is the degree to which the film, unwittingly, succeeds. Judith Butler's speculation that it may now be a matter of "letting that which cannot fully appear in any performance persist in its disruptive promise" is given forceful, if unconscious, weight by *Paris Is Burning*.[1]

I

Focusing on cross-dressing as a means of investigating the politics of culture, knowledge, and power, Livingston employs some of the common ethnographic devices for displaying community: inter-titles explaining specific lexical markers seemingly "unique" to this community – (but translatable nonetheless) – "reading," "shading," "mopping"; interviews with articulate informants; a significant change within the community under observation – the consciousness of AIDS; and voice-overs marking the consequences of that change. In presenting her community as both unique and comprehensible Livingston implicitly fetishizes her subjects, by transforming the "unknown" (and potentially anxiety-inducing "other") into the "known" (the reassuring familiar). Once fetishized, another displacement occurs from the performance to the film, and *Paris Is Burning* itself becomes the reassuring familiar, the fetish object. By "explaining" her subjects so (apparently) thoroughly Livingston encourages the spectator to believe s/he has mastered their drama, their pain, their art. She provides the spectator with a feeling of assurance, of competence as a "reader" of this "other" culture. The terms of that reading, however, bear further scrutiny – if only because they work to eclipse the fetishism of the image of the woman that motivates the drag performance itself. In other words, the film traces a series of displacements which reveal the *mise-en-abyme* of "woman as fetish."

In part a visual threnody for a pre-AIDS culture, the film is nostalgic for a future her informants had dreamed of in a more vital past. The loss of that future haunts the speakers' dreams of economic success and idealized femininity. (While the performances are also aimed at other idealized images – such as male business executives and military men – I am concerned here primarily with drag.) The impossibility of realizing these dreams frames the space of this particular theatre. The balls documented in *Paris* are masquerades of absence and lack which enact the masochistic power and genuine pleasure of symbolic identification so crucial to both capitalism and erotic desire.[2] Part of that symbolic identification is with the power connoted by whiteness (which is different from "identifying as white"); another part of that identification stems from a desire to reverse the coded power of visible and invisible markings.

The walkers admire "whiteness" in part because it is unmarked and therefore escapes political surveillance. For these men who are simultaneously over-seen and under-represented – they are overseen because they are represented as the needed-to-be-watched – appropriating whiteness can be a paradoxical gesture. On the one hand, it is complicitous with the notion of whiteness as an unmarked part of "ideal beauty" and on the other, the marked appropriation comments on that "normative" notion of beauty. But the force of feeling that one does not conform to that model, that one is always other-than the model, leads to a desire to revise and/or enhance one's own physical body so that it more closely imitates and conforms to that model.[3]

Imitation and conformity are motivated by more than a desire to "look like a model." Embedded within a complex community of familial, linguistic, economic, psychic, aesthetic, political, and erotic signifiers, "reading" the balls is tricky business. Livingston carefully explains the structures of the communities, the families, the hierarchies of the balls, and the common linguistic signs – shading, mopping, realness – which inform and define the competition. Participants are performing legends, mothers, up-and-coming legends, or children. They compete in contests whose names include Military Realness, Butch Queen Realness, Best Bangee Boy and Bangee Girl. They belong to houses, which, under the seemingly thin bond of fashion and style, knit members together into the fabric of family. Their family names are taken either from the stars of the fashion industry – St Laurent, Chanel, Armani – or from the most captivating member of the house – Pepper Labeija, Willi Ninja, Angie Xtravaganza – who serves as the mother of the family. In taking the corporate name/logo of the most expensive fashion designers as their own, the children both appropriate and mock the intentional "exclusiveness" of these labels. In adopting the name of the mother rather than the name of the father the houses valorize the femininity which they emulate in the balls themselves. The architecture of that femininity, however, is thoroughly masculine. And it thoroughly reflects the psychic-political structure of capitalism.

The driving force of an appropriative capitalism insists on affirming the "have-not" condition which motivates the desire to purchase a never-ending series of commodities. Economic "lack" everywhere infiltrates sexual and political lack in *Paris Is Burning*. The boasting pride of the children who have bought breasts for their mother condenses the political, economic, and psychic narratives. From no breasts to two breasts, Angie Xtravaganza displays the visible sign of the nurturing Symbolic Mother with obvious pride and joy. Told "no" by the law of the father so often, the children double the negative and turn it into a

positive. The children want to be mothered and to be given the nurtur-
ant pleasure associated with breasts; but they also want to *see* the
Mother and to participate in her construction and (re)birth. The layers
here are thick: ironic, ambivalent, and earnest; at once the invention of
this Mother is extraordinarily intricate. Freud believed that the male
child's desire to ingest the maternal breast was a formative influence on
his castration complex.[4] (His desire is projected and displaced onto her,
with appropriate shifts in body parts duly noted.) Although not completely inside the heterosexual narrative within which this psychoanalytic proposition rests (although neither completely outside of it), the
children of *Paris* reverse the assumptions of this narrative. Assured of
access to the breasts they purchased and thus own, the children blissfully keep the breasts before them while retaining the potent reassur-
ance of "her" (and thus their own) penis. Angie Xtravaganza's breasts
turn the silent, invisible "no" of the castrating father into the giddy and
visible "yes" of the Mother. The children of *Paris* accept the structure of
the Freudian narrative, in much the same way they accept the operative
power of whiteness, mimic it, and in that mimicry transform its defining
power.

The gender play operative within *Paris Is Burning*, therefore, involves
much more than cross-*dressing*. And the stakes are higher than most
theoretical speculation around gender generally allows. Driving the
mechanism of these performed identities is a notion of "the real."
Realness is determined by the ability to blend in, to not be noticed. Like
the performance of passing more generally, the performance at these
balls represents that which cannot be seen precisely by underlining that
which is seen.

The paradox of using visibility to highlight invisibility is complex and
quite often misfires. Passing performances in general seek to use one
form of invisibility to highlight a usually privileged form of visibility.
Gays and lesbians who choose to pass as straight, are employing the
(relative) invisibility of the marks of sexual preference. But this very
passing also highlights the "normative" and unmarked nature of heterosexuality. It is easy to pass as heterosexual because heterosexuality is
assumed. In other words, what is made visible is the unmarked nature
of heterosexual identity. The one who passes then does not "erase" the
mark of difference, rather the passer highlights the invisibility of the
mark of the Same. But increasingly the "privileged" form of visibility is
shifting. We are now witnessing the attempt of heterosexual men, for
example, to pass as gay. Matthew Barney's Fall 1991 show in New York
illustrated a significant moment in contemporary culture. Barney appropriated the tropes of (white) gay contemporary art as his signature
statement. Madonna's public flirtation with Sandra Bernhardt is another
instance of a straight woman attempting to pass as a lesbian. While the

political implications of these gestures tend to be deflated by the self-aggrandizing self-promotion which attends them, the philosophical and psychic performances necessary for these attempts to pass continue to provoke my interest. For if the ascendant term in the binary hetero-homo is beginning to shift, if only in these limited instances, perhaps too the binary visibility-invisibility will also shift.

The power of the "unseen" community lies in its ability to cohere outside the system of observation which seeks to patrol it. So the "in-jokes," the "secret" codes, the iconography of dress, movement, and speech which can be read by those within the community, but escape the interpretative power of those external to it, can create another expressive language which cannot be translated by those who are not familiar with the meanings of this intimate tongue. (This "separate" speech also makes members of these communities complain of claustro-phobia.) The risk of visibility then is the risk of any translation – a weaker version of the original script, the appropriation by (economically and artistically) powerful "others." The payoff of translation (and visi-bility) is more people will begin to speak in your tongue.

The story of feminist theory within the academy is a good illustration of the risks and the promises of translation and visibility. On the one hand, Tania Modleski can now write a book entitled *Feminism Without Women*; on the other, more students than ever before have heard of something called "the male gaze." Both facts continue to inscribe the gender binary. This binary is precisely what is at issue in *Paris Is Burning*. Passing *seems* to suggest a potential performative space in which the binary is broken down. But fundamental to passing is the binary of the seen and the unseen, the visible and the invisible. This binary functions like the binary of sexual difference. *Paris Is Burning* demonstrates how intimate the link is between the binaries. The walkers use one set of binaries to question the other. Before returning to the film, I want to interrogate the question of the stability of the binaries by recourse to another passing performance.

Adrian Piper's "calling card" performances seek to make visible what is taken to be invisible. Piper, who is a light-skinned African-American and sometimes passes as white (much to her dismay), created a business card which she "passes" out to people who pass over her racial differ-ence. Terse and formally polite, the card reads:

Dear Friend:
  I am black.
  I am sure that you did not realize this when you made/laughed at/agreed with that racist remark. In the past, I have attempted to alert white people to my racial identity in advance. Unfortunately, this invariably causes them to react to me as pushy, manipulative, or

socially inappropriate. Therefore, my policy is to assume that white people do not make these remarks, even when they believe there are no black people present, and to distribute this card when they do.

I regret any discomfort my presence is causing you, just as I am sure you regret the discomfort your racism is causing me.

Sincerely Yours,
Adrian Margaret Smith Piper[5]

Piper's text resists the disappearance of her difference by those who would pass her without her consent. Working on the opposite end of the visibility/invisibility continuum from the walkers in the balls, Piper's performances are aimed at re-establishing the force of that which is not registered within the given to be seen, her racial identity.

Piper's work consistently dramatizes the failure of the visible to represent race. Her performances seek ways to "supplement" the visual by marking what it excludes. Refusing to let her identity be a matter of its visible appearance, Piper has gone very far in imagining another form of identification between performers and spectators. By appropriating the tight square of the business/calling card, Piper suggests that the *business* of politicizing racial difference involves marking its *disappearance*. (The white liberal response to racial difference – "it doesn't matter what color you are, you are my friend" – can be seen as a way of ignoring the historical force of racism itself.) Piper's card then establishes, simultaneously, the failure of racial difference to appear within the narrow range of the visible and registers her refusal to let the visual field *fail* to secure it. The card itself ruptures the given to be seen and exposes the normative force of everyday blindness: if no one looks black, everyone is white.

The insecurity engendered by the disavowal of the visual field to perpetuate racial difference is an incredibly potent consequence of Piper's work. If racial difference is not registered visibly, where is it located? Is it a free floating signifier? How can one secure it? By marking her racial "otherness" in the landscape of the Same, Piper points to the universalizing mimetic "likeness" that the given to be seen attempts to secure. In denying that likeness, Piper makes the insecurity of vision and visibility apparent. Suggesting that location and identity are never *only* related to what can be seen, Piper's work forces spectators to look much more closely at their internal politics of location and racial difference than they are usually required to do.[6]

Within the communities recorded in *Paris*, however, the possibility of passing is seen as something to be exploited, not resisted. The extravagant costume and *personae* displayed at the balls are serious rehearsals for a much tougher walk – down the "mean streets" of New York City. The balls are opportunities to use theatre to imitate the theatricality of everyday life – a life which includes show girls, bangee boys, and business executives. It is the endless theatre of everyday life that determines the real: and this theatricality is soaked through with racial, sexual, and class bias.[7]

As one of the informants explains, to be able to look like a business executive is to be able to be a business executive. Within the impoverished logic of appearance, "opportunity" and "ability" can be connoted by the way one looks. But at the same time, the walker is *not* a business executive and the odds are that his performance of that job on the runway of the ball will be his only chance to experience it. The performances, then, enact simultaneously the desire to eliminate the distance between ontology and performance – and the reaffirmation of that distance.

The relative claims of the "realness" promised by Being and the "realness" created in performance are interrogated by the *filmic documentary* of these performances. This is worth remarking. As a documentary the film supports a belief in the "realness" of being, and as a representational genre, the film also supports a belief in the unavoidability of performance, artifice, mediation.

Realness, then, is not a static concept – anymore than race, sexuality, or identity are static. Dorian Corey, one of the wisest informants in the film, is a light-skinned African-American who dresses *à la* Marilyn Monroe in part because when he began to do drag performances the "show-girl look" was the apex of drag.[8] That "show-girl look" was emphatically white. The younger and darker-skinned teenagers who walk in the balls now dressed as "bangee girls" have a radically different image of what the ideal drag performance imitates. The performances can congenially inhabit the same frame, however, because they both appropriate the historical image of "the woman" and in that appropriation recirculate it (Figure 22).

Woman remains available to further recirculation in part because she is that which can never be internalized as identity for men and in part because each repetition of that image (re)marks its perpetual (re)construction. Woman is the figure of disguise, of masquerade. In imitating her, the cross-dresser makes visible his own desire to be disguised. Within the economy of patriarchal desire which frames – although it does not completely define – gay male cross-dressing, the figure of the woman is appropriated as a sign to validate male authority. His authority is determined by how fully he can "wear" her; in wearing her, however, he renders her actual presence unnecessary.[9] In this sense, gay male cross-dressing makes manifest the psychic structure of "traditional heterosexual culture" – which is to say, male homosocial culture. Woman is a necessary point of tension because she reflects and assures male authority. "She" disguises his desire for the phallus – and the

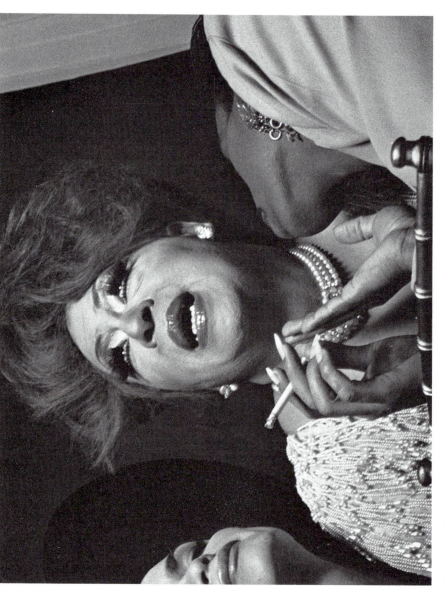

Figure 22 Film still of Angie Xtravaganza, Dorian Corey, and Willi Ninja from Jennie Livingston's *Paris Is Burning* (1991). (Photo: Michel Comte. Courtesy: Prestige, A Division of Miramax Films)

competition to wear her well merely makes room for the displacements operative in all erotic exchange.

A re-presented woman is always a copy of a copy; the "real" (of) woman cannot be represented because her function is to re-present man. She is the mirror and thus is never in it. Her narrowly defined but ubiquitous image represents the frenzy of man to see she who makes him him. (Woman is man's always-mother.) In the film, Willi Ninja teaches young women how to walk like women – to be "models." These walkers are in turn imitated by Ninja's compeers at the balls. A man teaches a woman how to walk and she models that walk for another man to imitate. Given the slippery politics of appearance, this walk contributes to the definition of what a woman "is." Homophobia demands that the woman continue to be placed between the bodies of the two men – but she is just a foil for the central relationship between the men. At the balls, he then displays that walk for the approval of other men.

As "mothers," women's bodies retain the possibility of being entered and evacuated by other bodies. As a Mother, she internalized him within her body – and women in general become for men always potential Symbolic Mothers. The tight literalness of the Western psyche seeks equations and equivalencies: women cannot themselves enter the body of men; they can internalize men but they cannot be internalized by men. Men's inability to absorb the woman fully accounts for the projective anxiety of castration which traditional heterosexual culture represses and gay male drag fetishizes. Much energy in both cultures is dedicated to keeping her image external, forever before their eyes. As a supplement within the field of the Same, the re-presentation of the woman is a substitute for a substitute, a fetish.[10] She is the *mise-en-abyme* of patriarchal representation for both heterosexual and gay male culture (insofar as it is useful to make the distinction between these cultures – heterosexual culture is mainly a male homosocial culture anyway).

Gay male cross-dressers *resist* the body of woman even while they make its constructedness visible. This is in part why the misogyny which underlies gay male cross-dressing is so painful to women. As Marilyn Frye puts it: "[G]ay men's effeminacy and donning of feminine apparel displays no love of or identification with women or the womanly. [. . .] It is a casual and cynical mockery of women."[11] But it is something more than that as well.

Within the film world of *Paris* walking in a ball is at once a celebration of one's grandest ambitions to charm, seduce, and attract, and an admission that the model one most admires is perennially hostile and impervious to such admiration. Masochism is an integral part of the spectacle; but it cuts both ways. The distance between the model and the walker – what the performance tries to narrow even while, necessarily, reaffirming – produces violence. The barely contained violence of the balls (vogueing itself is described as a "safe" gang war) comes from the profound display of the arbitrariness of this distance. Pain is never too far from the parade of costume and Protean self-invention demanded by the discriminating spectators/performers who watch the show – spectators who, no matter how critical (and competitive), are ever so much "safer" than the spectators on the street, the subway, the line for the movies.

The filmic spectators who watch *Paris Is Burning* have a different relation to the performance than the spectators/performers recorded within the film. Within the film, the spectators are also performers: the categories, like the boundaries around sexual difference, are extremely unstable. Underneath the image of the visible woman is a man, but it is extremely difficult to say what a man is. Underneath the film there is a performance but it is extremely difficult to say what the performance "means." In an effort to ease this difficulty, Livingston "fixes" her own spectator via the form of filmic address she employs. In keeping with the law of the genre of ethnographic film, Livingston addresses her spectator as external to the community. Ethnographic law insists that the film will function as the liminal figure who sutures "them" to "us." The film must then maintain the distinction between "them" and "us" so as to justify its address and its powerful liminality. But these very categories are severely questioned by the performance itself.

As Jackie Goldsby points out in her incisive review of *Paris*, Livingston "can tell this story because her identity is not implicated in it. [. . .] This is not to say that Livingston shouldn't have made the film, or that a 'black' film necessarily would have been different. It is to suggest, though, that the cultural and social privilege of the filmmaker is inscribed into the film however unobtrusive she strives to be" ("Queens of Language": 11). That cultural and social privilege is the privilege of a non-interrogated whiteness. The danger of this particular form of liminality is that it allows the white spectator to be flattered, rather than chastened, by the ideological critique of white capitalist culture embodied in the balls. The distinction between symbolic identification and identity is in danger of being lost by the form of spectatorial address Livingston employs. Some of the walkers want to *pass* as white, but they do not want to *be* white. This is a crucial difference.

As bell hooks remarks in her blistering review of the film, "Livingston does not oppose the way hegemonic whiteness 'represents' blackness, but rather assumes an imperial overseeing position that is no way progressive or counterhegemonic" ("Is Paris Burning?": 62). While hooks implicitly subscribes to the overly simple idea that reflexivity about whiteness would have "saved" the film from its appropriative hegemonic grasp, she forcefully denounces the uncritical praise of the film's methods. Her critique is severe but it should be noted that she is writing against the adoring voices of reviewers ranging from Vincent Canby to Essex Hemphill.[12] Hemphill, for example, remarks enthusiastically: "We are not exposed to any of Livingston's judgments, if she has any, of the subjects. The authentic voice of this community emerges unfettered" ("Paris Is Burning": 10). The wish to hear an authentic, single voice is very strong, but representation is never transparent. The desire for an "authentic" racial and sexual identity is similarly impossible to satisfy; the walkers accept that desire and stage its perpetual failure.

The specific and important achievement of *Paris* is that it opens up the possibility of seizing an appropriative epistemology not *about* cross-dressing but indebted to its wisdom. Livingston's film does not enact the radical epistemology of her subjects – it sticks too close to the rules of ethnographic documentary to experiment with criss-crossing filmic identities. To take the challenge of her subjects seriously, Livingston might have eagerly and restlessly ransacked the codes of the filmic real – the history film, the "realism of melodrama," the simulated-crime film, the sports replay – in order to find a filmic "match" for the represented real that her performers seek. But despite these limitations *Paris Is Burning* is still an important film – if only because it comes so close to being an astonishing documentary about something that may be unfilmable.

The balls Livingston documents and the film with which she documents them are precisely alike in their revulsion for and adoration of the *real*. Ontologically, cinema detests the real because it must remain a celluloid shadow of it, a trace of something always receding and absent. At the same time, cinema loves the real because in tracing and framing the real, it gains power and definition. Similarly, those who walk in the balls win for *imitating* – rather than being – the real. The walks both perpetuate the aspiration to be real and mark again the artifice that makes it, always, impossible to be real (and not only for the walkers). Cheryl Lynn's "Got to Be Real" haunts the sound-track and the camera restlessly wanders out of the clubs into the streets of mid-town and finds what normally would appear to be white, heterosexual couples chatting in well-coiffured hair and trim suits. The walkers want to believe that such people are real in order to have something to imitate *and* define themselves against. But realness has become such a fluid term that these heterosexual white couples seem exceptionally artificial. In fact, these couples appear to be more "unreal" than the walkers because they remain unaware of the artifice that the walkers have made hyper-visible. Framed within a film that is so relentlessly concerned with the fine gradations of the (relative) real, these couples have the same uncanny appearance as those who attend a costume ball without disguise.

Surrounded by masks, the "natural" appearance seems like the most effective illusion.

All film is preoccupied with the calibrations of illusion inherent in the real because ontologically film is excluded from the real – just as the walkers are excluded from "being" the real they perform at the ball. While the walkers are not excluded ontologically, the forces of class, racism, and homophobia conspire to make their political-social exclusion seem ontological. The art of the walkers, however, is to illustrate how capricious such exclusions are, and how falsely narrow the white hetero-sexual "real" is.

The balls aim to show that a flamboyant walk at the Imperial Elks Lodge is a ticket to passing for real outside of the club. Counter-intuitively, performing this real allows the walker to be passed over, not vulnerable to the hostile gaze of white heterosexual culture. The goal of the balls is to theatricalize the passage from excessive hyper-visibility attendant on the "other" in white, affluent culture to the "invisibility" accorded to white men within that same culture. The image of the woman is the figure for this theatricality because she is the currency with which men strive to out-purchase one another.

When the white couples appear in *Paris*, it is almost as if the film has become a commercial selling and exposing the commodity of white, heterosexual, and economic privilege. These couples signal the distance between the ball's dream of the real – a dream full of concentration, energy, and focus – and the surface casualness of these couples' real. This easy casualness is the inimitable kernel of the Real that eludes the walkers. The balls are the manifestation of the alarmingly powerful distance between symbolic identification and identity itself. The figure of the (white) woman as the cipher for that distance is then necessarily a figure of immense ambivalence. Had Livingston rigorously examined this subject she might have made an extraordinary film. The film's failure to take up that harder project is the failure to look closely at the political implications of appropriative epistemology and to examine the incredible allure of being unseen when visibility has meant (and continues to mean) violence, imprisonment, death.

II

My friend keeps telling me to be sure I keep saying I'm only writing about Livingston's film of the balls and I'm not writing about the balls themselves. My friend knows how tempted I am to take Livingston's film as a perfect unbiased record of the performances. That's where the hook of the film (and perhaps of most ethnographic film) breaks my skin. Like Essex Hemphill, I want a film that substitutes for the perform-ance itself – a transparent film that renders the performance in all its complexity. I know there's no such thing as transparent film, but that doesn't make my wish for it disappear. So my friend tries to remind me of the difference between what I know to be true and what I wish to be true. I half listen and half rant. I type and retype these old and new words, look at the clock, look at time moving across my own face. This typeface. The projector is still on.

I want the film to be transparent so I can explain in lavish detail how the performance makes equivalencies between mopping a St Laurent dress and "buying" breasts. Gender has a price tag – and once in the market, it can be bought and sold, manipulated by the surgeon's knife, deft clefts in the market of elegant signs. But there's something more behind my desire for the film to be "real." White women like myself have been encouraged to mistake performance for ontology – to believe that the role is real, and thus sufficient to constitute an identity, a sense of purpose, a reason for being. If performance can provide a substitute real then "identity" can truly be an invention – not something susceptible to some external facts (biological, sexual, economic) which prohibit our access to "femininity," "beauty," "glamour," "power," "wealth," or whatever it is we desire. But the only way we can see if performance is an adequate substitute for ontology is through the staging of performances. In that enactment, however, we make conscious again the difference between performance and ontology: precisely what motivates the performance is that which ontology – the question of being itself – will not and cannot answer. In the variations on that re-enactment, we can read the historical and political imperatives that prohibited Dorian Corey from seeing Lena Horne as his real idol twenty years ago, and allows someone today to see Patti La Belle as his. Are these the "facts" that cannot be flicked away with the surgeon's knife? Is imagination the "real" limit? Or history? Or our imagination of history?

Racism and homophobia are seen in *Paris* as more hostile than the forces of sexism – and this I believe is partially because the informants are men and less astute about the impact of sexism on identity than they are about the impact of racism and homophobia. Pepper Labeija hints as much when he says that he thinks having a sex-change operation is taking things "a little too far." After all, he points out, in many ways women have it a lot worse than men in this culture. But given the virulence of homophobia it may well be that for someone like Venus Xtravaganza surgically transforming her genitals promises a more satisfying life than desiring a man from within the caverns of a biologically male body. Surgery, for women – and increasingly for men – is an accepted way to achieve "self-improvement," that fundamental aspiration of the American mythos.

It is in the attitude toward self-invention that the relationship between the ideology of nation/culture and the ideology of gender can most clearly be seen. The stories told in *Paris* are compatible with the myths of American identity – myths which center on white men's struggle to invent and reinvent their identities in the moment. (The parallel myth for women involves the endless reinvention of their image because how she looks is (still) who she is.) Part of the appeal of *Paris* for a white, straight audience is its ability to absorb and tame the so-called Otherness of this part of Black and Latino gay male culture. The dreams of economic success, fame, and security articulated by the performers are exactly the same dreams of "most American men." The means by which these dreams are realized – self-invention, hard work, and ingenuity – are the same methods celebrated in the careers of Ragged Rick and *Rocky I* through *V*. For the American man, self-(re)invention is an integral part of the mythos of success.[13]

Overlaid on this mythos is the American philosophical predisposition toward pragmatism; the sense that philosophy and jurisprudence must, above all, be practical and concern themselves with the questions and problems of "the ordinary guy." Philosophical positions and judicial decisions must, in other words, be responsive to the real.

Given the accents on pragmatism within the US, the judicial stance toward difference, most recently underlined by *Bowers* v. *Hardwick* (1986), has a startlingly clear relation to the street life and culture of "the ordinary guy." *Bowers* v. *Hardwick* effectively eliminated the notion of privacy for homosexuals: the state is legally permitted to survey and prosecute sodomy between same sex partners, even in their own bedrooms. By legally eliminating privacy for homosexuals, the Supreme Court extends the runway of the ball. There is no legal boundary to the gaze of the state and the "enforcers" of the law. Thus, if a gay man can get home on the subway dressed as a woman without having his head bashed in, he wins because he has managed to escape scrutiny and notice. That's pragmatism and self-invention at once. That is America. And that is living and surviving based on appropriative knowledge.

But it is here too that the most troublesome aspect of Livingston's film is revealed. This is the same problem endemic to ethnography: once the subject is turned into the Subject-supposed-to-know, the subject is misrecognized. Lacan argued that "truth" emerged from the fact of this misrecognition, that what one knows, finally, is that misrecognition is a defining aspect of all true knowing. Certainly, this essay itself implicitly assumes that Livingston's misrecognition produces what I know, and my misrecognition of her work will motivate your response to these words. But what Lacan consistently understated and critical commentary continues to obscure, is that this misrecognition contains within it an affective power. On the one hand, it supports the impulse to fetishize, to transform the unknown (the thing one cannot recognize and therefore cannot imitate or own) into what one does know, can see, and securely own. One then represses the fact of the transformation, although it remains "known." As Freud put it in his brief article on fetishism one continually finds oneself saying, in effect, "I know very well, but just the same . . . "[14] And it is at the level of "just the same" that the fetish functions.

However, the affective power of misrecognition also promises the threat *and* joy of self-dissolution. Leo Bersani elaborates a psycho-analytic desire for "self shattering" and suggests that sexuality itself contains within it a kernel of masochism that is pleasurable precisely because one persists after the imagination of one's own shattering.[15] Often on the verge of being unbearable to ourselves, the ability to imagine our own dissolution is often pleasurable, if only because it reveals the tenacity of our imaginative will, as Western theology, litera-ture, and philosophy have demonstrated.[16] In other words, part of what motivates the misrecognition of the other is the real knowledge that one cannot see or recognize oneself. The failure to recognize one's internal other(s) is rehearsed and projected externally as the misrecognition of the external other. Thus psychic mimesis, an adequate reflection of the failure to see oneself, must be an integral part of "realistic" represen-tation – in ethnography, in literature, in love. To avoid the conquering impulses of fetishism, representation must mark the limits of its generic laws – limits which expose what cannot be seen, what will not appear within the representational frame. And Law itself, if it seeks to nurture sociality, must bow to the higher claims of privacy and individual freedom from surveillance.

Within these boundaries then, where does the power of *Paris Is Burning* lie? In framing the mimicry of all identity, Livingston's film documents the impossibility of securing the authentic view of anyone or anything. The film mimes the performance; the performance mimes the images of women; the images of women mime the fantasies of men; the fantasies of men mime the "real" which underscores all fantasy and so on. The balls intervene in the smooth reproduction of physical images by using mimicry and appropriation both to point out the constructed-ness of that image and to replicate its power. Unavoidably complicitous with the thing they try to denounce, the walkers – like other post-modern artists such as Cindy Sherman, Sherrie Levine, and Richard Prince – find themselves caught in the tight logic of the commodified sign.[17] It is virtually impossible to escape this logic and Livingston's lucrative film – to appropriate Foucault's description of Freud – would have to be invented if it had not already appeared.

III

If the challenge of *Paris* is to find a filmic equivalent for the appropriative knowledge of cross-dressing, what is the challenge for writing, for the critical-political economy of the sign? It must require more than the insistent mentioning of "my friend." Writing always requires scrutiny of the name; all signature is appropriation; writerly authority and identity are both announced by and through naming. By quoting the response of an unnamed authority in a text covered with the authoritative names of others – from Freud to bell hooks – I (feebly) attempt to re-mark the collaborative and appropriative nature of writing itself. "Venus Xtravaganza." "Willi Ninja." Names are the literal signs of appropriative knowledge. As metaphors of identity, these renamings serve to make present the absence of the "proper" name – for subjects and for objects. It is this absence which metaphor tries to hide.

By linking the appropriated, metaphorical name with the masquerade of stylized, performed identity, the balls underline the violence of language and, more specifically, the rhetoric of identity. Neither metaphor nor performance can summon the proper name which will reveal ourselves to ourselves. There is no transparent document which contains our image, our name. Always we are stuck trying to find ourselves within and through the realm of the Other, which is to say within the other-sign, the metaphor.

Between my own first and last names, my first name for my mother, my sur name his name, is the Symbolic identification that allows these words to be rewritten, written over, touched up, retouched, reprinted, revised. And here too is the inscription of violence. Circulated again in the economy of print, bleeding into another text, notating the choreography of another film. Falling in behind Barthes' *déjà-lu*, the always already read, the quoted words, the floating (phantasmatic?) friend. That's always the (small) authority of girl talk. Nothing ever set in stone; nothing ever rigid. Fluid they usually say. Liquid assets. Rigid is boy talk. Reprint as is. Girls can mimic boy talk. Boys can teach girls to talk and walk. James Joyce writing Molly's version of Bloom's (second) coming. Willi Ninja teaching the girls to swing their hips wide for the boys. Incomplete choreography, the stutter step before the music fades. The open hand writing; the emptiness of the word carving a space for others to inhabit.

The dramatic climax of *Paris Is Burning* is not, as the title suggests, the final and grandest ball of the season. (Another displacement of the proper name: the title "fails" to convey the film's subject.) It is rather the murder of Venus Xtravaganza. Petite and soft-spoken, the pre-transsexual Venus, dressed all in white and leaning back against a bed, says she wants only to be a "spoiled rich white girl" and live with the man she loves. As Venus speaks I am struck again with how deeply self-invention and reinvention structure the performance of identities. In abandoning the dream of being a spoiled white girl I paradoxically confirm the fact that I am spoiled enough and white enough to be able to afford to abandon it. Venus abandoned "being a man" in part because her version of masculinity gave her no currency (or even a negative currency, a perpetual debit) within the rigid economy of the sex-gender system. Through the single interview she conducts with Angie Xtravaganza, Livingston implies that Venus, found under a bed in a cheap hotel after four days, was murdered because she could not finally pass as a woman. Livingston wants that to be the message of her film – gender and sexuality are games played for keeps and no one who steps too far outside traditionally assigned roles is ever home free.

But it may well be that Venus was murdered precisely because she did pass. On the other side of the mirror which women are for men, women witness their own endless shattering. Never securely positioned within the embrace of heterosexuality or male homosexuality, the woman winds up *under* the bed, four days dead.

Paris, the city on the Seine. In the song Judy Collins sings her father always promised her they would live in France, go boating on the Seine, and she would learn to dance. (He never does take her there though.) In the myth, Paris is the one who must decide which of the three goddesses should get the enigmatically inscribed golden apple – "to the fairest" – thrown by Eris into the wedding feast of Thetis and Peleus. Eris' name announces the transformation of the unified circle of Eros to the singular "I" of Strife; that is why she alone among the divinities is not invited to the wedding. The apple is immediately given to Zeus who is asked to settle the question of rightful ownership – who should appropriate the apple? Zeus, a wise god, says Paris, the most handsome man, must be the judge. Pallas Athena promises Paris wisdom; Hera promises him power; but Aphrodite (Venus) promises that Helen, the most beautiful woman, will love him. Paris gives her the apple. She gives Paris Helen. And Troy burns.

From the Greek Aphrodite to the Roman Venus, the proper name is transformed. Textual emendation; sexual emendation. The proper name for woman may be always a transsexual, a sign forever "in process." The name of woman may always be susceptible to translation, reinterpretation, an endless cut in/to the mother tongue. Vulnerable to a master myth and inscribed within the narrative telos of Mastery, the image and the name of woman is always temporary, metaphoric, substitutive. In the advertisements for the film Venus' image is frozen on the film ads (Figure 23). Her singular display portends her final absence. Venus' leg is propped up, you can see up her dress. Covered in white, her genitals are on display as mystery, as disguise, as revision. Reprinted, blown up,

Figure 23 Film still of Venus Xtravaganza from Jennie Livingston's *Paris Is Burning* (1991). (Photo: Jennie Livingston. Courtesy: Prestige, A Division of Miramax Films)

cropped back, Venus' transformations are textual and sexual. The desire enunciated by *Paris* is that what the walkers want is a life *on* film: a life which records the subtle transformations of physical surface by manipulating the light, changing the shutter speed, cropping this or that unnecessary surface detail. Such a life guarantees the production of the walkers' endless re/presentation, a reproduction which promises perfect copies. In a climate which aggressively and violently associates "imperfect" desire with death, the frozen image of a perfect copy maintained in the perpetual present seems more than an appeal to "surface."

While always entering representation disguised as an other, these walkers remain invulnerable to surveillance as themselves. As the possibility of "privacy" continually recedes in this culture of the documenting camera and legislating lens, this strategy of mis/representing has its own brilliant and tragic logic.

Projecting "the woman" the walkers manage at once to be the screen and the creators of that image. "And were it not for the assistance of a projection screen – a dead cave – which provides some goal for representation, no doubt representation would fall short" (Irigaray, *Speculum*: 355). That dead cave is the "real" body of the woman – she who is actually screened out of representation to assure men of their image.

Film's own ontology, its need for dark rooms and bright light, mitigates against the demise of privacy and participates in creating the distinction between the real and the phantom. Film's history is implicated in the impoverished politics of appearance that fuel the balls. Like old lovers who leave smoke in your eyes, film must always leave a ghost on the screen. This time her name is Venus. She died because she thought if she were a beautiful woman, a man might love her. But that's against all the rules. Zeus to Paris: the golden apple is always given by men to other men.

5

Theatre and its mother: Tom Stoppard's *Hapgood*

> To produce is to materialize by force what belongs to another order, that of the secret; seduction removes from the order of the visible, while production constructs everything in full view, be it an object, a number, or a concept.
>
> (Baudrillard, *Seduction*: 34)

Half-way between seduction which removes the visible apparatus of desire and production which displays it, theatre operates in a curious psychic space. The "secret" of theatre's power is dependent upon the "truth" of its illusion. Enfolded within fiction, theatre seeks to display the line between visible and invisible power. Theatre has, then, an intimate relationship with the secret. And secrets contain within them the aroma of seduction.

When Freud decided that his patients' reports of sexual abuse could best be explained as indications of a seduction fantasy, the knotted relationship between the secret, the sexual, and the envy and abuse operative in relations of unequal power, became even more difficult to untangle.

The secret is a token in the currency of power and intelligence. Foucault's career can be seen as a long meditation on state secrets; and Freud's can be seen as a long meditation on erotic secrets. The relation between the state secret and the erotic secret is part of the subject matter of Tom Stoppard's play *Hapgood* (1988). Raiding the "secrets" of physics and intelligence officers, Stoppard's play is a densely layered "proof" about the visible and invisible relations which prevail in secrets, in love, in theatre, and in physics.

Memory: London 1988. Aldwych Theatre, second tier. Someone who was sitting in the seat I am now in has left behind behind a pair of opera glasses (amplification for the eyes). Using them for the first time, I see Felicity Kendal in close-up. Wearing a Burberry raincoat and carrying an umbrella, she emerges from a men's public shower in the first scene of Stoppard's spycatcher-quantum mechanics-thriller *Hapgood*.

Hapgood. I know the name but I can't remember how. Elizabeth Hapgood. Two or three years later I remember: Elizabeth Reynolds Hapgood, the English translator of Stanislavski. Stoppard's puns: the detective is the translator; the playwright is the physicist. The shower water is falling but the umbrella keeps her perfectly blonde hair perfectly dry. (And now, four years later, the umbrella seems like so much more than an umbrella. Derrida's *Eperons,* spurs towards Nietzsche's umbrella. The "bottlecap" on the end of Star Wars. The proliferation of condoms: from her head to his. Acid rain. "Drink It Dry." The dangers of wetness everywhere proclaimed. The end of the cold war. Casting away defensive shields. And adding others.)

Sight: in the first act, slides of London street maps are projected on the stage set. They change as the detective's target approaches the men's room at the public pool where the first scene takes place. The streets outside the Aldwych theatre are made to move within it. Through the play of projected light, the map of a solid city slides across the walls. The city moves and disappears, but the theatrical set is solid. Prospero's theatre in reverse: the city vanishes leaving not a rack behind, but the theatre set itself stays firm in its architectural rigidity.

The slides moving in the tray are like the shifting memories I now have of the performance. The play unfolds in my mind like an old movie, Super-8, a little grainy. At my elbow in my apartment in New York, the program, Stoppard's script, and three books of physics. (The subject supposed to know cannot reveal her props or the imputation of unity and coherence will not hold.) My memory like a dream, a hallucination, a hyper-real recollection. Kerner, the Russian physicist turned spy, says "the particle world is the dream world of the intelligence officer." What then is the dream world of the critic? The perfect interpretation. All part(icle)s made coherent. Beneath the echoing science of physics and the desire of the subject there is again the drama of interpretation.

Love: *Hapgood* is a play about the interpretation of erotic love. This interpretation is hedged in on all sides by enormous doubt. Love is compared to the "uncertainty" of the quantum. Both are given to sudden reversals and both defy prediction. The attempt to plot either, in theatre or in the scientific laboratory, leads one to beg for the certain wisdom of the other (the other subject is supposed to know). In this play, the figure who operates like a threshold linking the intelligence agency of spies who are physicists to the doubtful drama of love is the only female character in the play. The men call her, aptly, Mother.

Memory. Sight. Love. Again. Theatre's past, like the psychic subject's, can never be as secure as the architecture of its set, precisely because the very re-enactment of that past marks it as illusion. The impermanence of the past, like that of erotic love, provokes the subject to repeat an encounter that restages the loss of that "first" encounter. Symbolically, that "first" encounter is with the Mother. The attempt to re-place the Symbolic Mother is a necessary condition for the elaboration of crime, passion, and their revolutions – from Oedipus to Operation Rescue. Her lack-of-Being, her blankness within the phallocentric order, makes her the screen on which he can project an image of himself. In using her as his mirror, however, he seeks also to re-place her, to return to her, but from a different place. As he moves, however, so too does she. Just as it is impossible to coordinate the movements of the quantum in the time–space dyad so too is it impossible to fix the nature of erotic love. As a repetition, the performance of love both secures and makes unstable love's trajectory.

Memory. Sight. Love. Again. For the critic to return to the perform-ance is to restage and represent the drama of meaning's constellation and evaporation. It is to turn back again to the past that is already projected toward a different future.

I

I have that within which passes show.

(*Hamlet*)

Hamlet's problem remains the problem of modern theatre: how to dramatize the energy and ethics of action when the motivation for action is immaterial? During the Renaissance, immateriality was located within the figure of the ghost whose voice could not be located in a corporeal body. As a shadowy phantom, the ghost, part of both an interiority and an exteriority which escaped proof, was always subject to doubt.[1] In a post-psychoanalytic world, such ghosts are described as the symptoms of the unconscious. In the world of modern physics, immateriality is located in quantum laves which "conform" to Heisenberg's uncertainty principle. Each form of uncertainty is the result of the inexact match between vision and knowledge. It is within the limitation and freedom of this mismatch that most modern Western theatre occurs.

Two of the most astute readers of Shakespeare in this century, Beckett and Stoppard, have written plays with very different attitudes toward the immaterial motivations for action. Both take doubt as presence's necessary familiar; in their theatre the spectator can only glimpse "pres-ence" through the large lens of doubt. Beckett's *Waiting for Godot* erases the distinction between stage players and stage watchers. Both wait for the spectacle of presence wondering if they've missed it. Perhaps they are seated in the wrong place, perhaps they came on the wrong night, perhaps they ate too little or too much, perhaps their shoes are too tight and distracting, perhaps when they were playing with Lucky and Pozzo they should have been looking for Godot. Maybe they did see him but they can't remember for sure. So they ask someone. In Beckett's imagination, the mimetic stand-in for the critic, the subject supposed to know, is a little boy.

Beckett takes the condition of the theatrical spectator waiting for a powerful presence to appear – and worried about his or her ability to recognize it – and makes that wait and that doubt the drama his characters face within the play itself. Beckett makes clear that presence is doubt; presence is impossible without doubt; doubt is the signature of presence, rather than the security of re-presentation. Once the distinction between the stage watcher and the stage player is erased, locating spectacle on one side of the stage rather than the other seems to involve the laws of probability and physics, rather than the theory of metaphysics and catharsis. The watcher influences what is seen at least as much as the characters whom the watcher watches. Or to borrow the words of Niels Bohr, we are "both spectators and actors." Physicists and playwrights, then, are necessarily and unavoidably involved in both metaphysics and metatheatre. Experiments are designed to isolate how we understand our understanding, and how we perceive perception, when all that is certain is that neither can be certain.

Modern theatre makes up the truth because as Lacan reminds us truth is structured like a fiction. Part of the necessary energy of that fiction is to provide a perspective from which to see a past. As a performative genre dramatic theatre is anxious about its own legitimacy.

For Stoppard, the always unmarked history of performed theatre functions like a ghost – it haunts and taunts him. So he quotes, steals, parodies, robs, sends up, and revises the marked dramatic texts which comprise "theatre history." But Stoppard's very allusiveness heightens the sense of the absence he wants to overcome: the more plays he quotes, the more missing performances he makes apparent. **Theatre continually marks the perpetual disappearance of its own enactment.** "The theatre is born of its own disappearance, and the offspring of this movement has a name: man" (Derrida, *Writing*: 233). Where is the woman-mother in this view of reproduction?

II

Hapgood is an overt meditation on the nature of perception within the metaphysical structure of theatre and the physical structure of light. Physicists, spycatchers, and playwrights try to understand the uncertain actions of "turning" figures – turning particles, turning spies, turning characters. In tracking these turns, Stoppard discovers that the energy required to track their presence produces the anatomy of (a theatrical) presence which is made up of deception, doubles, and uncertainties.

His method is to proceed by metaphor and analogy. By making physics like spycatching, and theatre like physics, and the uncertainties generated by these systems akin to the uncertainties generated by erotic love, Stoppard creates theatre as an "open system" in which the collisions of energy and matter are made manifest.

The central riddle which led to the exuberant and dizzyingly elegant understanding of quantum mechanics – is light particle or wave energy? – can only be answered by accounting for the power of perception itself to transform the measure of matter.[2] In classical physics, measurement is thought to be "objective" and precise. Relied upon as an ideal law, measurement can be reproduced at different times and in varying spaces. If macroscopic instruments measure macroscopic objects this ideal is realizable. One can accurately weigh a 10-pound rock on one thousand bathroom scales without worrying how that measurement will change the weight of the rock. But in the world of microscopic and subatomic energy this ideally neutral measurement is impossible. Newton began by proposing that light must be made of particles because unlike sound, he thought, light does not seem to bend around solid walls. Energy in the form of waves bends around solid things and continues. Energy in the form of particles crashes into solid things and "stops." But as physicists tried to test Newton's theory they discovered that light does both. When it is not observed, light energy conforms to wave pattern (it sometimes does go around objects); when a physicist tries to discover *which* photons are waves, the waves disappear and light conforms to particle pattern. When the physicist does not try to measure which photons do what, light reverts to wave pattern. The attempt to measure quantum energy with macroscopic instruments transforms and "contaminates" the form of that energy. Observation and measurement themselves both absorb and emit energy; thus the act of observation transforms the activity observed.[3]

The theory of the quantum marks the transition from "objective" measurement to "uncertainty," from deterministic rules to probability and chance. Quantum mechanics erases the possibility of classical physics' belief in a mimetic relationship between matter and measurement. Within the quantum universe it is impossible to derive a physical "law" without accounting for the conditions of measurement and experimentation which produce that law. Merely by looking (?) at matter we alter its action. Quantum theory makes the transcendent representation of the Real impossible.

For Stoppard the allegory of particle and wave is fundamentally theatrical. Physicists, like theatrical spectators, see what they believe to be false – and in attempting to account for that falsity, they see the truth of disguise and discover the need to augment the theory of the real itself. For the physicist, that elaboration involves a complex theory of the rules of the universe. For the artist, that augmentation determines the orbit of imagination. For the actor, it maps the attempt to discover Presence within representation.

When spectators are not looking, actors rehearse. Since Stanislavski, when actors are observed carefully and perform well, they are said to have "presence." The actor achieves presence through performing as if another. Donning a disguise an actor creates a believable "self," one that is and is not the actor's "own" self. In *Hapgood*, Stoppard underlines his interest in this Method (of) acting through the inscription of name. His title character shares the name of Stanislavski's English translator and promoter, Elizabeth (Reynolds) Hapgood.

The plot of *Hapgood* is to determine whether or not a "turned" Russian physicist, Joe Kerner, has been turned again. Hapgood believes that her Kerner is a spy on Russia *for* Britain; but secrets are going in both directions and so it may be that Kerner is working for both the Russians and the British. Or, the source could be in the opposite direction. Ridley, the British spy, has a secret twin, he (or they) may be secretly working for the Russians as well as for Hapgood. The possibilities of the secret always lead to the possibilities of the double. The double agent, the double cross, the double image (the twins), the double nature of integers (which can carry either a positive or a negative value), are all scrutinized by Stoppard. But since this is a play, rather than a scientific experiment, Stoppard frames the whole puzzle within the psychic enigma of erotic love itself.

Like a musical composition with two main themes resolved in a third key, Stoppard's play requires that the spectator link the desire to know the "truth" about spies with the quest to measure the path of the quantum and the attempt to trust love. Just as physicists always get what they interrogate for in terms of light, so too does the person who wants to believe s/he is (be)loved, or unloved, discover "evidence" in the Other to uphold and/or discount that interpretation. The perception of the other is always enfolded within the frame of the perceiver. Distortion is the condition of seeing and it is this distortion which frames our awareness of the condition of matter. It is the recognition of this distortion (the theory of the effect of the act of observation on measurement) that allows us to glimpse how matter works, and to see what is the matter with us. Given Stoppard's obsession with puns, matter becomes the focal point of a series of interrelated questions – e.g. "what is the nature of matter" – "what is the matter" – "what matters most." And it is the job of "matter/mater/mother" to solve it.

Hapgood is the biological mother of Joseph, whose father is the turned joe, Kerner. Her biological maternity is a "secret," although it is a pretty open secret. Thus her code name "Mother," as a general appellation, is a true-fiction. Discerning the relationship between the fiction of truth and the truth of fiction is the labor of the intelligence industry and the playwright. How to discover the secret, the amplification of reality which exceeds the frame of the "known"? How to map and stage the passage of information one cannot see?

The parts of maps we see in act I scene i are "real" representations of the city, which move in time with the dialogue on radio – "OK, we have a blue Peugeot. . . . He's crossing the road. . . . [T]arget is approaching." An immaterial representation of a solid city frames the initial scene in which classified material vanishes, seemingly into thin air. This original loss, like the originary loss of Mother, determines the ensuing action. The inaugural gesture of modern theatre is the confrontation with its lost past.

A kind of shell game unfolds as men with and without briefcases and towels enter and leave the changing stalls, the showers, the offstage pool. Wates, an American intelligence officer, is positioned in the front of the maze, and serves as a surrogate pair of trained eyes. He sees and follows what the spectator cannot. Hapgood, covered up in a Burberry raincoat and nestled under a pink umbrella, is standing concealed under one of the running showers. When she emerges from her watery cell, the spectator, like an infant, is completely lost and lacks all orientation and sense of a center. In this confusion, the clarity of the image of the Mother (aided for sure by opera glasses) provokes the spectator-child's cathexis.

Scene ii has Kerner explaining to Blair, Hapgood's senior confidant and supervisor, the nature of quantum mechanics. He does so by employing Isaac Newton's metaphor for light in a slightly distorted form, "If your gun was a torch and light was bullets, you'd get [particle pattern.]" Kerner advises Blair to give up his belief in objective reality and to learn to appreciate the mysteries of the quantum. "The act of observing determines the reality," Kerner tells Blair. The idea that there may be some "objective" explanation for the behavior of spies is too naive a hope when the objective explanation for something as tiny (and as apparently mindless) as a photon is unknown. Kerner's link between the world of particles and the world of spies is the central metaphor of the play. To determine human behavior, to trap the movement of a spy, is to borrow the physicist's laboratory and conduct experiments. What gradually emerges as the experiments begin is that the behavior of spies is related to his notion of "allegiance," which is in turn the result of his beliefs about love. And those beliefs are fortified by experiments conducted in "the past," the thing that theatre can never make (re)appear. Theatrical performance is always bound to the present. For this reason, theatre continually marks the perpetual disappearance of its own enactment.

In using quantum mechanics as the central metaphor of his play, Stoppard considers science's relation to its past as a model that might allay his anxiety about the theatrical past. In physics, as in the theory (if not the practice) of law, precedents determine the logic of reading new "data." New results and new cases are meant to be understood in terms of known and established theorems or opinions. New science "builds" on established science. This is a deeply attractive idea to Stoppard for it implies that nothing "right" (and therefore, nothing real) is lost. But he finds, over and over again, that the theatrical past is more like a misunderstood quantum than a sturdy set of boards. In his previous play, *The Real Thing* (1981), Stoppard's playwright, Henry, may well have added theatrical performance to this list of things that are not "real":

> There is, I suppose, a world of objects which have a certain form, like this coffee mug. [. . .] But politics, justice, patriotism – they aren't even like coffee mugs. There's nothing real there separate from our perception of them.

> (II.v.)

Thus, *The Real Thing* disappears into *Hapgood*, but that disappearance is marked by the exact symmetry Stoppard creates between the two plays. Henry the playwright in love with the actress Annie stands behind Kerner the physicist in love with the spycatcher Hapgood. All four characters share a reality in which the inevitable (mis)perception of the real defines their work. Physics is theatre; theatre is physics; physics is spycatching; spycatching is physics. More than looking for equivalent metaphors, Stoppard stakes his faith on the power of the unmarked and unseen to "determine" the illusion of reality – and the reality of illusion. Since Shakespeare, western theatre's favorite metaphor for this dilemma is the illusion inspired by erotic love.

If *Rosencrantz and Guildenstern are Dead* can be seen as Stoppard's comic response to the tragedies of Shakespeare, *Hapgood* is his meditation on Shakespeare's comedies. The distance between love as the giddy emblem of the instability of reality, and quantum physics as the somber "proof" of that instability, is the distance between the exuberant optimism of the Renaissance and the alienated pessimism of postmodernity. But both Stoppard and Shakespeare agree that the consequences of this radical determinism (regardless of its cause) are never more fraught than in love and erotic desire.

Ridley, Kerner, and Blair all "love" Hapgood, but the nature of that love eludes definition. Stoppardian love is always subject to doubt and mistrust – except maybe between parents and children.[4] Among adults and especially between mothers and fathers there are positives and negatives; false claimants, mistakes, ciphers, stand-ins. In both *Hapgood* and *The Real Thing* – "affection . . . will not be gainsay'd." Whitman's wonder and doubt are shared by all of Stoppard's adult characters:

. . . the sense of what is real, the thought if after all it should
     prove unreal,
The doubts of day-time and the doubts of night-time, the curious
     whether and how,
Whether that which appears so is so, or is it all flashes and
     specks?

("There Was a Child Went Forth")

III

Erotic love is bedeviling because, despite its insistence on the body, it is immaterial. The illusion of love is given strength by the projection of what the interrogator hopes for. Love's witnesses are unreliable narrators because their perception determines love's "reality." In *Hapgood* each of the men's relation to Mother is complex, suspect, uncertain. Each gives a different version of who Hapgood is to them, and each calls her a different name. Hapgood has so many names she could be St Christopher's football team all by herself. She is: Elizabeth, Betty, Celia, Ma'm, Mum, Mother, Mamashuska, Auntie, Mrs Hapgood, Mrs Newton, Lilya, and Lilichka. (And for good measure she also travels on false passports.) Love of Mother is – or appears to be – a story from the past whose present re-enactment requires characters who have fictive and always sliding names.

Like a scientific theorem, this story from the past guides how the current, always shifting, relations are read. The past's inability to stay past, its continual re-emergence into the present, makes it peculiarly unfixed and alive. Turning back one necessarily sees a different future. Tracking the past is like following one of Kerner's uncertain electrons: "This is not because you aren't looking carefully enough, it is because there is *no such thing* as an electron with a definite position and a definite momentum; you fix one, you lose the other [. . .] it's the real world, it is awake." Once you think you have established how you love or see or remember someone else, they have moved.

"There is something appalling about love," Kerner tells Blair. "It uses up all one's moral judgment. Afterwards it's like returning to a system of values, or at least to the attempt." The test for love occurs only in the "afterwards" – in the endless drama of interpretation, and reinterpretation, in vision and revision. Like testing for particle or wave, love's "afterwards" determines what happened during the experiment – either it was "real" or it was an "illusion." Or a real illusion.

Kerner has decided – or wants to believe he has decided – Hapgood's love for him was a decoy, a fake, and that his for her was "the real thing." When Kerner is "blown" as her joe, Hapgood tells him "your career [as a spy] will be over . . . I won't need you anymore, I mean I'll need you again – oh *sugar*! – you know what I mean – do you want to marry me? I think I'd like to be married" (I.v.). Not surprisingly, Kerner casts a cold eye on Hapgood and says, "I'm not charmed by this. If I loved you it was so long ago I had to tell you in Russian and you kept the tape running." Hapgood protests and twice tells him she loved him. Kerner corrects her and says no, "You interrogated me."

But love is always an interrogation – a series of questions about the self and the other. For this reason love is also "feminine" – unfixed and unmarked until "afterwards." Erotic love is a question, occasionally an imperative, hardly ever an assurance. Like the woman, or the physicist tracking the quantum, love exists as a maybe, a conditional hypothesis, a doubt.

Presence is theatre's promise as well as its doubt, and in this theatre imitates love and its illusions. Rehearsing to create Presence always already compromises its power, makes it a trick, in much the way a Lothario who practices his lines in front of the mirror before offering them to her (his other mirror) risks being more of a narcissist than a lover. Kerner tells Blair, "I never saw Elizabeth sleeping. Interrogation hours, you know. She said, 'I want to *sleep* with you.' But she never did. And when I learned to read English books I realized that she never said it, either." Kerner is suspicious of Hapgood because she repeats phrases he later reads in English. Thus he concludes *she* never said them; she performed them as part of her spycatcher's script. Kerner's interpretation is based on rereading her performance in light of his mastery of English, an education in the language accomplished by reading "spy stories." In that reading, however, he sees himself as a (mere) character in Hapgood's plot. Looking for his "real" self, he keeps reading spy stories so he might reread their past. "Well, they're [detective novels] different you know. Not from each other naturally. I read in hope but they all surprise in the same way" (I.v.).[5] The repetitions of science are a comfort because they establish operative laws; the repetitions of literary genre are generative because they illustrate the seemingly infinite possibilities of new combinations for the same formulae; the repetitions of love, however, are dismaying because they seem to disprove authentic presence and compromise the ego's desire for singularity. Trapped like a particle in someone else's experiment, Kerner devotes himself to antiparticles. There he discovers that the other side of repetition is the possibility of reversal.

As a figure in Hapgood's plot Kerner is made to see that sometimes circumstances compel one to make up the truth. When he finds himself "performing" the truth about the Russians' discovery of their son Joe as part of the plot to trap Ridley, Kerner realizes that his lines are both "true" and useful for Hapgood's plot. (*Truth is structured like a fiction.*)

Finding himself in this true-fiction, Kerner begins to realize that Hapgood may well have been making up the truth when she said she loved him. Kerner's repetition of Hapgood's past performance of love, which at first he believed, then after reading doubted, allows him to see that the opposite conclusion (she really did love him) will also "solve" the problem. Just as the square root of sixteen is both positive and negative four, "making up the truth" can be motivated by a desire to delude and thereby remain hidden or a desire to tell the truth and thereby be discovered.

But truth without the successful solicitation of belief functions as a fiction.

In the final scene of the play, Kerner comes to say goodbye to Hapgood who is watching their son Joe and his St Christopher school-mates play football. Hapgood tells Kerner she has discovered he made up the truth about Joe. (The Russians "really" were threatening Kerner by using Joe to blackmail him.) In Hapgood's discovery of Kerner's true-fiction, she discovers Kerner himself. Finding himself recognized Kerner thinks perhaps Hapgood does love him, after all. Since his "lie" about Joe fits the necessity of the (false) plot, he used it to achieve the deception. But such a lie may nevertheless be true. Therefore, it may be that Hapgood's "lie" about loving Kerner was necessary for her spy-plot but it may nonetheless be true. Suddenly and newly absorbed by the game of football, the turned Joe turns again and does not return to Russia. Repetition, like spycatching, love, and football, must allow for the possibility of reversibility.

The structure of reversibility is built into Stoppard's play. While Kerner is trying to interpret the "afterwards" of his "love trap" with Hapgood as fictional, Ridley is trying to interpret his with her as true. While Kerner wants to believe Hapgood's love was a lie, Ridley wants to believe Hapgood's love was true. Kerner is the most romantic and imaginative character in the play, and Ridley is the most cynical. He openly jeers at the value of the secrets he risks his life for, and yet, he also continues to risk his life for them. Trying to be tough, mainly he wants to be loved, preferably by Mother. Ridley wants to believe Hapgood loves – or at least desires – him. Bluntly lusting after her, he admits that when they were "pretending to be lovers" in Athens he was having "the best time of [his] life" (I.v.). He would like that time to return, that pretense to be true. Hapgood, however, repeatedly tells Ridley he is not her type.

When Blair and Hapgood conclude that the puzzle about the material being passed can only be solved by either Ridley or Kerner being a double agent, or by twins, Hapgood proceeds as if she believes Ridley is the liar. Mother, under the guidance of Blair, reproduces another Hapgood, a secret twin, Celia Newton. With Mrs Newton she will attempt to trap

Ridley and his twin. But Ridley decides to do an experiment of his own; he proceeds as if Hapgood would not lie to him. Sometimes, he reminds himself when speaking to Mrs Newton, people do tell the truth – and he would prefer to believe that Hapgood would not lie to him. (As a double agent he, of course, lies to her.) If she has set him up, he tells Celia calmly, he will kill her.

Both Kerner and Ridley realize that they are not the only man in Hapgood's life. In addition to narrating a coherent story about their own relation to her, they must also explain Hapgood's relation to Paul Blair. Kerner is clearly jealous of it and when Hapgood asks him to marry her he refuses and says he believed she would marry Paul (I.v.). Ridley tells Celia that Hapgood is lusting after the dry Blair and that Blair is running her (in the way he believes she is running Kerner). In this, as in his assessment of Kerner's anti-particle trap, Ridley is right. Blair is "running" Hapgood, and the plot they set up together to ensnare Ridley, positions him in the role of pimp, as we shall see. In the scene of erotic desire certainty itself completely disappears. The fantasy of theatre suspends belief, even as it solicits it.

Ridley, believing he is with Celia, but continually desiring Hapgood, whom she looks uncannily like, is determined to prove his power. He wants to believe that Hapgood's performance of indifference is a lie and that underneath the performance she loves/desires him. He is right about Hapgood's performance, but he is wrong about what motivates it. He pushes himself on the "false" Hapgood, Celia, hoping to find his true love. Stoppard's stage directions are worth quoting in full:

> Ridley: (*Grabbing her*) *Who the hell are you?*
> Hapgood: I'm your dreamgirl, Ernie – Hapgood without the brains or the taste.
> (*She is without resistance, and he takes, without the niceties; his kiss looks as if it might draw blood.*)

Seduction, Baudrillard argues, is the realm of the reversible. Arguing that seduction is ruled by the feminine, Baudrillard claims that seduction manipulates appearances by mastering them. "Who the hell are you?" Ridley asks this enigmatic figure of criss-crossing signs lying, fully clothed, next to him. Hapgood, Mother, Celia, Elizabeth, Betty, Ma'm, Mum, Lilya, Mamashuska, Auntie, Mrs Hapgood, Mrs Newton answer "I'm your dreamgirl . . ." As phantom and dream, she can seduce him by doing/being nothing or everything. As a *dream/girl*, she ensnares him. Like the quantum whose coordinates cannot be fixed, the woman fascinates because "she" always recedes. Just as it is impossible to predict the movements of an electron, it is also impossible to say who she is – Hapgood, Auntie, Mrs Newton, the actress Felicity Kendal. Seduction gives her room to act *like* a woman, as distinct from acting *as* a man. The history of theatre makes apparent the fact that acting like a woman is a profession open to either gender.

Unable to fix Hapgood/Mother, her meaning is always elsewhere, encoded in the stories the male characters tell about her. She finds things for them – keys, rugby boots, computer disks, secret keys, but she remains unlocatable herself. She is the secret that cannot be cracked (as Mrs Newton, she continually describes Hapgood and her cohorts as "nutters.") She is the quantum which it is impossible to "see." So the men are seduced precisely because "she" is not there. Once they are seduced, she disappears (in strobe) and they contemplate each other. To modify Derrida's proposition: the theatre and its mother are born in their disappearance, and the offspring of their union are men. Seduced by Hapgood, Kerner falls to thinking of Blair; Blair thinks of Kerner; Ridley thinks of Blair. Her disappearance (re)produces them *as* men. This is her function as their mutual Mother.

The reproduction of men seems to rely on the repression of maternal origin. Elin Diamond's reading of Irigaray's *Speculum* brilliantly suggests theatre's own position within this truth-telling:

> Irigaray wittily retrieves and confirms Plato's worse fears about theatre, female duplicity, and by implication, maternity. Platonic philosophy wants to place man's origins, not in the dark, uncertain cave but in the recognition of the (Father's) light. The philosopher wants to forget – wants to prove illusory – his female origins. But the anarchic effect of that proof, in Irigaray's playfully serious rereading, is the discovery that his mother is a theatre.[6]

Mother is the code name for Stoppard's titular character. She is the threshold across which the bodies and minds of the male characters meet one another. She is their translator; but her own motivations are inscrutable. ("The real secrets," Blair instructs her, "are about intentions and deployment" (I.iii.).) Hapgood's "real" maternity is an open secret within the play if not within the spy empire and her role as surrogate Mother is confirmed by her ability to reproduce a twin sister – and a lemon for tea – with the same aplomb. If the men in the play are defined through their original relation with her, who is the original relation from which she seeks definition?

The play's deepest question is about her past, about theatre and its Mother. Stoppard's desire to locate and reference a theatrical past is related to the anxiety of Platonic philosophy: if the shadows in the cave must always be located outside the mother's body so too must theatrical projection occur across rather than within the female body. This same anxiety underscores Freud's and Lacan's insistence on arguing that the

Oedipal complex and Symbolic castration are the most formative psychic thresholds for the development of the psychic subject – rather than the more intuitively sensible idea that the separation from the Mother is the formative threshold.

Stoppard's meditation on the past is both metatheatrical and psychic. What he proposes in *Hapgood* is that each scene reflects and refracts the reading of a previous scene. For example, the fact that Newton/ Hapgood allows herself to be seduced by Ridley, can be seen as a confirmation of *Kerner's* hypothesis that Hapgood never loved him. For the sake of protecting a secret, Hapgood would be able to perform her part "without resistance," to pretend to love him, since she is doing so here. "As soon as a sign emerges, it begins by repeating itself" (Derrida, *Writing*: 297). The sign or action "repeats" in both the past and in the future. Even while the scene provides evidence for Kerner's hypothesis, it simultaneously encourages Ridley to believe that Hapgood does want him since Celia Newton, an iconic "echo" and double of/for Hapgood, is "without resistance." Ridley knows well enough that signs and images have a mimetic effect which other similar signs and images repeat. If he can get the sign-image called Celia to desire him, maybe this will allow the sign-image called Hapgood to repeat that desire. But the spectator, unlike Ridley, knows that Celia is Hapgood already and that the desired repetition requires an internal transference (Hapgood's resistance has to be converted into desire) rather than an external one (Celia has to make Hapgood repeat her act). This is an altogether more ambivalent affair then and the spectator must decide if "without resistance" is the same as "with desire." Is Ridley raping Hapgood? Is Celia seducing Ridley? Is Hapgood trapping Ridley's twin? As Aretha Franklin sang it: "Who's zooming who?" In love, as in physics, and maybe as in theatre, you get what you interrogate for. (One sees oneself in terms of the other; one sees the other in terms of one self. Love is blind, as the song sings.)

After Ridley "takes" Newton/Hapgood "without the niceties," Blair, restoring the performance of and to niceness, inquires of Ridley (or of his twin), "Surely you know Mrs Hapgood?" To which Ridley replies Hamlet-like, "I know her sister better." He who has had her "without the niceties" knows the woman who does not exist best. The radio crackles and Hapgood identifies herself with the name the men know her best by, "Mother."

"To produce is to materialize by force what belongs to another order, that of the secret; seduction removes from the order of the visible, while production constructs everything in full view, be it an object, a number, or a concept" (Baudrillard, *Seduction*: 34). The theatrical production wants simultaneously to seduce and to reveal. It finds itself using doubles and making up the truth and confronting again the secret force of the illusion of a (transparent) real. The figure which perpetually marks that continuing return to the real is the figure of the Mother. Her body, like the actor's, is always already doubled.

So too for the interpretative possibilities of Ripley's liaison with Newton/Hapgood. Is it a seduction scene? A rape scene? An illustration of a woman who lies back and thinks of England? As Freud's embrace of the seduction theory, and the legal history of rape cases makes clear, you get what you interrogate for. Desire *is* the other's interpretation of it. Ridley "seduces" (Mrs) Newton and "rapes" Hapgood. But Hapgood *becomes* Newton by performing the role of Ernie's "dream-girl" – by being "without resistance." Particles and waves live in every piece of light.

IV

Corporeal bodies amid real objects: realistic theatre employs properties which reproduce the effects of the real. These props index the failure of representation to reproduce the real. The real inhabits the space that representation cannot reproduce – and in this failure theatre relies on repetition and mimesis to produce substitutes for the real. Behind the effects of the real is a desire to experience a first cause, an origin, an authentic beginning which can only fail because the desire is experienced and understood from and through repetition. Diamond argues that the "experience of origin is always already mimicry, a representation of repetition. Hence mimesis without a true referent – mimesis without truth" (Diamond, "Mimesis": 64). Nonetheless *the desire* for a true referent *is* always already the true referent of mimetic theatre. The Symbolic Mother, for example, is a copy of something that never was truly there. And because she never was there, she'll never be forgotten.

V

Quantum mechanics' dilemma over light is also a dilemma about time. Equations in both classical dynamics and thermodynamics rely on a notion of reversible time, that is, the same formula can describe an object's motion whether it is moving forward or backward in time. This means that time itself conforms to its constant fixed measurement *and* that events in the future can be (theoretically) predicted. This further suggests that events in the past "contain" their futures. Freud's conception of the libido was based on thermodynamics; repetition compulsions could be "predicted" and traumatic events could be restaged because the psychic kernel of libidinal energy nestled within them remained the same, although it reappeared in different forms. Quantum physics introduces an element of "uncertainty" into all prediction, and speaks in terms of probabilities. But quantum mechanics, like classical dynamics and thermodynamics, assumes a reversible (and therefore regular and reliable) time. If time repeats itself absolutely (with no variation whatever) then, theoretically, an absolute repetition is possible and so too is a transparent representation/measurement. But philosophy, ideology, and theatre suggest otherwise.[7]

Ilya Prigogine and others have demonstrated, however, the appearance of a "second time" which may suggest a different way of thinking about time. Fundamental to the physics of a second time is the notion of irreversibility. For Prigogine, "life even in its simplest form presupposes a distinction between past and future" (*From Being to Becoming*: 213). This distinction informs the organization of what Prigogine has called "dissipative structures" – chemical systems which emerge under far-from-equilibrium conditions and which reorder themselves after crossing critical heat thresholds. These structures, which occur in open systems (exchanges of both energy and matter), do not conform to the laws of thermodynamics regarding linear entropy. These chemical structures, which are very large and occur over long periods of time, are organized in such a way as to incorporate a "sense of history" into their various arrangements and rearrangements over time. Thus, they may begin to indicate that chemistry, like biology, knows the past and adheres to evolution.

Dissipative structures organize and reorganize themselves under certain conditions depending on how they were organized in the past. In this limited sense, dissipative structures exhibit irreversibility; they assume a distinction between the past and the future. Unlike crystals which also exhibit nonlinearity, dissipative structures are organized via "memory"; after reaching a certain critical fluctuation length (called the nucleanation point) they exhibit highly organized broken symmetries before "calming down." In other words, as these structures pass through heat thresholds, they arrange themselves logically, although they do not achieve equilibrium. (The logic of these arrangements is derived from bifurcation theory in mathematics.)

These structures do not conform to the rules of entropy, and yet they too achieve order (not of equilibrium and not the "same" order over time). Dissipative structures seem to suggest the possibility that time is not always reversible, but rather additive, at the microscopic level. It is this "additive" notion of time that Prigogine and his colleagues believe may lead to the discovery of a "second time." If such a time were observable, then time may not be a neutral "constant" in the universe. Time itself may be a dissipating structure exhibiting significant fluctuations which correspond to a principle of order that is not entropic.

If, as Kerner tells Hapgood, the particle world is the dream world of the intelligence officer, dissipative structures seem to be keeping some feminist theorists awake, most notably Irigaray.[8] The structure of matter, within the language of science, and within the cultural unconscious, should matter to women, and not only because they are forever interrogated as may-be mothers. Irigaray suggests that

> feminine sexuality could perhaps better be brought into harmony – *if one must evoke a scientific model* – with what Prigogine calls dissipating structures that operate – via the exchange with the external world, structures that proceed through levels of energy. The organizational principle of these structures has nothing to do the search for equilibrium but with the crossing of thresholds.
>
> ("Subject": 81)

As the foundational figure of cultural reproduction and representation, the mother invades the threshold marking and unmarking the feminine body. As an always "dissipating structure," the mother *breaks* the smooth symmetry of paternal linearity and inheritance, the myth of historical determinism and progression, and the consolation of a coherent nonfluctuating time which artists call "immortality" and scientists and theologians call eternity.

Fluctuations, women, dissipating structures. The theatricality of motherhood, the "double" body that the law and science want to make into separate bodies in space/time, can "work" in the theatre because the body of the actor is similarly doubled (by the character the actor portrays). Excluding women from the stage, as many theatrical traditions did and some continue to do, is a way of limiting the double and quadruple effect of the woman-mother's acting body.

In *Hapgood*, however, the effort is to explode the limit – to make it impossible to see the distinction between the double and the triple turn. Stoppard's Mother multiplies in front of their moving eyes: Mother reproduces Joe, Celia, and "double" agents. Stoppard is trying to create a metatheatre in which continuity, rather than limitation and distinction, is the epistemological puzzle. He places Mother in a discursive laboratory in which the language of physics, law, politics, and spy novels all work to suggest the possibility that a continuous body, a body who crosses threshold boundaries (on false passports), is natural to logic – rather than a social and legal and psychic aberration.

"All the mystery in life turns out to be this same mystery, the join between things which are distinct and yet continuous, body and mind, free will and fate, living cells and life itself; the moment before the foetus" (I.v.). Kerner is waxing philosophical and instructing Hapgood, the mother of their child, about the continuous maternal body. Distinct yet continuous, modern theatre turns back to the moment before its own conception and finds the shadows flickering and fluctuating across performance history. The body it cannot see is the one it is enfolded within.

Hapgood tells Blair, "I already run the only intelligence network in the world which exhibits seasonal fluctuations and it's only a matter of time before someone works out it's the school holidays" (I.iii.). The regulated maternal body has to experience fluctuations in order to keep science guessing about "all the mystery in life" that can be solved with rigorous proofs. The logic of that cast of mind is to return to the "origin of the universe," and to "the moment before the foetus." The measuring mind, in so doing, seeks to make separate that which is continuous. This love of separation, rigid logic, again stumbles over the maternal and continuous body at the foot of the stage whose projections so thoroughly seduce him.

6

White men and pregnancy: discovering the body to be rescued

The anti-abortion demonstrations staged at medical clinics under the direction of the New Right group Operation Rescue are deeply revealing indications of the fraught relation between visibility, invisibility, and reproduction. The performances inspired by the abortion debates provide an instructive example with which to begin to explore the psychic and political investments in visibility and invisibility across both the representational and reproductive field.

The members of Operation Rescue, and the New Right more generally, are extraordinarily conscious of the power of media representation.[1] (On the Left, ACT-UP and to a lesser extent, the South Africa divestment movement display a similar sensitivity to representational power.) The members of Operation Rescue shrewdly understand the necessary requirements of making a spectacle *for* the sake of publicity. Knowing that the press corps would be in Atlanta for the Democratic National Convention in 1988, they targeted that city for their first national protest. In so doing, Operation Rescue simultaneously attacked Democrats who ran on pro-choice platforms, signaled a new political history for civil disobedience, and declared their antipathy to law, order, and the democratic way. They accomplished all of this by diverting the press' attention away from the pageantry of the orderly conventional convention toward the drama of clinic blockades, threats of imminent violence, and hundreds of arrests. By capturing the media's attention in Atlanta, Operation Rescue gained an enviable notoriety and revitalized the stagnating abortion debates. Therefore, those who want to launch a counter-argument about the politics of reproduction must assess how they relate to the politics of representation. As the debate about reproduction develops so too does an ideology of representation.

difficult to chart demographically in part because many participants remain anonymous (protesters are instructed to give their names as John or Jane Doe when they are arrested) and in part because "membership" can mean anything from participating in a single rescue to traveling throughout the country and performing rescues continually. But it seems clear that there is a surprisingly large number of men in the group – in 1989, Frances Wilkinson noted that 56 per cent of its members were men, the three highest paid staff members on a fifteen person payroll are men, and almost all of its members are white.[2]

It's difficult to build a critique of a group based on shifting numbers and demographic makeup. There is, however, a coherent ideology, most powerfully articulated by Terry himself, which guides Operation Rescue and which bears close scrutiny. Terry, the 33-year-old founder and director, believes "Most people – men and women included [since women are not necessarily included in the category 'most people' they must be marked] – are more comfortable following men into a highly volatile situation. It's human nature. It's history."[3] The "highly volatile situation" Terry refers to here is the "rescue."

The members of Operation Rescue pretend to believe that by staging demonstrations outside abortion clinics they will rescue the unborn. These rescues tend to be emotionally and often physically violent. Like most staged rescues, Operation Rescue's generate a feeling of terror, and thereby produce the feeling that one needs to be saved.

In creating an opportunity for "rescuing" the unborn, the demonstrations also catalyze the conversion narrative so crucial to Christian culture. Saving the unborn allows those who were "born again" to continue the missionary work which concludes all conversion experiences. But the women who walk into clinics often have more to fear from Operation Rescue than from doctors. Fewer than ten of the 1 million women who have abortions each year in the US die as a result of the procedure.[4] The number of actual "babies saved" by Operation Rescue is nowhere documented, but the demonstrations themselves are destructive and violent.

The rescues, theatrical performances of extraordinary boldness and violence, are largely sex-segregated. Many of them are doubly oppositional because pro-choice groups, composed largely of women, often attempt to stage counter-demonstrations at the same clinics. The Operation Rescue men confront the counter-demonstrators or, on occasion, the clinic workers, and form a wall, shoulder-to-shoulder, often screaming "dyke" or "whore" to any woman who walks across. (The ideas underlying these appellations are breathtakingly crude: all feminists are lesbians; all pregnant women contemplating abortion are sexually promiscuous.) When a pregnant woman attempts to enter the clinic, a male rescuer will yell out in a strange falsetto, "Mother, please don't murder me." Off to the side, most of the women from Operation Rescue form what is called a "Prayer Support Column": they chant hymns, stand still, try to maintain an air of "above the fray" about them, and keep their hands open and raised toward heaven. Another group of protesters carry placards with alternating images of the "innocent" and the "mutilated" fetus on them. The spatial separation between the men and the women rescuers mimics the situation often found in mainstream Western theatre: speaking men and observing women. This reinforces the idea that in any drama, including that of pregnancy, mainstream theatre will do all it can to insure that the main character remains an embryonic man.

Inside the clinic, a group of other people lock themselves to chairs in the waiting room, and if possible, to the desks of the clinic workers. While lying there waiting to be removed by police, they sing Christian hymns. The locks they use must be sawed off by police officers. While the flames from the electric saws fire, the rescuer calls on Jesus. In the meantime, another group of people sit or stand in the waiting rooms with open Bibles and read Scripture in soft voices. They sit very close to those waiting and try to provoke a conversation. When the police come to saw the locks off their colleagues, this group will often sing hymns.

At the heart of the New Right's relation to abortion is a psychic fear about *paternity*; this fear is repressed and displaced through a series of substitutions and disavowals that make the chain of significations in the demonstrations *productive* of an/other terror, the terror of absolute alterity, that is displaced onto the body of the pregnant woman trying to enter the abortion clinic. Conveying an ideological and religious belief about abortion, the blockades and demonstrations also frame and define a contested psychic arena between men and women.

Freud describes men's psychic relation to reproduction as an "anxiety" stemming from the inability to prove paternity; what we are witnessing now is a transformation of that psychic field. Paternity is now verifiable by science and thus subject to law. The men of the New Right, like most men, are uneasy and ambivalent about paternity's new visibility. In an effort to displace the profoundly important consequences of this visibility a new effort has been made to make the fetus visible.

Fetal imagery, a persistent and ubiquitous focus in the abortion debates, is important because it upsets the psychic terrain which formerly located all reproductive visibility exclusively with the body of the pregnant woman. Fetal imagery locates reproductive visibility as a term and an image independent of the woman's body. Once that independence is established, fetal imagery itself becomes vulnerable to all the potential manipulations of any signifying system. Within the strategy of Operation Rescue, two representations of the fetus continually work together in a complex dialogue. On the one hand, the "innocent" fetus is photographed, as Faye Ginsburg observes, "in warm amber tones, suffused with soft light, [and] rendered more mysterious by [its] separation from the mother's body." This image is juxtaposed with "gruesome, harshly lit, clinical shots of mutilated and bloody fetal remains" (*Contested Lives*: 105). The "innocent" image works to induce sympathy and protection while the mutilated one is a call to outrage and outrageous action.

In making the fetus the focus of the visible spectacle of the demonstrations, Operation Rescue subtly erases the pregnant woman herself. Detached from the mother, the image of the fetus is rendered as utterly alone and heartbreakingly innocent. Held aloft on sign posts outside of abortion clinics during Operation Rescue's demonstrations, the fetal image functions like a flag, a banner under which protecting "rescuers" march off to prevent the "slaughter of the innocent." But what happens, as in most wars, is a slaughter of a different order. Erasing the woman from the image has allowed the fetal form to become a token in a discourse of and about men. Cropped out of the picture, the pregnant woman's life and reasoning are rendered both invisible and irrelevant. By focusing on the fetus, Operation Rescue manages to ignore the pregnant woman. This literal ignore/ance of the pregnant woman limits sympathy for her situation and represses ethical uncertainty about her liberty; this same ignorance props up the righteous tone of the demonstrations.

Detached from the pregnant woman, the fetal form has become a sign that is already powerfully implicated in the political economy of capitalism and patriarchy. Take, for example, the recent Volvo television advertisement: a sonogram of a fetus fills the screen; on the sound track, the steady beating of a fetal heart – and then, as if on the sonogram monitor itself, computer print rolls up the television screen as a male voice-over intones: "Isn't it time for a Volvo?" Many parents experience their first feeling of "bonding" with the fetus when they see its sonogram.[5] Exploiting this feeling of protectiveness, Volvo uses the fetal form to make the same emotional plea as the anti-abortionists – protect this helpless, beautiful life. The means by which protection is assured, however, are dramatically different. The people representing Volvo want you to buy their safe car; the members of Operation Rescue want you to help outlaw abortion. In both instances, an implied moral threat is operative: not buying a Volvo will leave blood on one's hands. Not "rescuing" a fetus makes one a complicit murderer. Fetal imagery provokes both protectionist sentiment and the potential feeling of guilt in those who "bond" with it.

In a brilliant discussion of fetal imagery, Rosalind Petchesky argues:

"The fetal form" itself has, within the larger culture, acquired a

> symbolic import that condenses within it a series of losses – from
> sexual innocence to compliant women to American imperial might. It
> is not the image of a baby at all but of a tiny man, a homunculus.
>
> ("Fetal Images": 268)

In other words, the fetus is always already gendered – and not surprisingly, gendered male. The anti-abortion handbook, *Abortion: Questions
and Answers*, compiled by John Wilke, president of the National Right to
Life Committee, instructs anti-abortion activists to refer to the fetus "in
humanizing terms [. . .] such as 'this little guy.' "[6] The identification is
further highlighted within the demonstration as the man speaks both for
and as the fetus. As moral ideology is turned into political theatre, the
woman is again negated. The grown man speaks in full sentences,
ventriloquizing for the unborn child a fear of murder: the fetus is not
only sentient, he is Noam Chomsky's dream child – within the womb
the deep structure of language is up and running. The men who would
rescue place their own voices and heroism center stage, while the drama
of the pregnant woman remains invisible, unspoken, pushed to the
other side of the curtain that opens and closes on their own holy work.

By locating "maleness" within the image of the fetus, men displace
their new reproductive visibility onto representations of the hitherto
unseen "child," further strengthening the identification between the
fetus and the men of Operation Rescue. It is this identification which
justifies the belief that they must be noble advocates for "the pre-born
child," a point which also underlines the swift enactment of fetal rights
laws – most of which have been used to incarcerate pregnant women,
charging those who drink or take drugs with child abuse. In the meantime, however, child abuse outside the womb, often at the hands of
male guardians, beats its repetitious rhythm.[7] Under the banner of
protecting women and children, men continue to protect themselves.

The psychic economy of Operation Rescue's demonstrations enacts a
series of political displacements whose consequences have not been
sufficiently elaborated. The demonstrations aim to produce fear and
terror not *because* Operation Rescue is composed of "fanatics," as the
Left often too summarily assumes. The production of terror sets up a
more profound psychic theatre in which the potential power of pregnancy for women is converted back into the province of men's control.
This theatrical production of terror allows men (and their "female support column") to cast themselves in the role of "nurturing protectors"
thereby appropriating for themselves the traditional female roles of
emotionally sensitive being and of care-taker, while the pregnant
woman becomes the murdering, hateful mother.

The image of the fetus deflects attention from both the pregnant
woman and the father. The only part of the reproductive triangle in

need of rescuing becomes the tiny, "innocent" fetus. All of these displacements occur under a veil, in a kind of psychic and political theatre whose curtains are heavy and whose legally unnamed performers appear only behind scrims. The veil which sheathes the "innocent" fetus has an uncanny similarity to the veiled paternal phallus, Lacan's ubiquitous caul-baby-who-would-be-king. Unlike the hymen, this veil cannot be broken if patriarchy is to continue to be reproduced. What is required to interfere in its reproduction?

Values about reproduction govern ideas about representation and inflect the negative values associated with the nonreproductive and the unrepresentable. Homophobia, for example, stems partly from cultural discomfort with a nonreproductive sexuality. Sexual activity which leads only to more of the same activity (as against leading to procreation) is unattractive to the ideology of production and reproduction which suffuses late twentieth-century capitalism. While we've long recognized the connection between the fiscal economy of capital and the psychic economy of sexualities, the particular shape of this connection is now changing as we attempt to face the alarming specter of prodigious spending in both spheres. The national response to HIV infection and AIDS has unwittingly made clear the intimacy of the ideological relation between safe sex and safe spending. In a sexually grieving culture, conservative politicians exploited rampant homophobia under the guise of fiscal restraint to restrict the spending of the National Endowment for the Arts (NEA). Nonreproductive performance art dovetailed with the nonreproductive ontology of homosexuality: conservatives used one to attack the other. All four performers "defunded" during the NEA scandal in 1990 make work which incorporates a sympathetic, if not evangelical, attitude towards homosexuality.[8]

This same distrust and suspicion of the nonreproductive reifies the pregnant woman as the embodiment of "natural" desire, for both men and women within the patriarchal economy. The reification of the pregnant woman (furthered in part by limiting her visibility within representational systems) sets the dialectic between the good mother and the evil mother in motion, a cycle which once again represses the question of paternity within the abortion debates. (The woman who is not a mother is rendered valueless – or a "failed" woman, or a woman-soon-to-be-a-mother-we-hope. Given this economy, it is no accident that so many teenage girls with few other options "prove" their value by having babies.) Patriarchy oscillates between reverence for the "natural" maternal instinct and the terrifying specter of the monstrous, forever murdering/castrating, mother.

It is this dialectic that accounts for: (1) the need for "objective" men to determine the legal and financial parameters within which abortion is legitimate; and (2) the fraught relationship between abortion and racism, which is to say, as well, between abortion and money. Currently, Medicaid funds will pay 90 per cent of a voluntary sterilization procedure for a woman and will pay nothing for an abortion. While abortion has long existed, its particular relation to legality, funding, and publicity, has been a relationship dominated by the agenda of white men and secondarily by white women.[9]

In the US, traditional common law permitted abortions before quickening until 1845 when physicians led a campaign to restrict them. Intent on establishing medicine as a profession, the doctors wanted to outlaw untrained physicians, primarily midwives, from practicing medicine. By the turn of the century, almost all states had passed laws restricting abortion.[10] Thus, *Roe* v. *Wade* (1973) (re)legalized abortion for the first six months of pregnancy.

In turning back to an earlier "right," Justice Harry Blackmun, in writing *Roe*, declared that the court recognized "a right of personal privacy [. . .] [which has] some extension to activities relating to marriage; procreation; contraception; family relationships; and child rearing and education." While both Justices Stewart and Renquist agreed that the "liberties" protected by the Fourteenth Amendment (passed in 1868) cover more than those explicitly named in the Bill of Rights, by the time the court heard *Bowers* v. *Hardwick* in 1986, it did not believe that "privacy" or "liberty" extended to one's right to engage in nonreproductive sexuality. Arguing that the police had a right to arrest two consenting homosexual men who were in bed together at home in Georgia, the opinion notes that homosexuality is not protected by the Fourteenth Amendment. Heterosexual activity and its attendant reproductive consequences are a private liberty and homosexual activity which does not broach a reproductive consequence is subject to "prevailing moral standards." The threat of homosexuality is that it does not need a larger sociality than the actors who consent, thus the law seeks to make it an illegal activity, a pursuit explicitly regulated by the sociality of law and prevailing moral standards. Heterosexuality, firmly entrenched as the very ground of a reproducible sociality, must be protected from the "constraints" of a surveying law.

The members of Operation Rescue, however, want to resocialize the relation between the law and reproduction. They suggest that the "unnaturalness" of women who would abort is much the same "unnaturalness" as those who would engage in nonreproductive sexuality. (Not surprisingly, Randall Terry has vowed to outlaw contraception after abortion.) Arguing that abortion cannot be private, the members of Operation Rescue have rendered abortion a visible and public problem crying out for legislative reform. *Bowers* is a serious threat to those seeking to assure sexual object choice and reproductive choice. It may well be that the new abortion legislation will be crafted around the precedent against sexual (and by implication, reproductive) privacy established in *Bowers* v. *Hardwick*. Distracted by the explicit legislative interest in revising the abortion laws, the pro-choice people may fail to notice this open door. Conservatives who prefer that the Left remain divided into small and separate constituents benefit from the tendency to see *Bowers* exclusively as a "gay rights bill." It has a much wider net than that.

II

In Witchita, Kansas in the summer of 1991, Operation Rescue members added another act to their drama. They launched what has come to be called the Witchita Walk. Defying a court order to clear the entrance to three abortion clinics, Operation Rescue demonstrators crawled and/or took baby steps to the patiently waiting paddy wagon. The police allowed the demonstrators to proceed (legally, if they are "progressing toward the conveyance" the police are enjoined to wait): it took twenty-eight hours to remove all the demonstrators from the clinic entrances. Literally performing the part of sentient and calculating infants, the members of Operation Rescue put the law into a stupor for more than a full day.

Encamped in Witchita for three weeks, Operation Rescue took over the city and dominated the air and radio waves with their psychic theatre. The "Summer of Mercy" campaign marks a new level of drama in the abortion debates. As the legal battle unfolds, more of these powerful demonstrations are sure to occur. Alisa Solomon points out that Operation Rescue members are "as litigious as they are liturgical."[11] The demonstrations themselves are becoming progressively more intense and dramatic as the members of Operation Rescue seek to hold the attention of the media, the public, and the politicians.

Between 1987 and 1990, over 28,000 "rescuers" have been arrested; they refuse to give their real names – they call themselves "John Doe" or "Jane Doe" – and with this form of civil disobedience they clog the overcrowded courts and the prisons. Over 267 incidents of violence and disruption have been documented by the National Abortion Federation between 1987 and 1990. In 1989 alone, nine clinics were either bombed or set alight; the estimated cost of physical damage to clinics is $375,000.[12]

This visible violence masks the invisible violence of the psychic wrestle raised by the politics of reproduction. It is no accident that it is the man who mouths the words of the unborn child in Operation Rescue's demonstrations. For the effort is to make the "male seed" productive – a speaking seed, however infantilized. He addresses her repeatedly as "mother"; the appellation under which all adult women in this culture labor. His most urgent adult plea from his deepest passion is still "Mother, please don't murder me." These men are not, generally speaking, terrifically empowered.

Susan Faludi, who has written the best mainstream account of Operation Rescue, points out that these activists

> do not fit the stereotype of grizzled Christian elders. Almost all its leaders and nearly half its active participants are in their late twenties to mid-thirties. They are men who belong to the second half of the baby-boom generation, men who not only missed the political engagement of the sixties but were cheated out of that era's affluent bounty. They are downwardly mobile sons, condemned by the eighties economy to earning less than their fathers, unable to buy homes or support families. [. . .] These are men who are losing ground and at the same time see women gaining it – and suspect a connection.
>
> ("Where Did Randy Go Wrong?": 25)

In what sense, precisely, are these men losing ground? Faludi suggests that women's sexual liberation and the widespread availability of contraception, have given women much more control of their own sexuality than ever before. This control threatens paternity itself. Wilke, for example, warned that pro-choice women "do violence to marriage" because they "remove the right of a husband to protect the life of the child he has fathered in his wife's womb" (in Faludi, *Backlash*: 402). Along with suggesting that the fetus be referred to as "a little guy," Wilke proposed that the mother's womb be referred to as "a place of residence" (ibid.: 421). "Fathering" in Wilke's terms seems to be an independent masculine exercise requiring only the temporary use of the mother's womb. Insofar as the feminist movement made such thinking seem antiquated, many American men seemed at a loss. George Gilder put the tension of the shift with remarkable bluntness in his 1986 book *Men and Marriage*. Arguing that women's access to birth control and abortion depletes male power, Gilder concludes that the penis itself is reduced to "an empty plaything" (ibid.: 403). The failure of sexual desire and the reduction of reproductive power are always both political and psychic. The psychic anxiety is often assuaged by the exercise of political power. The intersection of the legal and psychic transformation of paternity is an integral part of the struggle over abortion rights.

In *Moses and Monotheism*, Freud defined paternity as "a hypothesis based on an inference and a premise."[13] At the origin of the patriarchal order, Freud argues, civilization "advances" because in honoring the paternal rather than the maternal line, civilization chooses "intellectuality over sensuality" as the means of establishing power. Since maternity is visible and "proved by the evidence of the senses," and paternity is an hypothesis based on an inference and a premise, the authority of the patriarchy depends on a hierarchical relationship between the visible and the invisible, with the invisible (paternity and an invisible God) being the ascendant term in the pair. Abstract thought must be made to be superior to matter/mater/mother. Law's abstractions, until recently, have proven to be patriarchy's best friend in the establishment and maintenance of this superiority.

As Foucault and Freud have, in their different ways, shown us: law needs invisibility to survey the visible; visibility inspires surveillance and submits to the gaze of the panoptic authority. Insofar as law involves the delicate negotiation of inferences and premises, the balance between hypothesis and contested evidence, it is aligned with the inferences and premises of paternity. What we are witnessing right now is perhaps the first serious threat to the shared sympathy between the law and paternity. Paternity too can now be a matter "proved by the evidence of the [scientific/legal] senses." Paternity – and male sexual potency and impotency which underlie it – is now both *more and less* than an inference and a premise. By making paternity visible civilization robs it of its complicity with the law. The new visibility of paternity feminizes it and submits it to the decisions and mediations of law. Rather than enjoying the freedom of doubt, paternity has moved into the realm of the verifiable. Verity thy name is woman; but it is in the realm of fiction and fantasy that freedom and power live.

As paternity becomes as visible as maternity and loses its ascendancy in the binary, the pressures brought to bear on it become more intense and more confining. In Prince George's County alone, Judge Gary Ross' paternity court processes over 150 paternity cases *a day*. In 1987, his court handled 1,757 cases and made the county second in the amount of money collected for child support in Maryland. In two years, Prince George County raised child support by $9 million from $13.5 million in fiscal 1985 to $22.5 million in 1987.[14] How has this happened? In the courtroom itself the medical technicians now conduct paternity tests. In every way, the establishment of paternity as something more and less than an inference and a premise, transforms the economy – psychic, fiscal, and political – of patriarchy.

Rather than seeing paternity's "doubtability" as *only* a source of psychic anxiety, as Freud argued, I am suggesting that the unverifiable status of paternity also provided justification for their role as policemen over women and criminals (leading some to think of female sexuality as criminality). This role in turn establishes men as "disinterested" and neutral arbitrators of law, including reproduction laws. The psychic "law of the father" is powerful precisely because while remaining unseen itself, it determines what is and what is not seen, what is and is not subject to visibility and the apparatus of surveillance. Now, paternity can itself become a subject of legal scrutiny and modulation.

III

Instead of staging themselves as fathers, the men of Operation Rescue project themselves as speaking-fetuses or nurturing "rescuers." They understand that their goal in the demonstration is to remain veiled *as* fathers. While I am not suggesting that we imitate the men of the New Right, I do believe that the power of a finely calibrated invisibility has been too quickly dismissed as a political strategy by the Left. Representational visibility as *the* goal for progressive, leftist representational politics, may overlook too much when it ignores the real traps within visibility itself. What the Operation Rescue blockades demonstrate is the need for a much more nuanced relation to visibility and invisibility within representation itself.

More than calling for a shrewd analysis of the "terms and structures of representation" I am suggesting that we rethink the entire visibility-power game itself. The relations between visibility and power are never only representational; representation is not a simple abacus adding and subtracting power from visible beads. To employ that much over-used Turnerian term, visibility and invisibility within representation are always liminal. To watch paternity enter this liminal zone is to see the disadvantages of staking too much on visibility as a means of achieving representational power. Visible to whom? Who is looking and who is seen?

I am not proposing here that women need to imitate men who do not appear in relation to paternity. I am suggesting, however, that in the reluctance to make paternity more than an inference and a premise, one of the logical appeals of invisibility is made comprehensible. The pregnant woman's very visibility has made her body the focus of his laws.

In the past decade, medical technology has made it possible to determine paternity within a range of about 96 to 98 per cent probability. Formerly, a simple blood test (used extensively through the 1970s) could reliably *eliminate* possible fathers, but it could not ascertain the correct father – since there are only six blood types many unrelated people share the same blood type. In the early and mid-1980s a new test called the human leucocyte (HLC) antigens test compared similarities between the child and the alleged father by concentrating on molecules which formed above blood cells. While it is still possible for unrelated people to have the same HLC types this was a far more reliable test than a simple blood test (there are many more possible HLC combinations than blood types). In the late 1980s the DNA test, which compares genetic material itself, became a relatively cheap (about $200) method for paternity testing. The chance of two unrelated people having the same DNA pattern has been calculated to be one in 30 billion.[15]

If DNA tests are allowed to be widely admissible, paternity trials will become a thing of the past – the test will make a trial unnecessary. Currently, in the US 285,000 paternity cases are filed each year; 60,000 of them are disputed.[16] The possibility of bringing a false claim against a putative father as well as the possibility of a father disputing a claim will be effectively eliminated by the DNA test. (Trials will be heard about the reliability of the test; different labs have different records of accuracy. But this will be a fundamentally different kind of trial than in the past. Perhaps what may emerge as a trial issue is the legality of forcing a man to undergo a paternity test against his will. Precedent may be established by cases in which rape victims are demanding that their alleged rapists undergo HIV tests.) However, the Supreme Court has not yet declared DNA tests admissible in paternity trials, and seems troubled by the test's threat to "the marital family." In fact, it is the sociality of the established family that the law wants to leave unsurveyed. This social family, interestingly enough, is not grounded in biological "proof."

In *Michael H.* v. *Gerald D.* (June, 1989) the Supreme Court upheld an 1872 California law stating that the husband of the mother can be "presumed" to be the child's legal father. I will describe this case at some length because it so dramatically illustrates the vested interests in keeping paternity and potency "an inference and a premise." The mother, Carole, was married to Gerald in 1981 when she became pregnant and gave birth to her daughter Victoria. However, she was estranged from Gerald for the first three years of Victoria's life (but still legally married) and was living off and on with three different men. One of these three was Michael H. In the case, Michael H. argued that he was the child's father – a DNA test demonstrated a 98.07 per cent chance that Michael is Victoria's father – and that he should be granted visitation rights because he had a "constitutionally protected liberty interest" in maintaining a relationship with his daughter. In 1984, Carole and Gerald were reconciled and they both opposed Michael's wish to visit Victoria. Gerald argued that as the husband of Carole when the child was conceived and born, he was "presumed" to be the child's father and thus the law should guarantee protection to "the marital family" against claims such as Michael's.[17] The majority of the court preferred to keep paternity "a hypothesis based on an inference and a premise" rather than something that could be proved by medical "senses." To do so, they had to uphold a law from 1872, a law written very much in the spirit of Freud's idea about the paternal hypothesis. Ruling against Michael, the court argued that the state can and should help foster the presumption that the husband is the father. Not surprisingly, Justice

William Brennan (that much-missed rational man) in his dissent argued that Justice Antonin Scalia, who wrote the decision, had a view of the Constitution which "is not the living charter I have taken to be our Constitution; it is instead a stagnant, archaic, hidebound document steeped in the prejudices and superstitions of a time long past."[18] As of this date no further challenges have been brought regarding the admissibility of DNA tests.

Michael H. v. *Gerald D.* is a case about competing claims to fatherhood; one claim is based on the integrity of biology and the other on the integrity of the marital family.[19] By giving credence to the marital over the biological, the court implicitly devalues the biological claim of paternity. This is consistent with the pattern of decisions governing competing claims between maternity and paternity. In the 1976 case of *Planned Parenthood* v. *Danforth* the Supreme Court held that it is not necessary for a woman to gain the consent of the biological father in order to have an abortion. Laurence Tribe summarizes the court's thinking:

> Of course, it would be ideal if both parties concurred in an abortion decision, but when the woman is unwilling to continue the pregnancy, a requirement of consent from the man would not facilitate *consensus*. It would simply transfer the power to decide from the woman, who has decided on an abortion, to the man, who has decided to stop her. Only one party can prevail in such a situation. Since the abortion at issue is one that would be legal if the man had no objection, the interest in the life of the fetus cannot justify ruling for the man.

> (*Abortion*: 198)

In other words, within the legal parameters of reproduction rights biological paternity comes in second place and this, I suspect, is the real outrage which fuels the abortion debates. In the only arena of law which gives "preferential" treatment to women, Operation Rescue seeks to have the abortion decisions overturned. On the one hand, women can use paternity tests to enjoin men to pay child support against their will; but men cannot enjoin women to bear children against their will.[20] It is this perceived inequality which accounts for what seem, at first glance, to be the bizarre affinities Randall Terry insists on making between the civil rights movement and Operation Rescue. After being arrested in Atlanta in 1988, Terry spent his time in prison reading the work of Martin Luther King, Jr. Since then Terry has repeatedly claimed that he is continuing the civil rights movement. "In many, many ways, the rescue really is like the civil rights movement. This is a civil rights movement, seeking to restore the civil rights of children, the right to life."[21]

Within the series of substitutions and displacements that align men with the fetus, Terry's belief that the rescue is part of the civil rights movement highlights the implicit agenda of Operation Rescue – that men must not be secondary partners in reproductive choices. Defiantly opposed to the law which would give them only secondary rights, Operation Rescue runs up court fines, frustrates the Internal Revenue Service, and clogs the courts with arrests that cannot be processed without the "name of the father."

Revising the ideological claims of the civil rights movement to make themselves heirs to it is a bold move. But even more extraordinary is Operation Rescue's current project of revising the legacy of the women's movement. In a remarkable editorial in the August/September 1990 *Rescue Report*, the newsletter of Operation Rescue, entitled, "What Ever Happened to the Women's Movement?," the anti-abortion group de-clares itself the rightful heir to the women's movement:

> What has happened to the women's movement? We have picked it up; we have become the true defenders of women in this generation by allowing women to be what God intended them to be. We are the ones who are intervening for women in the courts. We are the ones helping single women raise their families.

This "we" refers to men; they are the "we" who have become the protectors of women. The abortion debates are conversations among men about the bodies of women; when women enter the conversation as speakers they enter a conversation with well-defined parameters and rigid language. (Thus "pro-life" is countered with the rather weaker motto "pro-choice.") While there is nothing new about men determining the thoughts and actions of women – after all, this is what Virginia Woolf satirized so brilliantly in *A Room of One's Own* in 1929 – what is new and startling is the belief that in this gesture Operation Rescue has become the heir to the women's movement itself. In Witchita, many women among the Operation Rescue demonstrators wore tee-shirts with a small (baby) women's sign nestled within a bigger women's sign and accompanied by the words, "Equal Rights for Unborn Women." The more subversive among us may read this in a very French fashion – living women are not yet born or bearable within phallocentric represen-tation – but alas, the intention is quite the opposite. The unborn fetus can be part of a propaganda campaign for the newly emerging "femi-nist" turn of Operation Rescue.

It would be a mistake to read this turn as part of an ideological shift in the paternalistic thinking of Operation Rescue. It is part of their larger attempt to appropriate the signs of other "popular" movements. For Operation Rescue, the women's movement and the animal rights move-ments are equally ripe for appropriation. One of their other new tee-shirts borrows the motto of environmental groups who saved baby seals trapped in fishermen's nets. The shirt has an image of a circle with a line through it (stolen from *Ghostbusters*) and reads: "Save the Baby Humans."

By defining paternity as more and less than an inference and a premise, medicine and the law have rendered paternity feminine. To add insult to injury, the Law has had the temerity to give "real" women greater legal right to reproductive "freedom" than men. Under the threat of this feminization, Operation Rescue has ignored the law and revised the history of the civil rights and women's movements, and *Tootsie*-like its members have staged performances in which they take on the role of the "good mother" in order to perpetuate fear of the "murdering mother." Disguising the newly visible claims of paternity within the image of the fetal form, Operation Rescue has attempted to hide the fact that the baby it wants so desperately to rescue is that mythically innocent white man, still caught in the silent womb of the maternal body.

IV

As performance, Operation Rescue's demonstrations elucidate the political consequences of making the hitherto unseen visible. These consequences are bound up with reproductive visibility, but they are not limited to it. The connection between reproduction and representation is intractable. To control one is to control the other.

Randall Terry takes every opportunity offered him to explain that reproductive rights are only a small part of his overall plan to control representation and power-knowledge. "Ultimately my goal is to reform this culture [. . .] the arts, the media, the entertainment industries, medicine, sciences, education – to return to right and wrong, a Judeo-Christian base." He wants to ban all birth control, censor sex scenes in film, and eliminate pornography. He wants to influence the direction of scientific research and curricular organization. The object of scrutiny – the fetus, the woman – allows the subject who looks to continue to direct his own play. Becoming the visible father is the real anxiety – controlling maternity offsets it.

While I mentioned that 56 per cent of the members of Operation Rescue are men, I have not here considered what motivates the women of Operation Rescue. In focusing on men, I do not mean to imply that the complex relationship between patriarchy, paternity, and women is not itself worthy of careful scrutiny. There are real benefits for some women in the current order of things. And many women are complicitous with the system that "protects" their positions. My effort here, however, is to consider in some detail the ways in which what can and cannot be seen in the abortion debates everywhere relates to what can and cannot be seen within reproduction and representation.

The Real pregnant woman – and therefore the Real mother – will never be the "proper" subject of psychoanalysis because as an image who potentially contains the other within one continuous body, she wreaks havoc with the notion of symmetry and reciprocity fundamental to understanding the exchange of gaze and psychoanalysis's dream of the Social I. (She can only enter psychoanalysis and representation as a Symbolic Mother.) As an image which contains, simultaneously, the I and the not-I, the visibly pregnant woman's body contains two sets of eyes/I. In place of the split subject and the drama of lack, the pregnant woman raises the spectacle of a double-subject and the drama of over-whelming presence. Lest this sound overly romantic or "essentialist," I should stress that the visibility of pregnancy is never absolute, and precisely because of this non-absolute visibility, almost all women are seen as potential mothers.

Classical psychoanalysis cannot adequately "see" the woman-mother because she threatens to make visible the real repression of psycho-analytic theory, the limit of the reciprocal gaze. She internalizes the eyes of the other; men cannot repeat that internalization or bear its return. Operation Rescue attempts to remove the skin of the pregnant woman to reveal the eyes of her internal other, the "independent" fetus. By displaying the fetus as the single image of pregnancy, Operation Rescue attempts to ignore the dilemma of the expectant mother entirely. More complexly, the members of Operation Rescue seek to erase the increas-ing visibility of paternity itself – a visibility the men of the New Right are reluctant to champion.

While Operation Rescue is extreme in its methods, its members merely make manifest a persistent and pervasive fascination to see and thus to control the woman's body. Increasingly, that means both the inside and outside image of her body. In excessively marking the boundaries of the woman's *body*, precisely in order to make it thoroughly visible, patriarchal culture seeks to make *her* subject to legal, artistic, and psychic surveillance.[22]

While the male psychic subject uses the woman's body as the focus of the erotic/medical/social spectacle, his own, once again, goes unmarked. The anti-abortion demonstrations of Operation Rescue make clear what is at stake in the conflicting political field of visibility. Often the one who never appears is the one running the show.

7

The ontology of performance: representation without reproduction

Performance's only life is in the present. Performance cannot be saved, recorded, documented, or otherwise participate in the circulation of representations *of* representations: once it does so, it becomes something other than performance. To the degree that performance attempts to enter the economy of reproduction it betrays and lessens the promise of its own ontology. Performance's being, like the ontology of subjectivity proposed here, becomes itself through disappearance.

The pressures brought to bear on performance to succumb to the laws of the reproductive economy are enormous. For only rarely in this culture is the "now" to which performance addresses its deepest questions valued. (This is why the now is supplemented and buttressed by the documenting camera, the video archive.) Performance occurs over a time which will not be repeated. It can be performed again, but this repetition itself marks it as "different." The document of a performance then is only a spur to memory, an encouragement of memory to become present.

The other arts, especially painting and photography, are drawn increasingly toward performance. The French-born artist Sophie Calle, for example, has photographed the galleries of the Isabella Stewart Gardner Museum in Boston. Several valuable paintings were stolen from the museum in 1990. Calle interviewed various visitors and members of the museum staff, asking them to describe the stolen paintings. She then transcribed these texts and placed them next to the photographs of the galleries. Her work suggests that the descriptions and memories of the paintings constitute their continuing "presence," despite the absence of the paintings themselves. Calle gestures toward a notion of the interactive exchange between the art object and the viewer. While such exchanges are often recorded as the stated goals of museums and galleries, the institutional effect of the gallery often seems to put the masterpiece under house arrest, controlling all conflicting and unprofessional commentary about it. The speech act of memory and description (Austin's constative utterance) becomes a performative expression when Calle places these commentaries within the representation of the museum. The descriptions fill in, and thus supplement (add to, defer, and displace) the stolen paintings. The fact that these descriptions vary considerably – even at times wildly – only lends credence to the fact that the interaction between the art object and the spectator is, essentially, performative – and therefore resistant to the claims of validity and accuracy endemic to the discourse of reproduction. While the art historian of painting must ask if the reproduction is accurate and clear, Calle asks where seeing and memory forget the object itself and enter the subject's own set of personal meanings and associations. Further her work suggests that the forgetting (or stealing) of the object is a fundamental energy of its descriptive recovering. The description itself does not reproduce the object, it rather helps us to restage and restate the effort to remember what is lost. The descriptions remind us how loss acquires meaning and generates recovery – not only of and for the object, but for the one who remembers. The disappearance of the object is fundamental to performance; it rehearses and repeats the disappearance of the subject who longs always to be remembered.

For her contribution to the *Dislocations* show at the Museum of Modern Art in New York in 1991, Calle used the same idea but this time she asked curators, guards, and restorers to describe paintings that were on loan from the permanent collection. She also asked them to draw small pictures of their memories of the paintings. She then arranged the texts and pictures according to the exact dimensions of the circulating paintings and placed them on the wall where the actual paintings usually hang. Calle calls her piece *Ghosts*, and as the visitor discovers Calle's work spread throughout the museum, it is as if Calle's own eye is following and tracking the viewer as she makes her way through the museum.[1] Moreover, Calle's work seems to disappear because it is dispersed throughout the "permanent collection" – a collection which circulates despite its "permanence." Calle's artistic contribution is a kind of self-concealment in which she offers the words of others about other works of art under her own artistic signature. By making visible her attempt to offer what she does not have, what cannot be seen, Calle subverts the goal of museum display. She exposes what the museum does not have and cannot offer and uses that absence to generate her own work. By placing memories in the place of paintings, Calle asks that the ghosts of memory be seen as equivalent to "the permanent collection" of "great works." One senses that if she asked the same people over and over about the same paintings, each time they would describe a slightly different painting. In this sense, Calle demonstrates the performative quality of all seeing.

I

Performance in a strict ontological sense is nonreproductive. It is this quality which makes performance the runt of the litter of contemporary art. Performance clogs the smooth machinery of reproductive representation necessary to the circulation of capital. Perhaps nowhere was the affinity between the ideology of capitalism and art made more manifest than in the debates about the funding policies for the National Endowment for the Arts (NEA).[2] Targeting both photography and performance art, conservative politicians sought to prevent endorsing the "real" bodies implicated and made visible by these art forms.

Performance implicates the real through the presence of living bodies. In performance art spectatorship there is an element of consumption: there are no left-overs, the gazing spectator must try to take everything in. Without a copy, live performance plunges into visibility – in a maniacally charged present – and disappears into memory, into the realm of invisibility and the unconscious where it eludes regulation and control. Performance resists the balanced circulations of finance. It saves nothing; it only spends. While photography is vulnerable to charges of counterfeiting and copying, performance art is vulnerable to charges of valuelessness and emptiness. Performance indicates the possibility of revaluing that emptiness; this potential revaluation gives performance art its distinctive oppositional edge.[3]

To attempt to write about the undocumentable event of performance is to invoke the rules of the written document and thereby alter the event itself. Just as quantum physics discovered that macro-instruments cannot measure microscopic particles without transforming those particles, so too must performance critics realize that the labor to write about performance (and thus to "preserve" it) is also a labor that fundamentally alters the event. It does no good, however, to simply refuse to write about performance because of this inescapable transformation. The challenge raised by the ontological claims of performance for writing is to re-mark again the performative possibilities of writing itself. The act of writing toward disappearance, rather than the act of writing toward preservation, must remember that the after-effect of disappearance is the experience of subjectivity itself.

This is the project of Roland Barthes in both *Camera Lucida* and *Roland Barthes by Roland Barthes*. It is also his project in *Empire of Signs*, but in this book he takes the memory of a city in which he no longer is, a city from which he disappears, as the motivation for the search for a disappearing performative writing. The trace left by that script is the meeting-point of a mutual disappearance; shared subjectivity is possible for Barthes because two people can recognize the same Impossible. To live for a love whose goal is to share the Impossible is both a humbling project and an exceedingly ambitious one, for it seeks to find connection only in that which is no longer there. Memory. Sight. Love. It must involve a full seeing of the Other's absence (the ambitious part), a seeing which also entails the acknowledgment of the Other's presence (the humbling part). For to acknowledge the Other's (always partial) presence is to acknowledge one's own (always partial) absence.

In the field of linguistics, the performative speech act shares with the ontology of performance the inability to be reproduced or repeated. "Being an individual and historical act, a performative utterance cannot be repeated. Each reproduction is a new act performed by someone who is qualified. Otherwise, the reproduction of the performative utterance by someone else necessarily transforms it into a constative utterance."[4]

Writing, an activity which relies on the reproduction of the Same (the three letters *cat* will repeatedly signify the four-legged furry animal with whiskers) for the production of meaning, can broach the frame of performance but cannot mimic an art that is nonreproductive. The mimicry of speech and writing, the strange process by which we put words in each other's mouths and others' words in our own, relies on a substitutional economy in which equivalencies are assumed and re-established. Performance refuses this system of exchange and resists the circulatory economy fundamental to it. Performance honors the idea that a limited number of people in a specific time/space frame can have an experience of value which leaves no visible trace afterward. Writing about it necessarily cancels the "tracelessness" inaugurated within this performative promise. Performance's independence from mass reproduction, technologically, economically, and linguistically, is its greatest strength. But buffeted by the encroaching ideologies of capital and reproduction, it frequently devalues this strength. Writing about performance often, unwittingly, encourages this weakness and falls in behind the drive of the document/ary. Performance's challenge to writing is to discover a way for repeated words to become performative utterances, rather than, as Benveniste warned, constative utterances.

The distinction between performative and constative utterances was proposed by J. L. Austin in *How To Do Things With Words*.[5] Austin argued that speech had both a constative element (describing things in the world) and a performative element (to say something is to *do* or make something, e.g. "I promise," "I bet," "I beg"). Performative speech acts refer only to themselves, they *enact* the activity the speech signifies. For Derrida, performative writing promises fidelity only to the utterance of the promise: I promise to utter this promise.[6] The performative is important to Derrida precisely because it displays language's independence from the referent outside of itself. Thus, for Derrida the performative enacts the now of writing in the present time.[7]

Tania Modleski has rehearsed Derrida's relation to Austin and argues that "feminist critical writing is simultaneously performative and utopian" ("Some Functions": 15). That is, feminist critical writing is an enactment of belief in a better future; the act of writing brings that future closer.[8] Modleski goes further too and says that women's relation to the performative mode of writing and speech is especially intense because women are not assured the luxury of making linguistic promises within phallogocentrism, since all too often she *is* what is promised. Commenting on Shoshana Felman's account of the "scandal of the speaking body," a scandal Felman elucidates through a reading of Molière's *Dom Juan*, Modleski argues that the scandal has different affects and effects for women than for men. "[T]he real, historical scandal to which feminism addresses itself is surely not to be equated with the writer at the center of discourse, but the woman who remains outside of it, not with the 'speaking body,' but with the 'mute body' " (ibid.: 19). Feminist critical writing, Modleski argues, "works toward a time when the traditionally mute body, 'the mother,' will be given the same access to 'the names' – language and speech – that men have enjoyed" (ibid.: 15).

If Modleski is accurate in suggesting that the opposition for feminists who write is between the "speaking bodies" of men and the "mute bodies" of women, for performance the opposition is between "the body in pleasure" and, to invoke the title of Elaine Scarry's book, "the body in pain." In moving from the grammar of words to the grammar of the body, one moves from the realm of metaphor to the realm of metonymy. For performance art itself however, the referent is always the agonizingly relevant body of the performer. Metaphor works to secure a vertical hierarchy of value and is reproductive; it works by erasing dissimilarity and negating difference; it turns two into one. Metonymy is additive and associative; it works to secure a horizontal axis of contiguity and displacement. "The kettle is boiling" is a sentence which assumes that water is contiguous with the kettle. The point is not that the kettle is *like* water (as in the metaphorical love is like a rose), but rather the kettle is boiling *because* the water inside the kettle is. In performance, the body is metonymic of self, of character, of voice, of "presence." But in the plenitude of its apparent visibility and availability, the performer actually disappears and represents something else – dance, movement, sound, character, "art." As we discovered in relation to Cindy Sherman's self-portraits, the very effort to make the female body appear involves the addition of something other than "the body." That "addition" becomes the object of the spectator's gaze, in much the way the supplement functions to secure and displace the fixed meaning of the (floating) signifier. Just as her body remains unseen as "in itself it really is," so too does the sign fail to reproduce the referent. Performance uses the performer's body to pose a question about the inability to secure the relation between subjectivity and the body *per se*; performance uses the body to frame the lack of Being promised by and through the body – that which cannot appear without a supplement.

In employing the body metonymically, performance is capable of resisting the reproduction of metaphor, and the metaphor I'm most keenly interested in resisting is the metaphor of gender, a metaphor which upholds the vertical hierarchy of value through systematic marking of the positive and the negative. In order to enact this marking, the metaphor of gender presupposes unified bodies which are biologically different. More specifically, these unified bodies are different in "one" aspect of the body, that is to say, difference is located in the genitals.

As MacCannell points out about Lacan's story of the "laws of urinary segregation" (*Ecrits*: 151), same sex bathrooms are social institutions which further the metaphorical work of hiding gender/genital difference. The genitals themselves are forever hidden within metaphor, and metaphor, as a "cultural worker," continually converts difference into the Same. The joined task of metaphor and culture is to reproduce itself; it accomplishes this by turning two (or more) into one.[9] By valuing one gender and marking it (with the phallus) culture reproduces one sex and one gender, the hommo-sexual.

If this is true then women should simply disappear – but they don't. Or do they? If women are not reproduced within metaphor or culture, how do they survive? If it is a question of survival, why would white women (apparently visible cultural workers) participate in the reproduction of their own negation? What aspects of the bodies and languages of women remain outside metaphor and inside the historical real? Or to put it somewhat differently, how do women reproduce and represent themselves within the figures and metaphors of hommosexual representation and culture? Are they perhaps surviving in another (auto)reproductive system?

"What founds our *gender economy* (division of the sexes and their mutual evaluation) is the exclusion of *the mother*, more specifically her body, more precisely yet, her *genitals*. These cannot, must not be *seen*" (original emphasis; MacCannell, *Figuring Lacan*: 106). The discursive and iconic "nothingness" of the Mother's genitals is what culture and metaphor cannot face. They must be effaced in order to allow the phallus to operate as that which always marks, values, and wounds. Castration is a response to **this** blindness to the mother's genitals. In "The Uncanny" Freud suggests that the fear of blindness is a displacement of the deeper fear of castration but surely it works the other way as well, or maybe even more strongly. Averting the eyes from the "nothing" of the mother's genitals is the blindness which fuels castration. This is the blindness of Oedipus. Is blindness necessary to the anti-Oedipus? To Electra? Does metonymy need blindness as keenly as metaphor does?

Cultural orders rely on the renunciation of conscious desire and pleasure and *promise* a reward for this renunciation. MacCannell refers to this as "the positive promise of castration" and locates it in the idea of "value" itself – the desire to be valued by the Other. (For Lacan, value is recognition by the Other.) The hope of becoming valued prompts the subject to make sacrifices, and especially to forgo conscious pleasure. This willingness to renounce pleasure implies that the Symbolic Order is moral and that the subject obeys an (inner) Law which affords the subject a veil of dignity. Why only the veil of dignity as against dignity itself? Because the fundamental Other (the one who governs "the other scene" which ghosts the conscious scene) is the Symbolic Mother. She is the Ideal Other for whom the subject wants to be dignified; but she cannot appear within the phallic representational economy which is predicated on the disappearance of her Being.[10] The psychic subject performs for a phantom who allows the subject veils and curtains – rather than satisfaction.

Performance approaches the Real through resisting the metaphorical reduction of the two into the one. But in moving from the aims of metaphor, reproduction, and pleasure to those of metonymy, displacement, and pain, performance marks the body itself as loss. Performance is the attempt to value that which is nonreproductive, nonmetaphorical. This is enacted through the staging of the drama of misrecognition (twins, actors within characters enacting other characters, doubles, crimes, secrets, etc.) which sometimes produces the recognition of the desire to be seen *by* (and within) the other. Thus for the spectator the performance spectacle is itself a projection of the scenario in which her own desire takes place.

More specifically, a genre of performance art called "hardship art" or "ordeal art" attempts to invoke a distinction between presence and representation by using the singular body as a metonymy for the apparently nonreciprocal experience of pain. This performance calls witnesses to the singularity of the individual's death and asks the spectator to do the impossible – to share that death by rehearsing for it. (It is for this reason that performance shares a fundamental bond with ritual. The Catholic Mass, for example, is the ritualized performative promise to remember and to rehearse for the Other's death.) The promise evoked by this performance then is to learn to value what is lost, to learn not the meaning but the value of what cannot be reproduced or seen (again). It begins with the knowledge of its own failure, that it cannot *be* achieved.

II

Angelika Festa creates performance pieces in which she appears in order to disappear (Figure 24). Her appearance is always extraordinary: she suspends herself from poles; she sits fully dressed in well-excavated graves attended by a fish; she stands still on a crowded corner of downtown New York (8th and Broadway) in a red rabbit suit holding two loaves of bread; wearing a mirror mask, a black, vaguely antiquarian dress, with hands and feet painted white, she holds a white bowl of fruit and stands on the side of a country road. The more dramatic the appearance, the more disturbing the disappearance. As performances which are contingent upon disappearance, Festa's work traces the passing of the woman's body from visibility to invisibility, and back again. What becomes apparent in these performances is the labor and pain of this endless and liminal passing.

In her 1987 performance called – appropriately – *Untitled Dance (with fish and others)*, at The Experimental Intermedia Foundation in New York, Festa literally hung suspended from a pole for twenty-four hours (Figure 25).[11] The performance took place between noon on Saturday May 30 and noon on Sunday 31. The pole was positioned between two wooden supports at about an 80° angle and Festa hung suspended from it, her body wrapped to the pole with white sheets, her face and weight leaning toward the floor. Her eyes were covered with silver tape and thus looked, in all senses, beyond the spectator. About two and a half feet from the bottom of the pole was a small black cushion which supported her bare feet. Her feet in turn were projected onto a screen behind her to the left in close-up. The projection enlarged them so much that they seemed to be as large as the rest of Festa's body. On a video monitor in front of Festa and to the left, a video tape loop of the embryology of a fish played continuously. Finally, on a smaller monitor facing Festa a time-elapsed video documenting the dance (re)played and re(in)flected the entire performance.

The images of death, birth, and resurrection are visually overlaid; Festa's point is that they are philosophically (and mythologically) inseparable. The work is primarily a spectacle of pain; while I do not wish to minimize this aspect of the performance, I will begin by discussing some of the broad claims which frame *Untitled*. The performance seeks to display the lack of difference between some of Western metaphysics' tacit oppositions – birth and death, time and space, spectacle and secret. By suspending herself between two poles (two polarities), Festa's performances suggest that it is only within the space *between* oppositions that "a woman" can be represented. Such representation is, therefore and necessarily, extremely up-in-the-air, almost impossible to map or lay claim to. It is in a space in which there is no ground, a space in which (bare)feet cannot touch the ground.

The iconography of the performance is self-contradictory: each position is undermined by a succeeding one. Festa's wrapped body itself seems to evoke images of dead mummies and full cocoons. Reading the

Figure 24 Angelika Festa, *You Are Obsessive, Eat Something* (1984). (Photo: Claudine Ascher. Courtesy: Angelika Festa)

Figure 25 Angelika Festa, *Untitled Dance (with fish and others)* (1987). (Photo: Hubert Hohn. Courtesy: Angelika Festa)

image one can say something like: the fecundity of the central image is an image of History-as-Death (the mummy) and Future-as-Unborn (the cocoon). The twenty-four-hour performance defines the Present (Festa's body) as that which continually suspends and thus prohibits the intrusive return of that death and the appealing possibility of that birth. The Present is that which can tolerate neither death nor birth but can only exist because of these two "originary" acts. Both are required for the Present to be present, for it to exist in the suspended animation between the Past and the Future.

But this truism is undercut by another part of the performance: the fish tape stops at precisely the moment the fish breaks out of the embryo; then the tape begins again. The tape thus revises the definition of History offered by the central image (History-as-Death). History is figured by the tape as an endless embryology whose import is not in the breaking out of – (the ubiquitous claim to historical "transformation") – but rather in the continual repetition of the cycle of that mutation which produces birth. ("Be fruitful and multiply" is wittily made literal by the repeated projection of the tape loop.)

The third image then undercuts the first two. The projected images of Festa's feet seem to be an half-ironic, half-devout allusion to the history of representations of the bloody feet of the crucified Christ (Figure 26). On the one hand, (one foot?) the projections are like photographic "details" of Mannerist paintings and on the other, they seem to "ground" the performance; because of their size they demand more of the spectator's attention. The spatial arrangement of the room – with Festa in the middle, the feet-screen behind her and to the left, the fish tape in front of her also on the left, and the time-elapsed mini-monitor directly in front of her and raised, forces the spectator constantly to look *away from* Festa's suspended body. In order to look at the projected feet, one has to look "beyond" Festa; in order to look at the fish embryo tape or the video monitor recording the performance itself, one has to turn one's back to her. That these projected images seem to be consumable while the center image is, as it were, a "blind" image, suggests that it is only through the second-order of re/presentation that we "see" anything. Festa's body (and particularly her eyes) is averted from the spectator's ability to comprehend, to see and thus to seize.

The failure to see the eye/I locates Festa's suspended body for the spectator. The spectator's inability to meet the eye *defines* the other's body as lost; the pain of this loss is underlined by the corollary recognition that the represented body is so manifestly and painfully there, for both Festa and the spectator. Festa cannot see her body because her eyes are taped shut; the spectator cannot see Festa and must gaze instead at the wrapped shell of a lost eyeless body. As with Wallace Stevens: "The

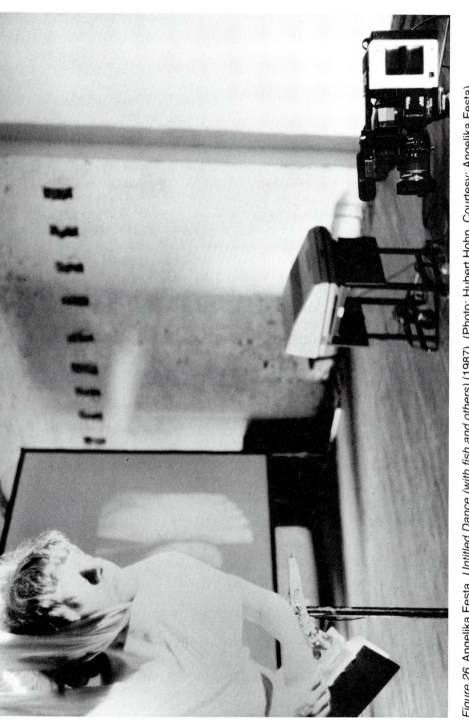

Figure 26 Angelika Festa, *Untitled Dance (with fish and others)* (1987). (Photo: Hubert Hohn. Courtesy: Angelika Festa)

body is no body to be seen/But is an eye that studies its black lid" – and its *back* lid – the Nietzschean *hinterfrage* (Stevens, "Stars at Tallapoosa").

What is the back question for women? Back against the wall. Back off. Back out. About face. Lorna Simpson's photography has recently raised the question of the relation between the about face and the black face. In *Guarded Conditions*, for example, Simpson reassembles the polaroid fragmented images of a black woman's body (Figure 27). Her back faces the viewer; because the images are segmented in three sections vertically and repeated serially in six horizontal panels, the effort to see her without effacing her is made impossible. While Simpson's work is overtly about the documentary tradition of photography, a tradition which has strong ties to the discourse and techniques of criminality, in *Guarded Conditions* she also poses a deeper psychoanalytic response to the violence of perception itself. At the bottom of the image march these words: "Sex Attacks/Skin Attacks/Sex Attacks/Skin Attacks." Racial and sexual violence are an integral part of seeing the African-American woman. Her response to a perception which seeks her disappearance or her containment within the discursive frames of criminality or pathology, is to turn her back. In the middle of her back, the woman clenches her fists and repeats the pose of Mapplethorpe's male model in *Leland Richard* (1980), discussed in chapter 2. Whereas for Mapplethorpe the model's clenched fist is a gesture toward self-imaging (his fist is like Mapplethorpe's holding the time-release shutter), in Simpson's work, the fist is a response to the sexual and racial attacks indexed as the very ground upon which her image rests. As in the work of Festa, the effort to read the image of the represented woman's body in Simpson's photography requires a bilingual approach to word and image, to what can and cannot be seen. The back registers the effacement of the subject within a linguistic and visual field which requires her to be either the Same or the containable, ever fixed, Other. To attack that, Simpson suggests, we need to see and to read other/wise.

Sight is both an image and a word; the gaze is possible both because of the enunciations of articulate eyes *and* because the subject finds a position to see within the optics and grammar of language. In denying this position to the spectator Festa and Simpson also stop the usual enunciative claims of the critic. While the gaze fosters what Lacan calls "the belong to me aspect so reminiscent of property" (*Four Fundamental Concepts*: 81) and leads the looker to desire mastery of the image, the pain inscribed in Festa's performance makes the viewer feel masterless. In Simpson's work, the "belong to me aspect" of the documentary tradition – and the narrative of mastery integral to it – is far too close to the "belong to me aspect" of slavery, domestic work, and the history of sexual labor to be greeted with anything other than a fist, a turned back,

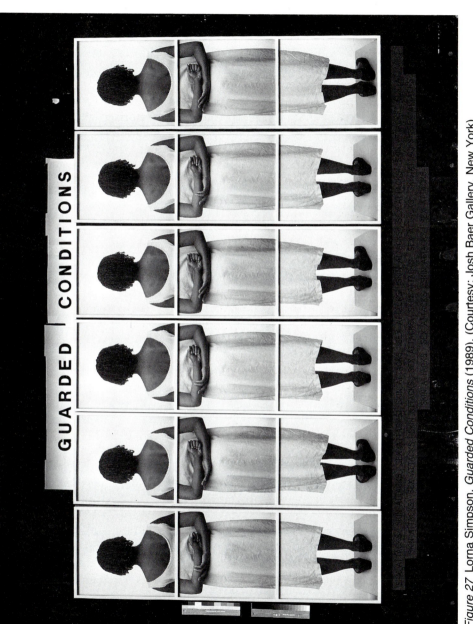

Figure 27 Lorna Simpson, *Guarded Conditions* (1989). (Courtesy: Josh Baer Gallery, New York)

and an awareness of her own "guarded condition" within visual representation.[12]

Unmoored from the traditional position of authority guaranteed by the conventions of address operative in the documentary tradition of the photograph, a tradition which functions to assure that the given to be seen *belongs* to the field of knowledge of the one who looks, Simpson's photographs call for a form of reading based on fragments, serialization, and the acknowledgment that what is shown is not what one wants to see. In this loss of security, the spectator feels an inner splitting between the spectacle of pain she witnesses but cannot locate and the inner pain she cannot express. But she also feels relief to recognize the historical Real which is not displayed but is nonetheless conveyed within Simpson's work.

In Festa's work, a similar splitting occurs. *Untitled* is an elaborate pun on the notion of women's strength. The "labor" of the performance alludes to the labor of the delivery room – and the white sheets and red headdress are puns on the colors of the birthing process – the white light in the center of pain and the red blood which tears open that light.[13] The projected feet wryly raise the issue of the fetishized female body – the part (erotically) substituted for the w/hole – which the performance as a whole – seeks to confront. As one tries to find a way to read this suspended and yet completely controlled and confined body, images of other women tied up flood one's eyes. Images as absurdly comic as the damsel Nell tied to the railroad ties waiting for Dudley Doright to beat the clock and save her, and as harrowing as the traditional burning of martyrs and witches, coexist with more common images of women tied to white hospital beds in the name of "curing hysteria," force-feeding anorexics, or whatever medical malaise by which women have been painfully dominated and by which we continue to be perversely enthralled.

The austere minimalism of this piece (complete silence, one performer, no overt action), actually incites the spectator toward list-making of this type. The lists become dizzyingly similar until one finds it almost impossible to distinguish between Nell screaming on the railroad tracks and the hysteric screaming in the hospital. The riddle is as much about figuring out how they became separated as about how Festa puts them back together.

The anorexic who is obsessed by the image of a slender self, Nell who is the epitome of cross-cutting neck-wrenching cartoon drama, the martyr and witch whose public hanging/burning is dramatized as a lesson in moral certitude – either on the part of the victim-martyr or on the part of the witch's executioner – are each defined in terms of what they are not – healthy, heroic, or legitimately powerful. That these terms are themselves slippery, radically subjective, and historically malleable emphasizes the importance of the maintenance of a fluid and relative perceptual power. These images re-enact the subjective and inventive perception which defines The Fall more profoundly than the fertile ground which the story usually insists is the significant loss. The image of the woman is without property; she is groundless. But since she is "not all," that is not all there is to the story. Emphasizing the importance of perceptual transformation which accompanied the loss of prime real estate in the Garden, Festa's work implicitly underlines this clause – "The eyes of both of them were opened" (*Genesis* 3, 7) – as the most compelling consequence detailed in this narrative of origin.

The belief that perception can be made endlessly new is one of the fundamental drives of all visual arts. But in most theatre, the *opposition* between watching and doing is broken down; the distinction is often made to seem ethically immaterial.[14] Festa, whose eyes are covered with tape throughout the performance, questions the traditional complicity of this visual exchange. Her eyes are completely averted and the more one tries to "see" her the more one realizes that "seeing her" requires that one be seen. In all of these images there is a peculiar sense in which their drama hinges absolutely on the sense of seeing oneself and of being seen as Other. Unlike Rainer's film *The Man Who Envied Women* in which the female protagonist cannot be seen, here the female protagonist cannot see. In the absence of that customary visual exchange, the spectator can see only her own desire to be seen. The satisfaction of desire in this spectacle is thwarted perpetually because Festa is so busy conferring with some region of her own embryology that she cannot participate in her half of the exchange; the spectator has to play both parts – she has to become the spectator of her own performance because Festa will not fulfill the invitation her performance issues. In this sense, Festa's work operates on the other side of the same continuum as Rainer's. Whereas in the film Trisha becomes a kind of spectator, here the spectator becomes a kind of performer.

But while Festa successfully eliminates the ethical complicity between watching and doing associated with most theatre, she does not create an ethically neutral performance. Festa's body is displayed in a completely private (in the sense of enclosed) manner in a public spectacle. She becomes a kind of sacrificial object completely vulnerable to the spectator's gaze. As I watch Festa's exhaustion and pain, I feel cannibalistic, awful, guilty, "sick." But after a while another more complicated response emerges. There is something almost obscenely arrogant in Festa's invitation to this display. It is manifest in the "imitative" aspect of her allusions to Christ's resurrection and his bloody feet, and latently present in the endurance she demands of both her spectator and herself.

This arrogance, which she freely acknowledges and makes blatantly obvious, in some senses, "cancels" my cannibalism. While all this addition and subtraction is going on in my accountant-eyes, I begin to realize that this too is superficial. The performance resides somewhere else – somewhere in the reckoning itself and not at all in the sums and differences of our difficult relationship to it. But this thought does not allow me to completely or easily inhabit a land of equality or democracy, although I believe that is part of what is intended. I feel instead the terribly oppressive physical, psychic, and visual cost of this exchange. If Festa's work can be seen as a hypothesis about the possibility of human communication, it is an uncompromising one. There is no meeting-place here in which one can escape the imposing shadow of those (bloody) feet: if History is figured in the tape loop as a repetitious birth cycle, the Future is figured as an unrelenting cycle of death. Where e. e. cummings writes: "we can never be born enough," Festa counters: "we can never die sufficiently enough." This sense of the ubiquitousness of death and dying is not completely oppressive, however (although at times it comes close to that) – because the performance also insists on the possibility of resurrection. By making death multiple and repetitious, Festa also makes it less absolute – and implicitly, less sacred – not so much the exclusive province of the gods.

My hesitation about this aspect of Festa's work stems not from the latent romance of death (that's common enough), but rather from her apparent belief (or perhaps "faith" is a better word) that this suspension/surrender of her own ego can be accomplished *in* a performance. It is this belief/faith which makes Festa's work so extravagantly literal. Festa's piece is contingent upon the possibility of creating a narrative which reverses the narrative direction of The Fall; beginning with the post-lapsarian second-order of Representation, Festa's *Untitled* attempts to give birth – through an intense process of physical and mental labor – to a direct and unmediated Presentation-of-Presence. That this Presence is registered through the body of a woman *in pain* is the one concession Festa makes to the pervasiveness (and the persuasiveness) of post-lapsarian perception and Being. Enormously and stunningly ambitious, Festa's performances leave both the spectator and the performer so exhausted that one cannot help but wonder if the pleasure of presence and plenitude is worth having if this is the only way to achieve it.

In the spectacle of endurance, discipline, and semi-madness that this work evokes, an inversion of the characteristic paradigms of performative exchange occurs. In the spectacle of fatigue, endurance, and depletion, Festa asks the spectator to undergo first a parallel movement and then an opposite one. The spectator's second "performance" is a movement of accretion, excess, and the recognition of the plenitude of one's physical freedom in contrast to the confinement and pain of the performer's displayed body.

III

In *The History of Sexuality* Foucault argues that "the agency of domination does not reside in the one who speaks (for it is he who is constrained), but in the one who listens and says nothing; not in the one who knows and answers, but in the one who questions and is not supposed to know" (*Sexuality*: 64). He is describing the power-knowledge fulcrum which sustains the Roman Catholic confessional, but as with most of Foucault's work, it resonates in other areas as well.

As a description of the power relationships operative in many forms of performance Foucault's observation suggests the degree to which the silent spectator dominates and controls the exchange. (As Dustin Hoffman made so clear in *Tootsie*, the performer is always in the female position in relation to power.) Women and performers, more often than not, are "scripted" to "sell" or "confess" something to someone who is in the position to buy or forgive.

Much Western theatre evokes desire based upon and stimulated by the inequality between performer and spectator – and by the (potential) domination of the silent spectator. That this model of desire is apparently so compatible with (traditional accounts of) "male" desire is no accident.[15] But more centrally this account of desire between speaker/performer and listener/spectator reveals how dependent these positions are upon visibility and a coherent point of view. A visible and easily located point of view provides the spectator with a stable point upon which to turn on the machinery of projection, identification, and (inevitable) objectification. Performers and their critics must begin to redesign this stable set of assumptions about the positions of the theatrical exchange.

The question raised by Festa's work is the extent to which interest in visual or psychic aversion signals an interest in refusing to participate in a representational economy at all. By virtue of having spectators she accepts at least the initial dualism necessary to all exchange. But Festa's performances are so profoundly "solo" pieces that this work is obviously not "a solution" to the problem of women's representation.

Festa addresses the female spectator; her work does not speak about men, but rather about the loss and grief attendant upon the recognition of the chasm between presence and re-presentation. By taking the notion that women are not visible within the dominant narratives of history and the contemporary customs of performance literally, Festa prompts new considerations about the central "absence" integral to the representation of women in patriarchy. Part of the function of women's absence is to perpetuate and maintain the presence of male desire as desire – as unsatisfied quest. Since the female body and the female character cannot be "staged" or "seen" within representational mediums without challenging the hegemony of male desire, it can be effective politically and aesthetically to deny representing the female body (imagistically, psychically). The belief, the leap of faith, is that this denial will bring about a new form of representation itself (I'm thinking only half jokingly of the sex strike in *Lysistrata*: no sex till the war ends). Festa's performance work underlines the suspension of the female body between the polarities of presence and absence, and insists that "the woman" can exist only *between* these categories of analysis.

Redesigning the relationship between self and other, subject and object, sound and image, man and woman, spectator and performer, is enormously difficult. More difficult still is withdrawing from representation altogether. I am not advocating that kind of retreat or hoping for that kind of silence (since that is the position assigned to women in language with such ease). The task, in other words, is to make counterfeit the currency of our representational economy – not by refusing to participate in it at all, but rather by making work in which the costs of women's perpetual aversion are clearly measured. Such forms of accounting might begin to interfere with the structure of hommo-sexual desire which informs most forms of representation.

IV

Behind the fact of hommo-sexual desire and representation the question of the link between representation and reproduction remains. This question can be re-posed by returning to Austin's contention that a performative utterance cannot be reproduced or represented.

For Lacan, the inauguration of language is simultaneous with the inauguration of desire, a desire which is always painful because it cannot be satisfied. The potential mitigation of this pain is also dependent upon language; one must seek a cure from the wound of words *in* other words – in the words of the other, in the promise of what Stevens calls "the completely answering voice" ("The Sail of Ulysses," in *The Palm at the End*: 389). But this mitigation of pain is always deferred by the *promise* of relief (Austin's performative), as against relief itself, because the other's words substitute for other words in an endless *mise-en-abyme* of metaphorical exchange. Thus the linguistic economy, like the financial economy, is a ledger of substitutions, in which addition and subtraction (the plus and the minus) accord value to the "right" words at the right time. One is always offering what one does not have because what one wants is what one does not have – and for Lacan, "feelings are always reciprocal," if never "equal."[16] Exchanging what one does not

have for what one desires (and therefore does not have) puts us in the
realm of the negative and the possibility of what Felman calls "radical
negativity" (*The Literary Speech Act*: 143).

While feminist theorists have been repeatedly cautioned about becoming stuck in what Sue-Ellen Case describes as "the negative stasis of
what cannot be seen," I think radical negativity is valuable, in part
because it resists reproduction.[17] Felman remarks: "radical negativity is
what constitutes in fact the *analytic* or *performative* dimension of thought:
at once what *makes it an act*" (original emphases; ibid.: 143). As an act,
the performance of negativity does not make a claim to truth or accuracy. Performance seeks a kind of psychic and political efficacy, which is
to say, performance makes a claim about the Real-impossible. As such,
the performative utterances of negativity cannot be absorbed by history
because their affects/effects, like the constative utterances about stolen
paintings which Sophie Calle turns into performatives by framing them
in the gallery, are always changing, varied and resolutely unstatic
objects. "*What history cannot assimilate*," Felman argues, "*is thus the
implicitly analytical dimension of all radical or fecund thoughts*, of all new
theories: the 'force' of their 'performance' (always somewhat subversive) and their 'residual smile' (always somewhere self-subversive)"
(original emphases; ibid.).

The residual smile is the place of play within performance and within
theory. Within play the failure to meet, the impossibility of understanding, is comic rather than tragic. The stakes are lower, as the saying goes.
Within the relatively determined limits of theory, the stakes are low
indeed.

Or are they?

The performance of theory, the act of moving the "as if" into the
indicative "is," like the act of moving descriptions of paintings into the
frames of the stolen or lent canvases, is to replot the relation between
perceiver and object, between self and other. In substituting the subject's memory of the object for the object itself, Calle begins to redesign
the order of the museum and the representational field. Institutions
whose only function is to preserve and honor objects – traditional
museums, archives, banks, and to some degree, universities – are
intimately involved in the reproduction of the sterilizing binaries of
self/other, possession/dispossession, men/women which are increasingly inadequate formulas for representation. These binaries and their
institutional upholders fail to account for that which cannot appear
between these tight "equations" but which nonetheless inform them.

These institutions must invent an economy not based on preservation
but one which is answerable to the consequences of disappearance. The
savings and loan institutions in the US have lost the customer's belief in
the promise of security. Museums whose collections include objects

taken/purchased/obtained from cultures who are now asking (and expecting) their return must confront the legacy of their appropriative history in a much more nuanced and complex way than currently prevails. Finally, universities whose domain is the reproduction of knowledge must re-view the theoretical enterprise by which the object surveyed is reproduced as property with (theoretical) value.

Afterword: notes on hope
– for my students

The uncertainty principle fundamental to physics is based on the failure of the empirical to secure the real. *Fort. Da.* Testing for the quantum is a hazard of probabilities if not fortunes, best guesses of events before and after the leap. The measurement of the quantum's movement in time/ space cannot be securely repeated within the logic of empirical representation. (Nor can the boson's, the quark's, or the gluon's.) Like performance, the quantum cannot be preserved, recalled, measured, and evaluated by recourse to representation's insurance policies. Always insecure, the nervous system of matter is reflected in the nervous condition of psychic being.[1]

Performance art usually occurs in the suspension between the "real" physical matter of "the performing body" and the psychic experience of what it is to be em-bodied. Like a rackety bridge swaying under too much weight, performance keeps one anchor on the side of the corporeal (the body Real) and one on the side of the psychic Real. Performance boldly and precariously declares that Being is performed (and made temporarily visible) in that suspended in-between.[2]

Performance commentators tend to open their critical cameras and set up their tripods on one side or the other – the "physical" readers are usually trained in movement analysis and/or history, and the "psychic" readers are usually trained in Freudian and Lacanian psychoanalytic theory (although rarely in practice). Perhaps it would be worthwhile to experiment with the possibility of a different notion of the relation between these two camps. It might be fruitful to take the body as always both psychic and material/physical: this would necessitate a combined critical methodology. One could employ both physics and psychoanalysis to read the body's movements and paralytic pauses.

But before one can speak of a psychoanalytic physics or a physics of psychoanalysis one must first recognize how each system "proves" the impossibility of seizing the Real. At the risk of redundancy: this is not to say that the real does not exist. It does. But it is to say that it cannot be seen, arrested, fixed with the "slower" I/eye. "Love's interpretation exists only in the afterwards." Within psychoanalysis, this impossible-to-seize-real complicates the notion of the symptom. The symptom's meaning emerges in relation to the psychoanalytic dialogue: it is not so much that the dialogue produces the symptom's meaning, but rather the dialogue creates a stage upon which the symptom's meaning can be amplified. This amplification distorts the sound the symptom makes – but it does provide a hearing. (There is no "pure" hearing without distortion anywhere, any time.) Lacan summarizes the point of Freud's career by remarking that "Freud took it upon himself to show us there are illnesses which speak" ("Intervention in Transference": 94). All symptoms, like all words, are metaphors, substitutes for unportable things. Sometimes particular metaphors are loudly obvious, other times they appear to be transparent, fully representative of the real they seek to convey. The meaning of a word/symptom is not, and cannot be, singular or stable: the meaning changes according to the context in which it appears and speaks. Symptoms like words are repetitious, undecidable, resistant to singular interpretations. The self-reproducing symptom creates a permeable and fluid set of meanings.

> The hysterical symptom does not carry this meaning with it, but the meaning is lent to it, welded on to it, as it were; and in every instance the meaning can be a different one, according to the nature of the suppressed thoughts which are struggling for expression.
>
> (Sigmund Freud, *Dora*: 57)

The symptom, then, is an interpretation, a substitutive metaphor, written within the syntax of a physical body, with which the patient explains herself to herself. She then submits her interpretation of the symptom by performing and re-enacting it for the doctor. When Freud describes Dora's hysterical symptoms, he remarks that Dora's body lays hold of the symptom to create an utterance of its own. That utterance, however, is heard fully for the "first" time within the drama of Freud's script. It would not or could not "speak" to Herr K. in the way that it spoke to Freud. In the same way that the quantum "jumps" when it is observed, the symptom undergoes a transformation when the counter-transference is activated. In the sociality of the production of meaning, words and symptoms mutate as they pass across the thresholds housing us in different bodies, separate selves. That mutation solicits a diagnosis from the other.

When patients speak of "dreaming for the doctor," they point to the way in which the psychoanalytic dialogue generates particular "data." The enabling assumption of psychoanalysis, the leap of faith which makes it possible, is that such data are always already there, unmarked but powerfully defining. The talking cure can be said to "heal" the utterances *it* produces. The "healing" comes through re-marking and re-making the symptoms. There is no such thing as a symptomless body, no such thing as a nonmetaphorical language. The "cure" readjusts and realigns the patient's interpretation of the symptoms, but it does not eliminate all symptoms. The symptomatic utterance created within the psychoanalytic dialogue is heard within the terms of that discourse. (Part of the power of symptoms, the energy that keeps them active, comes from their repression. Once amplified, they change.) Outside of that room, the symptom produces other utterances – expressions that are not vulnerable or susceptible (depending on one's perspective) to that healing.

This is worth pausing over because it points to the limits and possibilities of my own critical methodology. The idea that Operation Rescue's political ambitions and performance ideology can be adequately explained by a psychoanalytic reading of the visibility of paternity strains credulity. I am well aware of this. Nonetheless, a political analysis of Operation Rescue that ignores or overlooks the psychoanalytic displacements involved in the struggle for reproductive rights, is also inadequate. As a symptom of the fraught relations between men and women within cultural production and reproduction, the performances of Operation Rescue are repetitious signs whose meanings shift and merge according to "the suppressed thoughts which are struggling for expression" in an uncertain political, legal, economic, sexual, and psychic field. While the excellent work of Faye Ginsburg, Kristin Luker, Lawrence Tribe, Susan Faludi, and Rosalind Petchesky, has addressed and defined the political, legal, and economic struggle operative in the abortion debates, relatively little attention has been given to offering psychoanalytic analyses.

This is not surprising. The debate is so politically and legally urgent that one hesitates to bother spending energy and time creating something with apparently so little direct utility value. The ideology of reproduction informs critical work no less than it informs sociality. Theory and practice should commingle and reproduce a coherent practice. (When two become one, who is the one they become?) The notion that fetal imagery functions as a way of masking the new visibility of paternity hardly helps one protect the crumbling legal protection of *Roe v. Wade*. Nor does it provide a way of stopping Randall Terry's quest to become a radical reformer of moral life. Both of these things need to be done. However, it would be naive to suppose that these political goals can be straightforwardly achieved. Soaked through with ambivalence and uncertainty, the legal quagmire that constitutes reproductive rights in the United States reflects the immense disjuncture between the concept of a continuous body, which is enacted within the very image of a visibly pregnant woman, and a legal and psychic discourse dedicated to defining separations, distinguishing split subjects, and settling schisms. This yawning incoherence, which is simultaneously psychic and philosophical as Patricia Williams has powerfully argued, will continue to trouble the political realization of reproductive rights while it remains unmarked. My psychoanalytic reading of Operation Rescue is an attempt to mark the obscured power of unmarked reproductive visibility of men.

For the sake of clarity: the uncertainty at the heart of the abortion debates does not stem from hesitation about the legal right to abortion. "The Gallup Poll reports that nearly eight out of ten Americans have supported legal abortion since 1975" (Faludi, *Backlash*: 532). Rather uncertainty emerges because one feels the inadequacy of the join between "real" visibly pregnant women and legal and psychic representations of resolutely singular and/or split subjects. The fear is that if the gap is so large here, the join between what is real and what is representational must be enormous everywhere. In an effort to suture it back together, we fiddle and poke and tinker with legal contracts, psychic symptoms, political platforms, moral issues. These fiddlings distract us from the central failure of discursive representation – the illegibility of the materiality of a pregnant body within a visual economy which everywhere marks the boundary between self and other. Embodied in and by what is and is not one body, the visibly pregnant woman makes the possibility of a continuous subject/ivity real. This possibility is everywhere repressed by the institutional arrangements of law, medicine, and politics – all of which presuppose singular social subjects as the foundational units of their discursive economics. (They assume fluency in singularity rather than sociality.) Those who are working for reproductive rights and those who work against them also presuppose this framework. I fear that in accepting this notion of the subject, without also continually re-marking it, we accept the symptoms that it (re)produces. Psychoanalytic readings of the symptoms of anxiety, in this case the performances of Operation Rescue, can perhaps be used as an impetus to reanimate (certainly not replace) political movements. Or so I hope.

The failure of discursive, legal, and psychic representation to convey a continuous subject points as well to the limitations of visibility politics as a way to secure political power for the under-represented. All human subjects, not only visibly pregnant women, are continuous. Identities continue across and exceed the political and discursive boundaries of sexual preference, racial markings, age, physical abilities, economic class and so on. It serves certain interests, however, to insist that selves are distinguishable from others and that these distinctions have separate names – many of these "new" names are cobbled together with hyphens and dashes – marks indicating the suspension that new/old "identities" are asked to straddle. The visibly pregnant woman embodies the literal swelling of that proliferating hyphen. This is why she is, always already, an unresolved figure which Law continually recalculates: is the hyphen a posititive or a negative? Does one add or subtract? Is she a double subject or a half-subject? (Who controls her other half?)

The debate over abortion rights is an extreme example of the violent struggle that comes from our continuing commitment to categories of isolation, separation, and division. In order to conceive of the continuous subject we need to return to the schism between the real and the representational, the lacuna between body and being.

Nothing in *Unmarked* escapes the anxiety raised by the gap between the discursive construct "the body" and the affective experience of embodiment. To entertain psychoanalysis as fully as I do here is to accept a certain fiction of the Real. Yet I want to believe that something of what I "really mean" is conveyed by the marks I make all over these pages. I actively repress my knowledge of the hole in the signifier: I know very well but just the same. (Kafka: "I write to forget.") The paradox of this book – a series of marks about the possible virtues of being unmarked – might be a fruitful one. The argument cannot be made in writing for in recording it I destroy precisely what I want to affirm. *Fort. Da.* The leap of the quantum. The undocumentable performance. But the failure to "make" the argument (to re-produce it) does not, I hope, entirely invalidate its appeal. I hope instead that it challenges the means by which the logical success of arguments are judged. My wager is that a combined methodology of psychics and psychoanalysis is and will be fundamental to that logical re-evaluation. For physics and psychoanalysis can teach political ideology the generative powers of doubt and uncertainty.

Psychoanalysis has always been troubled by the body, continuous and split. (In fact, psychoanalysis can be said to be the science of body trouble, a hypothesis about the the trouble of bodies living with and in "souls" – this is the embodied psychic subject which psychoanalysis interprets.) Freud, in seeing the patient's body as a screen which he could read, also saw that screen as a mirror of his own body. There is no apprehension of the body of the other without a corresponding (re)vision of one's own. These revisions constitute the energetic force of sexual/textual/commodity desire. Transference for Freud was a restaging of the patient's role in his or her earlier primary relationships. In mapping the transference, counter-transference is activated: Freud sees the patient's history in terms of his own. The doctor's counter-transference re-enacts his primary relation with someone other than the patient, and the patient's transference re-enacts something of his or hers with someone other than the doctor. The re-enactment staged with the psychoanalytic session is a *mise-en-abyme* of never previously existing relations. To paraphrase Paul Simon, post-psychoanalytically, these are the days of meta-phors and substitutes.

The mutual performances of these absences constitute our only poss-ible relations with one another, inside and outside the psychoanalytic room. While the psychoanalytic dialogue is "about" the two people physically present in the room, it is also, more profoundly, about the relationship each has with the phantom bodies who will not quit the room. They cannot quit the room for they are "in" the bodies of those sitting in the room. The work of the transference "goes on invisibly behind the progress of the treatment, and [its] effects are 'not suscep-tible to definite proof' " (Lacan, citing Freud's *Dora*, in his "Intervention in Transference": 102).

The phantom Real emerges in the negative or "failed" transference of *Dora*. It is not coincidental that this phantom emerges in a psycho-analytic dialogue dedicated to elucidating the relation between hysteria and female sexuality. What is the phantom of her body, for him? Is her body more vulnerable to ghosts than his? Or is it merely that he houses his ghosts in her body? Or is it that all bodies are reluctant ghosts of other bodies?

In his essay "Mourning and Melancholia," Freud suggests that the subject responds to loss by internalizing the lost other. The incorpor-ation of the lost other both disavows the loss and deepens the grief. Judith Butler has recently argued that this incorporation happens across genders – in other words, when the girl child "loses" the beloved father she incorporates him. After this internalization, her own gender can no longer be self-identical, but is rather "doubled." It is the same for boys and mothers ("Imitation and Gender Insubordination": 26–7). Our "own" body, then, is the one we have and the history of the ones we've lost. Our body is both internal and external; invisible and visible; sick and well; living and dead. Noncontinuous, full of jerks and rears, the body moves, like an awkward dancer trying to partner someone she can never see or lay hold of.[3]

Within the radical contingency of this psychic and material Real, subjectivity is performed. This subjectivity is encoded as always already gendered. And always already more insecure for and about women. Representation functions to make gender, and sexual difference more generally, secure and securely singular – which is to say, masculine. (She ghosts him.) Representation tries to overlook the discontinuity between subjectivity and the gendered, sexual body, and attempts to suture the gap between subjectivity and the Real. The common desire to look to representation to confirm one's reality is never satisfied; for representation cannot reproduce the Real. This keeps us looking – and keeps us hoping. And so we are, most of the time, kept. More particu-larly, we are kept suspended between the depressing loop of disappointment and the aspiring arc of hope. (We shall return to this roller-coaster shortly.)

It is not enough, however, to notice this suspension as part of the "psychopathology of everyday life." For some bodies are always more secure than others. The institutionalized forces of misogyny, racism, and economic injustice (to rehearse just the short list) register real effects across different bodies. The means of propping up and recognizing the corpo-Real are unequally distributed. So some bodies become *apparently* more valuable legally, psychically "healthier," aesthetically more appealing, and seemingly more Real than other bodies. The particular bodies which appear to matter more change across history, class, race, age, aesthetics, and gender (again, a short list of variables).

Overlooking the absolute contingency of the Real has been a hallmark of Western politics and epistemology. This strategic ignorance has made it habitually possible for Western power-knowledge to perform a distinctively acquisitive role in the script of history. The consequences of this acquisitive posture are profound at both the micro and macro levels of the encounter between self and other. These encounters are the "atoms" which constitute power-knowledge. To restage these performances it is necessary to turn more directly to the scenario of the classroom.

I

How can one create a performative pedagogy in the West which refuses the acquisitive model of power-knowledge operative everywhere in institutions of "higher learning"? How can one invent a pedagogy *for* disappearance and loss and not *for* acquisition and control? How can one teach the generative power of misunderstanding in a way they will (almost) understand? And who are "they" anyway?

The pedagogical class, like any performance event, is a collaboration. Each person is part of the group and each a part from it. Collectively the class creates "a piece." The piece is a statement about each one's relation – political, psychic, performative, affective, geographical, economic, physical, aural – to the animation of "the material." In the mutual making of the class, the sociality of performance is manifest. There is always at least one who makes the doing and always at least one who makes the looking, at least for a moment. Communication cannot escape this binary. But it must continually be provoked out of its fixity: the static positions in the binary must be mobilized and made continually to disappear. In the performance of that disappearance, the interpretation of power changes. Less monolithic, more local, and in perpetual motion, a continually performed power can be the "subject" of pedagogical discourse. The new relations which emerge "after" the sources of power are multiply enacted (after the counter-transference is made conscious, after the means of measurement are acknowledged) risk becoming new monoliths themselves. Therefore, these moments of clarity must also disappear, which they do effortlessly because the overwhelming tendency of power is to obscure itself. The point is to demonstrate how new relations continually emerge by making the sources of power evaporate and re-emerge, elsewhere.[4]

These relations are not, and can no longer be, anchored on a notion of "understanding." They must rather be founded on the recognition of the impossibility of such "true seeing." Pedagogy must involve training in the patient acceptance of the perpetual failure of in/sight.

The widespread belief in the possibility of understanding has committed us, however unwittingly, to a concomitant narrative of betrayal, disappointment, and rage. Expecting understanding and always failing to feel and see it, we accuse the other of inadequacy, of blindness, of neglect. The acceleration of ethnic and racial violence may be due in part to the misplaced desire to believe in the (false) promise of understanding. It is perhaps past time that we begin to attempt to see the inevitability of misunderstanding as generative and hopeful, as opportunities for conversation (and maybe a little further down the line for comedy as well), rather than as a betrayal of a promise. Or to put it slightly differently, perhaps the best possibility for "understanding" racial, sexual, and ethnic difference lies in the *active* acceptance of the inevitability of misunderstanding.

Misunderstanding as a political and pedagogical telos can be a dangerous proposition, for it invites the belligerent refusal to learn or move at all. This is not what I am arguing for. *It is in the attempt to walk (and live) on the rackety bridge between self and other – and not the attempt to arrive at one side or the other – that we discover real hope.* That walk is our always suspended performance – in the classroom, in the political field, in relation to one another and to ourselves. The inevitability of our failure to remain walking *on* the bridge (when the storms come we keep rushing for the deceptive "safety" of one side or the other) guarantees only the necessity of hope.

He sits there again in our class. Sullen. Eyes downcast. He says he doesn't have any, no more hope, not any more. Not now. It's all gone to hell – the little time, the infected body, the imploding space. Sometimes he yells at us and sometimes we just look at him with nothing to say. He makes things – videos, poems, letters – that explain in meticulous detail why he has had to leave Hope. Like the familiar stories of beseeching lovers narrating their past, his story, history, is full of lies, lacunae, sutured narratives. It's all composite – a strange autobiographical fairy tale. It repeats in an exact fashion all the conventions of traditional Romance – his youth, her seduction, his dreams, her abrupt betrayals, his warnings to her, her indifference to them. But still he clung to Hope. He did not know what the alternative was. So he loved and he loved and he loved some more. And she teased him – threw him high in the air and listened to the sound of his laughter breaking across the sky.

Sometimes she caught him in the soft down of her expansive lap, other times she watched him fall hard onto the unyielding cement ground. Once she threw him so high he thought he was free – unbounded, beautiful, a form of ecstasy. He tasted the air rushing around him and he smelled the very top of a forest of fir trees, and he felt the strange nothingness of the bottom of a pale cloud. He was, at last, deliriously happy, in a state of bliss. And as he tumbled down so full of gratitude and love and wonder at his own ability to see and feel and smell such an exquisite array of sensations he thought of all the questions he would put to her, how he would ask her why the nothingness of the cloud felt, of all things, tender; why the pocket of air above the fir trees felt damp and the air between the clouds so dry. He was busy thinking of all he would tell her and all he would ask her. He was preoccupied with feeling how his lungs were screaming and how his throat was full of half-formed words so he hardly noticed how fast he was falling. And this time when she did not catch him when he fell, his body shattered in a thousand pieces and he lay there on the cement for a very long time. After the doctors came and the stitches were stitched and the bones were set and the medications given, she returned. She offered him her breast to succor him, but he would not, not this time, take it. So she offered him her stories but her words were like dry pellets that would not enter his newly non-porous body. They fell next to him but could not slide through his ear. So she offered him her silence, but to him it was a deafening din. He told her to go. He told her he had to recover without her. As he waited and watched his body's health return, he resolved to strengthen his will to live without her.

When we first met, now a long time ago, it was clear that none of us bothered at all about the Truth. We banked everything on the interpretative possibilities offered by the constructions of his/stories. ("Love's interpretation exists only in the afterwards" – in this Afterword?) We agreed we would be safe as long as we did not allow him to cast us in the role of Hope. No, we would be the stitching inside his lip and not the one who threw him in the air.

But we live in a city full of fainting buildings. Like Victorian women with tight corsets the buildings swoon in the late afternoon. At tea-time, they tumble down. So we study the instability of architecture, the failure of brick and board to remain vertical bone. Beneath these city streets abandoned postal tubes sit rotting. Pneumatic bodies wheezing with memories of the days fat letters sped through them. We research every scrap of information we can find about them. The severed connection, the broken line. Did the tubes ever burst with too many letters, too many words, whizzing through their pneumatic bodies? Why were they abandoned? Did the words become too heavy to carry? The post traveled thirty miles per hour below the streets and now the letters (if they arrive at all) lumber across the street surface at eight miles per hour (Willensky and White, *AIA Guide to New York*: 901). Abandoning the tubes, the post, the phone, the electronic mail materializes and vanishes screen to screen and the fax reproduces itself across telephone lines (fiber optics? textured seeing?). But he ignores all these possibilities, trusts nothing but himself, and hand delivers his letters to us. They always arrive, palm to palm. In his time.

His letters burn our eyes. Not so much because of what is in them, but for what is left out. As they burn, the light changes and we pretend we are fishermen hauling in that netted light, hand over hand. In order to write them, what does he have to pretend to be? A Venetian scribe in the days of Ficino? Looking for "the body of life," in the alchemist's cure – pure knowledge mixed with occult chemicals? A man out of time. Words looking for the right response/dent.

His letters are like stage directions for a play that has not been written. We cannot decipher them. He performs them for us. We watch intently and then try to say what we saw. The conversation goes round and round the fear like an abandoned merry-go-round with the motor running. Together we change the letters, make them ours, no longer the "original" ones he offered as condensations of other letters, someone else's plays. Once the letters are our own, we generate other interpretative possibilities. Sometimes we laugh. And sometimes when it all seems overwhelming we sit for a long time saying nothing.

And in this silent space he re-enacts his decision to abandon Hope. We no longer even pretend to be the stitching in his lip. We know we are no longer safe. We too have now lost Hope. But his vitality demands that we perform Hope, so that his rejection can confirm his strength. We take the part required and give him what we no longer have. We hand him our lost Hope (open palms) and in seeing our loss he finds a reflection of his own. We give him what none of us has. We search for other interpretations, other parts to play in his/story, his drama, the one still unwritten, but by now thoroughly blocked.

Progressive critics who worry so loudly and strenuously about "appropriation" forget that sometimes one *wants* certain terrible things to be appropriated. The absolute limit of appropriation is death; murderers appropriate life but they cannot take death away from one's suddenly and dismayingly singular body. Old stories, old scripts. Wanting only not to live the moment, the fact, of death. His. Each our own. The endless repetition of the always failed refusal of that moment is the wound theology tries to recuperate and historiography tries to salve.

On the pages here, there are several deaths. Deaths in theory. And Real-deaths. Venus Xtravaganza died; she was murdered in "real life." Her death is recorded and discussed in Livingston's film *Paris*; I use it for a theoretical point. Sex and death. Her death generates the tension in *Paris*, and fuels my concluding argument. The people who loved Venus could rightly object to such appropriation. (Even if you didn't love her, you could object.) Surely her life had more value than the punctuation of a filmic commentary, had more value than Livingston's record. The demands of representation, the laws of the current Western genre of knowing, require an endless list of objects – human and otherwise – to acquire as our own. And when we submit to this law, as even here I have and do, we forfeit a certain claim to the purely ethical. Robert Lowell: "[M]y eyes have seen what my hand did." And what we live with instead is the uncertainty of the ethical. *Fort. Da.* (We take his letters and make them our own. We try to hold him to us as if to erase Hope's brutal dropping. But every embrace reminds him of the one he missed. And knowing all of this changes nothing.)

Radiology reports of the "chronic" cancer, the recurring illness, the incurable disease, are always only tentatively clear. There is no such thing as permanent remission. Every three months another test. We have only begun to approach writing these bodies – the ones hanging on our bones like shabby coats, too big to be warm, too warm to be comfortable, too comfortable to be alert in.[5] The uncertainty of this body challenges the fundamental binary of Western culture – the living and the dead. But this binary is itself crumbling. Legislatively, psychically, and emotionally, we are beginning to face the uncertainty of our notion of when and how the body lives and dies, who does and does not inhabit it, who can and cannot speak for it when it is beyond the comforting amplifications of metaphor. Pure symptom, sometimes the body's Being insists on an end to interpretative possibilities. And so sometimes the body goes. Disappears. But the witness remains. Formerly mute objects become articulate. The old shirt recalls the riot of color he provoked in her face. The coffee cup with the broken handle hums a w/holy different hymn. The performance of grief reanimates the symptoms of his life, animate and disappearing, material and visible.

When David Wojnarowicz speaks of the pre-invented world, he refers to the world that sees us before we grasp it.[6] In that seeing we become trans/fixed. To abandon the pre-invented world totally is Impossible. But to move toward a vision in which such abandonment might be a regular possibility, like an airplane flight leaving Bombay and arriving in London, is worthwhile. Hand over hand hauling in the netted light, the holes in the representational, the holes in the visible. "Have you a match for my two?" "Go fish." The rules of this game are well known: one person wins the game and the others lose it. But if we say that symmetry emerges in the mutual acknowledgment of its impossibility we could maybe play the game differently. This time, let's play without the cards. Without the dealer. Just us, the cloth and the table. (The green station wagon is long gone: the family has a different body. The auto/mobiles still travel, but the silences exist in denser cartographies.)

He continues to come. We imagine the cards. We write the letters; we read the books, this book. Nothing changes. And we begin to see that everything is, therefore, different. We continue to meet. We change the titles of our card games and keep playing. Hope keeps throwing us up and dropping us down. The time keeps moving and promising us new histories and we keep reproducing the same collapsing cities.

We perform Hope but we do not perhaps believe enough in her any longer. What would it take to *be* her rather than (merely?) enact her, resist her, flirt with her? Maybe he can reject us so endlessly because we make it easy for him? What would it take to rewrite his/story? Invent a different city? Discover stronger bones?

Perhaps Yvonne Rainer's notion of a filmic architecture could be reinvigorated for performance. Non-possessable, fluid, full of uncertain architecture, and temporary sets, performance's relation to the Real is as precarious and as temporary as the Guerrilla Girls' fading posters barely legible under other scraps of paper. Performance's potency comes from its temporariness, it's "one time only" life. The ontology of performance maps a gateway across a different order of production and reproduction. It suggests that matter (and the Real) is created out of nothing – "the nothing that is not there and the nothing that is" (Wallace Stevens). This reproduction works according to the invisible calculus of multiple offerings of what one does not have. This then as a coda, a prolegomenon for another book, other words, other eyes. This then in Hope, the hope we fake and perform and the hope we thereby make and have. Hope's power is measured in this faking. Each performance registers how much we want to believe what we know we see is not all we really have, all we really are. That negation reveals the generative possibility of the "not all" that keeps us hoping. Maybe next time I'll love/be/loved; maybe next time I'll write a better book; maybe next time my I will see.

ONE VERSION OF ANOTHER HIS/TORY

Begin with a repetition:
"For physics and psychoanalysis can teach political ideology the generative powers of doubt and uncertainty."
   Offer paradigmatic example:
When Anita Hill tangled with the Senate during the Clarence Thomas

confirmation hearings in Fall 1991, she explained that she wound up in Washington DC after saying that she would "neither confirm nor deny" her knowledge of rumors that Thomas had "tolerated or participated in" sexually harassing behavior during the time they worked together at the Equal Employment Opportunity Commission in the 1970s. She was asked by a Senate aide if she would "neither confirm nor deny" her knowledge of the allegations or of the behavior. She indicated it was the behavior. The subsequent hearings and extensive media coverage were a lopsided attempt to discover if various people could confirm or deny her allegations about Thomas. On the asymmetrical stage constructed to hear Hill's carefully worded story, distortion and static sufficient enough to mute her sounds allowed the Senate to confirm Thomas as a Supreme Court Justice.[7]

Offer interpretation of paradigmatic example:
The power of Hill's initial decision to say she would neither confirm nor deny her knowledge of Thomas' behavior was enormous. The provocation of the doubt raised by her refusal to declare her knowledge of his innocence was overwhelming and potentially historically transforming. The "leak" to the press created a rupture in the smooth reproduction and transformation of *hommo-sexual* power, however fleetingly. In the gap revealed in that leaking rupture, the unmarked frame of political power was thrown into high relief. Suddenly all the world seemed to see that white men with economic privilege run things – and more importantly, that this may not be the only possible way to run things. Articulate, self-assured, and thoroughly sincere, Anita Hill's performance made it stunningly clear how thoroughly unusual it was to hear *anyone* in Washington, let alone an African-American woman, speak with conviction, care, and force.

Link example with larger point:
Hill's appearance in Washington radically questioned and punctured the unmarked power of normative whiteness and masculinity in a way that Thomas' first round of confirmation hearings only tentatively and glancingly approached. The asymmetry of power operative between Thomas, who was her boss at the time under discussion, and Hill, was mirrored in the structure of the hearings and the rules of evidence and argument admitted there. Hill could not have "won" within the terms of the pre-existing rules of discursive power in either context. But she could and did illustrate the pervasiveness of those structural asymmetries in our experience of dominant power. She performed and recalled the pain these asymmetries engender – in the moment and over time.

Draw conclusion:
The real relationship between Hill and Thomas in the early 1980s will never be re-presented. The "truth" of their relation can neither be confirmed nor denied (within the existing rules of interpretative

"proof"). Like the relation which adheres between the real and the representational, something which can neither be confirmed nor denied, can nonetheless be convincing and "true." The uncertainty created by this logic is immensely powerful. It suggests another way of thinking about the relation between representation and the real.

The New Right continues to assert a causal relation between representation and real behavior. For example, Jesse Helms argued that a photograph of men in leather jackets kissing encourages viewers to become homosexual (see Phelan, "Money Talks, Again"). The Left must deny such crude readings of the relation between the real and the representational. Even as this causal reading is denied, however, the Left must confirm some link between representation and the real. Both the Right and the Left believe that transforming representation brings about changes in the real. While the Left must deny the causal logic the Right wants to assert, it cannot and should not deny all links between the real and the representational. The Left must develop a way of talking about the way that representation and the real are related that does not lead to the simple logic of cause and effect, to a simple notion of mimetic resemblance which so quickly becomes "me-ism." (If my imagistic-like is not represented the work is limited and not "about" me.)

In the provocation of Hill's refusal to confirm or deny her knowledge, an asymmetrical hearing was constructed to produce either denial or confirmation. But interestingly enough, the hearings may have only been a public witnessing of the gap between legal rules of proof and the logic of belief. While the hearings illustrated the provocation of a refusal to confirm or deny, they also made visible the limits of the methodology by which "proof" is made visible.

Similarly, those concerned with understanding the relation between the real and the representational must also recognize that our failing eyes may be insufficient organs for measuring the terms and meanings of the transformative alchemy between them. The transformative possibilities of the Real, we may have to trust, while unable to be fully confirmed within the field of the visible (or the empirical), cannot be permanently denied. It is in doubt. That's why we must keep performing and transforming the interpretations of this relation. Doubt may be the best guarantee of real presence. *Fort. Da.* The generation and reproduction of this doubt may be the most significant achievement of the unmarked performance of the Real.

Notes

1 BROKEN SYMMETRIES: MEMORY, SIGHT, LOVE

1 Julia Kristeva, "Ellipsis on Dread and the Specular Seduction," quoted in Jacqueline Rose, *Sexuality in the Field of Vision*: 141.
2 The best discussion of Lacanian doubt can be found in Joan Copjec, "Vampires, Breast-Feeding and Anxiety."
3 The two most relevant meditations on the contemporary legal real in the United States are Jane Gaines' fascinating essay, "Dead Ringer: Jacqueline Onassis and the Look-alike" which examines a case of a model, Barbara Reynolds, who appears in an ad for Christian Dior. The model's "art" is her ability to look like Onassis. Onassis sued Dior and the ad agency for using her image without permission. Gaines formulates the questions raised by this case in terms of the "right" to appropriate/exploit/protect what both Onassis and Reynolds already own – their image. Patricia Williams' provocative book *The Alchemy of Race and Rights* examines the legal real in terms of the historical force of racist marks defining citizenry. While there are serious problems with Williams' work as "legal theory," hers is an extraordinarily enabling book. Williams reimagines the categories and interests by which the legal real is constituted and maintained.
4 The best essay on feminism and the theatrical real is Elin Diamond's "Mimesis, Mimicry and the True-Real." She re-reads Irigaray's re-reading of Plato and suggests that there is no original without a notion of a mimetic copy – including the "original" Mother. Lynda Hill's "Staging Hurston's Life and Work" considers the tricky politics of race and representation in relation to Zora Neale Hurston's attempt to reproduce "authentic folk" community and contemporary drama's attempt to restage the story of her life and work "authentically."
5 The best discussion of the Lacanian Real can be found in *October* 58: "Rendering the Real A Special Issue," guest editor Parveen Adams. Also see Slavoj Žižek, *The Sublime Object of Ideology*. Throughout this book, the Lacanian Real shall be distinguished from other versions of the real by use of the upper-case R.
6 In the vast library of autobiographical criticism see Phillip Lejeune, *On Autobiography* and Bella Brodzki and Celeste Schenck (eds), *Life/Lines*, for preliminary discussions of how the real defines the autobiographical.
7 Slavoj Žižek tells the tale of the reception of *Rashomon* (1950). Kurosawa's film was hailed as the "classic" Japanese film throughout the United States and Europe and won the 1951 Golden Lion in Venice. But it failed terribly in

Japan because it was considered "too European." Each culture employed the frame of the Other to define its relation to the representational text – not surprisingly the frame of the Other brought these others to opposite conclusions about the "same" representational text. Slavoj Žižek, "Lacan's Return to the Cartesian *Cogito*," a talk delivered in the English Department, New York University, December 1991.

8 This notion of the importance of the phantasmatic, however, also led Freud to abandon the seduction theory in favor of the Oedipal complex. In other words, the fantasy was ascribed to the child – despite "evidence" that the adult was indeed seducing the child. In abandoning the seduction theory, Freud was favoring the phantasmatic over the "evidence of the senses." For him, as we shall see in Chapter 6, the "evidence of the senses" (sensuality) is inferior to abstract and immaterial reasoning (intellectuality). In other words, the Oedipal complex, insofar as it remains phantasmatic, reproduces patriarchal reasoning in which "abstraction" is superior to visible evidence. The consequences of this shift, however, also perpetuated the idea that women (who were usually the patients recalling these seductions) were neurotics – while Oedipus remained a hero, however tragic.

9 Roy Schafer has clearly set this process forth in his essay "Narration in the Psychoanalytic Dialogue."

10 For an excellent discussion of the philosophical underpinnings of political identities see Diana Fuss, *Essentially Speaking*.

11 This term is borrowed from Luce Irigaray who develops it in *Speculum of the Other Woman*.

12 To the degree that the ethnic or racial "other" (not the norm and thus remarkable) is also always already feminized, the same risk is encountered. Visibility reproduces the self-same and converts the other into a fetish, a phallic substitute. The other is a metaphor understood within the pre-existing grammar and frame of the given to be seen.

13 Fuss sees this problem as the result of "an essentialist/constructivist" divide. I see it as a mistrust of the immaterial, a deep doubt about the "real" power of the unconscious and the unseen. Lynda Hart's essay "Identity and Seduction: Lesbians in the Mainstream" is a powerful analysis of the distinction between identity and (symbolic) identification. She constructs her argument around *Anniversary Waltz*, a dense performance by Peggy Shaw and Lois Weaver, which in every way collapses the distinctions between the real (it "really" was their anniversary that motivated the performance) and the representational (who is the couple they show?).

14 It is worth accenting, however, the real success of visibility politics. Curriculums from kindergarten to college are undergoing revision to reflect more adequately the achievements of non-European and non-white contributions to history and culture, largely because of the political-academic pressure brought to bear on "white" education by progressives. In addition, more attention and money have been given to HIV research, largely because ACT-UP (AIDS Coalition To Unleash Power) has made itself a visible force to be reckoned with. Pro-choice rallies draw more members from more diverse communities as the Supreme Court whittles reproductive rights down to a tiny nub, largely because feminists have identified abortion as the most visible arena for political struggle in the US.

    While these are not in any way pragmatic achievements to belittle, neither are they all one could hope for. To take just one example, the epistemological structure of white, European power-knowledge is able to incorporate at the level of content a certain amount of "new information" about non-whites and non-Europeans. But the model by which this information is represented contains within it an implicit system of evaluation and way of perceiving which remains intact. Other ways of viewing the reproductive rights debates are discussed in Chapter 6.

15 Piper's *Cornered* (1989), a video tape, is available from Visual Data Bank, Chicago.

16 The phrase "the Real impossible" is Žižek's who develops it in *The Sublime Object of Ideology*.

17 See Baudrillard's *Simulations*; the phrase "the precession of simulacra" is the title of an essay excerpted from that book and reprinted in *Art After Modernism*, ed. Brian Wallis.

18 Harold Bloom, "Agon: Revisionism and Critical Personality": 44.

19 This is because (in part) the camera mirrors the misperception of the eye, upon which it is modeled.

20 Please note this is from Lacan's *Le Séminaire I: Les Ecrits techniques de Freud*, and not *Ecrits: a Selection*, the English translation of several of Lacan's essays.

21 For good discussions of this definition by the negative see Teresa de Lauretis' "Technology of Gender," and Stephen Heath's "Narrative Space" in *Questions of Cinema*. Also, any good art history textbook should have a preliminary discussion of negative space.

22 Marianne Moore, "He 'Digesth Hard' Yron," *A Marianne Moore Reader*: 24.

23 See Norman Bryson, "The Gaze in the Expanded Field": 98.

24 From the catalog of the show Derrida curated for the Louvre (October 1990–January 1991), *Memoires d'aveugle: l'autoportrait et autres ruines* (translated title, *Memories of the Blind: Self-Portrait and Other Ruins*). See also Meyer Raphael Rubinstein's excellent review of the show, "Sight Unseen."

25 See Joan Copjec's article "The Orthopsychic Subject" for a full discussion.

26 Diana Fuss has a good discussion of Lacan's notion of the "essence" of woman in *Essentially Speaking*: 6–12.

27 This may well have something to do with why drag continues to exert such a powerful allure within gay male communities. Rendered non-phallic and effeminate by heterosexual culture, drag enacts an appropriation not only of the image of the woman but also of the phallic function. However, the very frame of most drag performance – camp, excess, "fantastic-ness" – also emphasizes the constructed nature of the phallic function and "subverts" it by revealing its arbitrariness.

28 The shift in emphasis from the man in Freud's work to the castrated subject in Lacan's anticipates the similar shift in emphasis between modernity's fascination with the man and postmodernity's fascination with the woman. It is wise to be suspicious of both shifts.

29 Copjec, "Orthopsychic": 70. Rose, *Sexuality in the Field of Vision*, esp. "The Imaginary": 167–96.

30 I have in mind here a version of Freud's notion of the "symmetry" of the perversions. In *Three Essays*, Freud carefully demonstrates how, for example, the masochist is also a sadist; the voyeur also an exhibitionist. The reciprocal nature of desire is what I am trying to suggest here.

31 See Rose, *Sexuality in the Field of Vision*: 190–4 for a full discussion.

32 In this sense, Hollywood cinema's fascination with the voyeur – most notably in the films of Hitchcock – confirms the voyeur's desire to be seen looking. The architecture of both the Hollywood and pornographic movie house in the US also assures the voyeuristic spectator that s/he will also be "caught looking."

33 This is a paraphrase of Lacan's "The mirror stage as formative of the function

of the I," in *Ecrits*: 1–7. While much of this is by now well known it may be worthwhile to stress again here the ocular ground of the desire to speak.

34 For Lacan's reading of Freud's *fort/da* game see his "The Function of Language in Psychoanalysis," in *The Language of the Self*, ed. Wilden, esp. pp. 83–7. Freud's analysis of the game appears in *Beyond the Pleasure Principle*: 12–17.

35 An integral part of the Symbolic is the knowledge of the loss of the Imaginary and the impossible realization of the Real. Both are present within the Symbolic in much the way a frame is present in cinema.

36 MacCannell's superb treatment of Lacan's metaphor-economy can be found in *Figuring Lacan*: 90–120.

37 Norman Bryson, "The Gaze in the Expanded Field," in *Vision and Visuality*, ed. Foster.

38 Similarly, Edward Said's anatomy of the Occident's various sightings of the Orient in Orientalism repeatedly discovers that the more the East is seen, described, cataloged, studied, the more the construction of Western knowledge and desire is secured and left unmarked. Through recourse to the visible other, the looker is both mirrored and screened. Within Western representation, the frequent (and narrow) visibility of the other is often used as a means of controlling those with less power.

39 Lacan puts it bluntly: "[I]f beyond appearance there is nothing in itself, there is the gaze," in *Four Fundamental Concepts*: 103.

40 For the particular politics of how the visibility/invisibility paradigm works in relation to African-American women see Michele Wallace, *Invisibility Blues*.

41 For an excellent discussion of the legal barriers involved in thinking of a pregnant woman as a continuous body see Patricia Williams' *The Alchemy of Race and Rights*, especially her stunning reading of the Baby M. case, pp. 224–30. It might be useful to remark that the case investigates the notion of the reproductive "same," but this time through the legal "right" (to stretch logic and the United States' Constitution) of Stern to father his "likeness." In other words, the reasoning of Judge Harvey Sorkow's decision in favor of the Sterns is Lacanian. But whereas Lacan speaks of (paternal) "desires," Sorkow legislates (paternal) "rights." Both maintain the Law of the Father and rely on the "castration" of the woman-mother (both Mary Beth Whitehead and the nonreproductive Elizabeth Stern).

42 This is "after" Rilke. His text reads:

> In solchen Nächten wächst mein Schwesterlein,
> das vor mir war and vor mir starb, ganz Klein.
> Veil solche Nächte waren schon selther:
> Sie muß schön schön sein. Bald wird irgendwer sein frein.
>
> ("Aus einer Sturmaacht," from *Das Buch der Bilder)*

2 DEVELOPING THE NEGATIVE: MAPPLETHORPE, SCHOR, AND SHERMAN

1 When Aristotle speaks of the pleasure of imitation in the *Poetics*, he is quick to acknowledge that that pleasure derives equally from the pleasure of seeing something again, and seeing something for the first time and recognizing it as an imitation. In other words, imitation is pleasing whether or not one has seen the model and whether or not the model is "real." Just as the primal scene is equally powerful whether seen or imagined, so too, for Aristotle, is the imitation-effect.

2 Virginia Woolf to Gerald Brenan: "It's an interesting question – what one tries to do, in writing a letter – partly of course to give back a reflection of the other person" (October 4, 1929); *The Letters of Virginia Woolf*, vol. IV: 98.

3 See *Classic Essays on Photography*, ed. Alan Trachtenberg for representative examples of this discussion.

4 See Rosalind Krauss, *The Originality of the Avant-Garde and Other Modernist Myths*, esp. pp. 86–118 and 131–50.

5 See Elizabeth Hollander, "Notes on Being an Artist's Model," for a preliminary attempt to describe what the art of modeling for painters requires, from a model-philosopher's point of view.

6 For a fine analysis of Mapplethorpe's long interest in the photograph as object see Richard Marshall.

7 This is the connection between Mapplethorpe's "art" photography and fashion photography. Unable to touch the model's skin, the looker settles for the touch of the fabric that the model wears – and so the spectator buys the clothes the fashion model wears.

8 See David Cook and Arthur Kroker, *The Postmodern Scene: Excremental Culture and Hyper-Aesthetics*: 23–5.

9 Risking redundancy and paranoia I want to state baldly: I am talking about the *virus* – and not about repetitive ("promiscuous") sexual activity – which is another topic altogether.

10 Marvell, "Eyes and Tears," *The Complete Poems*, ed. Donno: 52–4.

11 For more on the relationship between the penis and the phallus in art history see Mira Schor's "Representations of the Penis."

12 See my essays "Money Talks" and "Money Talks, Again" for a full discussion of the controversy.

13 See Geoffrey Hartman, *Saving the Text*: 106.

14 See her long meditation, "Plato's *Hystera*," in *Speculum*: 243–364, esp. 355–7.

15 See Kobena Mercer, "Looking for Trouble," for an intriguing discussion of Mapplethorpe, race, and gay male sexuality.

16 Mira Schor points out this link in her essay, "Representations of the Penis."

17 This fact was perhaps never more powerfully manifest than in the trial of Dennis Barrie, the Cincinnati gallery director who arranged to display Mapplethorpe's controversial *Perfect Moment* show in a city which outlaws pornography. On his trial for obscenity in October 1990, the lawyers for Barrie pounded home the idea that Mapplethorpe was an artist (and therefore not a "pornographer" unworthy of Federal funding) precisely because of the *formal* qualities of his work. The defense lawyers had art historians come to the court and talk about symmetry. The strategy worked; Barrie was acquitted. For a full discussion of the implications see my essay, "Money Talks, Again."

18 An adequate discussion of the differences operative in Mapplethorpe's photographs of women is impossible here. But speaking very generally, with the exception of his photographs of Patti Smith, most of Mapplethorpe's portraits of women tend to be almost too appreciative; they lack the struggle on the surface of the image which vibrates in his photographs of men. In other words, his women seem strangely asexual. They tend to turn into beautiful, fashionable, perfectly lit "objects."

19 The painting also inspired Schor to investigate the potency of the visual representations of penises in Western painting. Her essay "Representations of the Penis" is an interesting account of other "penis pictures."

20 Gerald Stern in a poem called "Little White Sister" speaks of a betraying ear,

and there is something of a similar accusation in Schor's image. Stern describes an enslavement to a small ear greedy for loving lies:

> My ear betrayed me, my little white sister
> glued to the side of my head, a shiny snail
> twisted everywhere to catch the slightest
> murmur of love, the smallest sobbing and breathing.
> It wasn't the heart, stuck inside the chest
> like a bloody bird, and it wasn't the brain,
> dying itself from love; it was that messenger,
> laughing as she whispered the soft words,
> making kissing sounds with her red lips,
> moaning with pleasure for the last indignity.

21 For a brilliant reading of Chicago's work, see Hortense Spillers, "Interstices: A Small Drama of Words," in *Pleasure and Danger*, ed. Vance.

22 For another example of the relation between painting and reproduction see Joyce Kozloff's collection of paintings, *Patterns of Desire*. See my discussion of Kozloff, "Crimes of Passion."

23 Schor's work also reveals the sexual politics operative in the ascendancy of the word over the image, an ascendancy which leads to the valuation of word-based images created by artists such as Barbara Kruger and Jenny Holzer. It is not for nothing that our most "powerful" readers are working in the aesthetic tradition outlined by Heidegger, Hegel, Freud, Lacan, Derrida, and Bloom. The thread that runs through this critical work, Schor suggests, will never be able to correctly write/right the woman, for she remains marginal to the issues central to these inquiries.

24 See my "Money Talks" and "Money Talks, Again" for a fuller discussion of Serrano's relation to the National Endowment for the Arts débâcle.

25 Schor is explicitly engaged in an effort to regender painting. Her 1989 essay "Figure/Ground" argues that the widely acclaimed "end of painting" reflects a fear of the feminine, a fear of flow.

26 Interview with Sherman quoted in Els Barents, *Cindy Sherman*: 11.

27 Marius De Zayas, "Photography and Artistic-Photography": 130.

28 See Jean Baudrillard, "The Precession of Simulacra," esp. p. 256.

29 Joan Riviere, "Womanliness as Masquerade."

30 See Mary Ann Doane's "Film and the Masquerade: Theorizing the Female Spectator," and Sue-Ellen Case's "Toward a Butch-Femme Aesthetic," in *Making a Spectacle*, ed. Hart. For a discussion of feminist mimicry see Luce Irigaray, *Speculum*, and Elin Diamond, "Mimesis, Mimicry and the True-Real."

31 Irigaray, *Speculum*. Note well that Irigaray's project involves a scrutiny of "the one" as the foundational goal of Western metaphysics. It is the insistence on the virtue of "one" that makes (sexual) difference impossible – that makes woman conform to the law of the Same. Photography, insofar as it refuses to valorize the "one," can be seen as a wedge into the system of representation which elevates the one (the original). This is partially why photography is still regarded as a degraded art form – which is to say, a feminine art form.

3 SPATIAL ENVY: YVONNE RAINER'S
THE MAN WHO ENVIED WOMEN

1 See Kaja Silverman *The Acoustic Mirror* for a comprehensive discussion of the possibilities of spectatorial identification with sound rather than image in cinema. In this book, Silverman has an extensive and illuminating analysis of Rainer's previous film, *Journeys from Berlin/1971* (1979).

2 *The Man Who Envied Women*, 16 mm, color, 125 min. Distributed by First Run Features, 153 Waverly Place, New York, NY 10014 and CFDC, 67A Portland Street, Toronto, Ontario M5V 2M9. All quotes unless otherwise noted are from the film.

3 The script for *The Man Who Envied Women* is published in Yvonne Rainer, *The Films of Yvonne Rainer*.

4 In this regard, Rainer anticipates de Lauretis' theoretical notion of "space-off" developed in the first chapter of her book *Technologies of Gender*.

5 The paper has now changed its schedule and the "Hers" column alternates with the "About Men" column in the Sunday magazine. The differently inflected titles, however, prohibit belief that *The Times* has discovered a gender-neutral format.

6 See Roland Barthes' *The Pleasure of the Text*.

7 See Mikhail Bakhtin, *The Dialogic Imagination*, ed. Holquist, especially the final essay, "Discourse in the Novel." "Heteroglossia" is defined and discussed on p. 263 and following.

8 Raynal read the film script which indicates that this scene was to be "a minimalist song and dance." On the day of the scheduled shooting she came wearing a dancing gown.

9 See Raymond Bellour, "The Unattainable Text" for a full discussion.

10 See, for example, Sue-Ellen Case, "Toward a Butch-Femme Aesthetic," in *Making a Spectacle*, ed. Hart, and Teresa de Lauretis, "Film and the Primal Fantasy – One More Time: On Sheila McLaughlin's *She Must Be Seeing Things*" on the under-represented lesbian subject position in accounts of cinematic spectatorship. For accounts of feminist film theory's inability to recognize racial difference see Jane Gaines, "White Privilege and Looking Relations: Race and Gender in Feminist Film Theory."

11 The most promising of these seems to me to be Trinh Minh-Ha's *Woman, Native, Other*, and the anthology *Blackframes*, ed. Mbye B. Cham and Claire Andrade-Watkins. The collection *How Do I Look? Queer Film and Video*, ed. Bad Object-Choices, adds a very useful perspective on the elusive connection between the "otherness" of race and the "otherness" of queer sexual identity.

4 THE GOLDEN APPLE: JENNIE LIVINGSTON'S
PARIS IS BURNING

1 See Judith Butler, "Imitation and Gender Insubordination," in *Inside/Out: Lesbian Theories, Gay Theories*, ed. Fuss, p. 29.

2 Slavoj Žižek argues in *The Sublime Object of Ideology*: "[I]n symbolic identification we identify ourselves with the other precisely at a point at which he is inimitable, at the point which eludes resemblance" (p. 109).

3 For a very important reading of the (colonial) politics of mimicry and ambivalence see Homi Bhabha, "Of Mimicry and Men: The Ambivalence of Colonial Discourse" and "Signs Taken for Wonders: Questions of Ambivalence and Authority under a Tree Outside Delhi, May 1987." It is stunning to recognize the similarity of situation and psychic-political response in the post-colonial

"hybrid" Bhabha describes and the "transsexual" at the Harlem drag balls documented by Livingston.

4 The best discussion of this can be found in Luce Irigaray's *Speculum*: 58.

5 Reprinted in Darcy Grimaldo Grigsby, "Dilemmas of Visibility: Contemporary Women Artists' Representations of Female Bodies": 608.

6 Alas, even this work can be absorbed by the marketplace. Piper recently recounted that about a year ago when she was introduced to someone at an art opening, there was a long pause and then the person said "I'm trying to think of a racist remark so I can get one of the cards." Since then, Piper says, she has stopped handing out the cards.

7 See Butler, "Imitation and Gender Insubordination" for a fuller discussion of this theatricality; and see Carole-Anne Tyler, "Boys Will Be Girls: the Politics of Gay Drag," also in *Inside/Out*, for a fuller discussion of how racial, sexual, and class bias inform drag performances.

8 It may well be that as the *internalized* homophobia of gay male culture abates – as it seems now to be doing – the appeal of the "show-girl woman" will decrease. In other words, the appeal of hyper-femininity may diminish as same sex relations seem more pervasive and less unusual. Perhaps this is happening with the category "best bangee girl."

9 For a different emphasis on this erasure of the "actual" woman see my essay, "Feminist Theory, Poststructuralism, and Performance."

10 For Freud the fetish functions as a phallic substitute. For Lacan, woman must turn herself into the phallus in order to signify the desire of the Other, the man. "Paradoxical as this formulation might seem, I would say that it is in order to be the phallus, that is to say, the signifier of desire of the Other, that the woman will reject an essential part of her femininity, notably all its attributes through masquerade. It is for what she is not that she expects to be desired as well as loved" (Jacques Lacan, "God and the *Jouissance* of The Woman," in *Feminine Sexuality: Jacques Lacan and the "école freudienne,"* ed. Rose and Mitchell: 84). These walkers exhibit the same relation to the masquerade, and to the attendant expectation that this masquerade will bring them love.

11 Marilyn Frye, *The Politics of Reality*, quoted in bell hooks, "Is Paris Burning?": 61.

12 A brief list: Vincent Canby, "Paris Is Burning," *The New York Times*, March 13, 1991: C13; Quentin Crisp, "Paris Is Burning," *The New York Times*, April 7, 1991: sec. 2: 20; Georgia Brown, "Paris Is Burning," *The Village Voice*, March 19, 1991: 54; Essex Hemphill, "Paris Is Burning," *Guardian*, July 3, 1991: 10–11.

13 This compatibility is reflected in the financial success of the film as well. In its first weekend limited release (23 screens in 17 cities) the film grossed more than $310,000. See Lewis Beale, "*Paris* has Box-office Appeal."

14 Sigmund Freud, "Fetishism", in *The Standard Edition of the Complete Psychological Works of Sigmund Freud*, ed. and trans. James Strachey in collaboration with Anna Freud, vol. 21, London: Hogarth Press (1953–66); New York: Macmillan (1953–74): 152–7.

15 In Leo Bersani, *The Freudian Body*.

16 See Richard Poirier, "Writing Off the Self," for a full discussion of the philosophical and literary history of the imagination of self-dissolution.

17 See Craig Owens, "The Allegorical Impulse," for a fuller discussion of these artists.

5 THEATRE AND ITS MOTHER: TOM STOPPARD'S *HAPGOOD*

1 For excellent discussions of the doubt accompanying the establishment of Renaissance subjectivity see Anne Ferry's *The "Inward" Language* and

Stephen Greenblatt's *Renaissance Self-Fashioning*.

2 My description of quantum mechanics throughout this chapter comes from (in order of increasing difficulty): Frank Wilczek and Betsy Devine, *Longing for the Harmonies: Themes and Variations from Modern Physics*; Richard P. Feynman, *QED: The Strange Theory of Light and Matter*; and Ilya Prigogine, *From Being to Becoming: Time and Complexity in the Physical Sciences*.

3 The scientific marvel is the change from wave to particle. I recognize that my description makes it sound as if the act of observation is what is stupefying. I can only plead the plea of the non-scientist always marveling at the "wrong" mystery. This plea is an endnote because I hate to give further weight to the distinction between scientists and non-scientists.

4 For Lacan (as for Freud but without the accents) it is the love between parents and children that structures the sense of loss for both. (Inaugural castration for the child, the continuation of castration for the parents.) But Stoppard shares with Lacan and Freud an interest in making manifest the childlike elements of adult love. It may be said that the difference between Stoppard and Lacan comes from Stoppard's hope that there "really is" a place of fullness, plenitude, and love and Lacan's insistence that such a dream is a symptom of the pervasive force of castration.

5 Stoppard may be trying to make a connection between the law of the literary genre and the law of a "representative ensemble" in physics. In *From Being to Becoming* Prigogine offers Gibbs' definition of a representative ensemble: "We may imagine a great number of systems of the same nature, but differing in the configurations and velocities which they have at a given instant, and differing not merely infinitesimally, but it may be so as to embrace every conceivable combination of configurations and velocities . . ." (p. 23). A representative ensemble begins with different original conditions but has the same Hamiltonian (the equation which determines the energy of the system across time) and is subject to the same constraints. A "detective story" begins with different crimes but produces the same result – the crime is solved within the constraints of the novel's duration.

6 Elin Diamond, "Mimesis, Mimicry and the True-Real": 64.

7 The source of theatre's fascination is precisely the disappointment of its apparent repeatability. The power of this disappointment (and the illusion its fulfillment would support) served as the fundamental ideological orientation of Brecht's theory and theatre, and as the galvanizing force of Artaud's insistence that theatre is, ontologically, cruel. Kierkegaard's most Nietzschean text, *Repetition*, imagines Constantin Constantius' disappointment in theatre's failed repetition as the dramatic catastrophe responsible for the birth of his belief in eternal renewal. It may be worth noting how amenable theatre is to the theological question of repetition and eternity since Western theatre's "origin" was also theological. See Jacques Derrida's "The Theatre of Cruelty."

8 See Naomi Schor's useful account of Irigaray's relation to physics in "This Essentialism Which is Not One: Coming to Grips with Irigaray."

6 WHITE MEN AND PREGNANCY: DISCOVERING THE BODY TO BE RESCUED

1 Faye Ginsburg, "Saving America's Souls: Operation Rescue's Crusade Against Abortion."

2 Cited in Frances Wilkinson, "The Gospel According to Randall Terry," *Rolling Stone* (October 5, 1989): 85–9.

3 Terry quoted in Frances Wilkinson, op. cit. All quotes from Terry, unless

otherwise noted, are from this essay.

4 See Laurence Tribe, *Abortion: the Clash of Absolutes*: 207.

5 See Rosalind Petchesky, "Fetal Images: the Power of Visual Culture in the Politics of Reproduction."

6 Quoted in Faludi, *Backlash*: 421. In naming the fetus male, the Right participates in and perpetuates the idea that sons are more valuable than daughters.

7 See Tribe, *Abortion: the Clash of Absolutes*: 235–7 for a discussion of the court's reluctance to impose state responsibility for child abuse, and its haste to provide fetal protection.

8 For a detailed discussion of the connection between safe sex, safe spending, and performance see my essay "Money Talks, Again."

9 It is worth noting that there are very real historical and political determinants that have fed the idea that abortion can be seen as a form of race/ethnic genocide. Just as the New Right has used alternating images of the innocent fetus and the mutilated fetus, the racial politics of the abortion rights campaign has been haunted by the specter of enforced sterilization. For a harrowing account of this history, see Angela Davis, "Racism, Birth Control and Reproductive Rights," in *Women, Race and Class*. The continuing failure to distinguish adequately the difference between being pro-abortion *rights* and pro-abortion has severely undermined the campaign for reproductive freedom. Currently, there is a serious danger that something akin to enforced abortion is occurring with HIV-infected pregnant women, particularly among the poor and non-white. For fuller treatment of the racial politics involved in reproductive technologies see Marlene Gerber Fried (ed.), *From Abortion to Reproductive Freedom: Transforming a Movement*.

10 See Paul Sachdev (ed.), *International Handbook on Abortion*: 476.

11 Alisa Solomon, "Oppression Theology": 35.

12 The National Abortion Federation: 1436 U St, Suite 103, Washington, DC 20009. It should be noted that 267 is actually fewer incidents than the previous three years (1984–6) when 413 incidents were reported. But before 1987, there were no "blockades" and therefore no subsequent arrests for blockading.

13 Sigmund Freud, *Moses and Monotheism*, in *The Standard Edition of the Complete Psychological Works of Sigmund Freud*, ed. and tr. James Strachey, vol. 23: 113–14.

14 Debbie Price, "Prince George's Paternity Court Delivers Results."

15 See Lis Wiehl, "DNA Test Dooms Paternity Trials, Lawyers Say."

16 ibid.

17 Ruth Marcus, "States Can 'Presume' Husband is Child's Father."

18 Quoted in ibid.

19 In the Baby M. case, the marital family of the Sterns was valued over the biological claim of Mary Beth Whitehead, the surrogate mother. But interestingly, the judge did give Whitehead visitation rights. Visitation rights were not extended to Michael H. Thus the court's thinking seems to go like this: marital family with biological tie to child who wants child first priority; biological mother second claim; biological father third claim.

20 Spatial limitations make it impossible for me to discuss fully the logic of the "consent" requirement in relation to parents, as against "fathers." In other words, while the biological father's permission to abort is not required, in the case of teenage pregnancy the consent of a parent, or a judicial *pater familias*, is required (see *Hodgson* v. *Minnesota* and *Ohio* v. *Akron Center for Reproductive Health* (1990). In effect, the pregnant woman is still required to enter a public discussion about her reproduction – with the doctor; the teenager is required to enter a discussion with the doctor, a parent, or a judge. The potential

interest in the abortifacient known as RU-486 is keen in part because eventually this has far greater potential to become a medical technology capable of restoring some privacy to the pregnant woman. (It is not yet private, however; the pill must be administered under a doctor's care and requires three visits to the doctor's office.) See Tribe (pp. 215–20) for a full discussion.

21 Randall Terry on video-taped interview with Julie Gustafason, October 1988; quoted in Ginsburg, "Saving America's Souls": 26.

22 For a brilliant reading of law's inability to think of a continuous body see Patricia Williams, *The Alchemy of Race and Rights*.

7 THE ONTOLOGY OF PERFORMANCE: REPRESENTATION WITHOUT REPRODUCTION

1 This notion of following and tracking was a fundamental aspect of Calle's earlier performance pieces. See Jean Baudrillard *Suite Venitienne/Sophie Calle, Please Follow Me*, for documentation of Calle's surveillance of a stranger.

2 See my essays "Money Talks" and "Money Talks, Again" for a full elaboration.

3 Of course not all performance art has an oppositional edge. The ontological claims of performance art are what I am addressing here, and not the politics of ambition.

4 Emile Benveniste, *Problems in General Linguistics*, quoted in Shoshana Felman, *The Literary Speech Act*: 21.

5 J. L. Austin, *How To Do Things With Words*, 2nd edn. Derrida's rereading of Austin also comes from an interest in the performative element within language.

6 Jacques Derrida, "Signature, Event, Context."

7 See Felman, *The Literary Speech Act*, for a dazzling reading of Austin.

8 See my essay, "Reciting the Citation of Others" for a full discussion of Modleski's essay and performance.

9 Juliet MacCannell, *Figuring Lacan: Criticism and the Cultural Unconscious*, esp. pp. 90–117.

10 The disappearance of the Mother's Being also accounts for the (relative) success of the visibility of the anti-abortion groups. The smooth displacement of the image of the Mother to the hyper-visible image of the hitherto unseen fetus, is accomplished precisely because the Being of the Mother is what is always already excluded within representational economies. See Chapter 6 in this volume for further elaboration of this point.

11 Some of the description of this performance first appeared in my essay "Feminist Theory, Poststructuralism, and Performance."

12 For an excellent discussion of these guarded conditions in television, fiction, and critical theory for the African-American woman see Michele Wallace's *Invisibility Blues*.

13 Festa actually began the *Untitled* performance wearing a white rabbit headdress, which is lighter and cooler than the red; she has on other occasions worn the red one and the themes of "red" and "white" are constant preoccupations of her work. The heat during *Untitled* (in the nineties) was intense enough that she was eventually persuaded to abandon the white headdress.

14 This is one of the reasons "shock" is such a limited aesthetic for theatre. It is hard to be shocked by one's own behavior/desire, although easy to be by someone else's.

15 In fact it may account for the intense male homoeroticism of so much of theatrical history.

16 Lacan, no citation, quoted in Felman, *The Literary Speech Act*: 29.
17 Sue-Ellen Case, "Introduction," in *Performing Feminisms*, ed. Case: 13. For other warnings about the negativity of feminist theory see: Linda Alcoff, "Cultural Feminism versus Poststructuralism: The Identity Crisis in Feminist Theory"; Laura Kipnis, "Feminism: the Political Conscience of Post-modernism?"; in *Universal Abandon?*, ed. Ross; and Janet Bergstrom and Mary Ann Doane, "The Female Spectator: Contexts and Directions," *Camera Obscura* (20–21) May-September 1989.

8 AFTERWORD: NOTES ON HOPE

1 Michael Taussig has developed the concept of the nervous system, political terror, and mimesis in his collection of essays, *The Nervous System*.
2 Notions of "between-ness" and "liminality" are fundamental aspects of Richard Schechner's performance theory. In *Between Theater and Anthropology*, Schechner credits the late anthropologist Victor Turner's work on liminality as a foundational insight for his own subsequent understanding of the "points of contact" between ritual and performance art. My point here is somewhat different. While Schechner refers positively to the power of performance to "invent" the real, I am arguing that actually performance admits and tries to face the impossibility of seizing/seeing the real anywhere anytime. Please note that this is not to say that the real does not exist, for surely it does. But it is to say that it cannot be arrested, seen, or seized. Performance's inability to be captured or documented within the re-enactments promised by the copy is part of what makes it, per force, face the impossibility of seizing the Real. Schechner's argument and my own are compatible insofar as one accepts the idea that the real "invented" (or more precisely, rediscovered) by performance is the impossi-bility of its representation. Just as an individual cannot secure self-seeing, neither can the Real. It is only fair to note, however, that I believe most days Schechner himself would reject this claim of compatibility. He values perform-ance's ability to invent new-Reals; I value performance's admission of the impossibility of securing the Real.
3 This is partially because she cannot lay hold of herself either since the self–other dyad is itself both internal and external. Butler argues: "In my view, the self only becomes a self on the condition that it has suffered a separation (grammar fails us here, for the it only becomes differentiated through that separation), a loss which is *suspended* and provisionally resolved through a melancholic incor-poration of some Other. That Other installed in the self thus establishes the permanent incapacity of that self to achieve self-identity; it is as it were always already disrupted by that Other; the disruption of the Other at the heart of the self is the very condition of the self's possibility" (emphasis added; "Imitation and Gender Insubordination": 27). Here, as elsewhere with Butler, one can see the way in which she enfolds Lacan within Freud: her parenthetical remark is the anchoring point of Lacan's Mirror Phase – it is language which is the loss that makes Being a reflective possibility and that reflective "mirror" which castrates being from "just" Being. I emphasize her notion of "a loss which is suspended" only to stress that it is *the self* who is always already in loss and always already lost who is (endlessly) suspended.
4 It is not so much that alternative power systems are impossible to perform for more than a minute or two. But it is to underline how quickly hierarchies of power reassert themselves even in communities dedicated to dissolving hierarchies altogether. An organization with a progressive, egalitarian ideol-ogy such as ACT-UP faces power struggles not terribly dissimilar to the

struggles of Operation Rescue. It is a mistake, in other words, to assume that we have done with issues of power-knowledge when we invent and perform alternative communities. All of this discussion is indebted to Foucault's notion of power-knowledge.

5 A text such as William Styron's *Darkness Visible* is exactly not the thing I have in mind. He uses illnesses to establish the certainty of "bad medicine." And thus the integrity of his body is re-established by the "triumph" of its essential "goodness" over the badness of medical opinion. Allon White's extraordinary memoir, "Too Close to the Bone" comes close to the kind of "writing the body" I mean. Michael Lynch's "Last Onsets: Teaching with AIDS" and Eve Sedgwick's fascinating "A Poem is Being Written" have moments in which they find a way for writing to accept the uncertainty of the body's ontology. For Sedgwick that uncertainty is best expressed in the dis/junctures between secrets and sexual expressions, while for Lynch that uncertainty is most fully expressed in the desire to remain healthy while "understanding" the route of his disease – within his own body and within the social body of his classroom. But both Lynch and Sedgwick fall back from this task in order to achieve a more traditional "literary critical aim." They use their bodies to read literature and implicitly valorize literary texts above their physical performances in and through their own bodies. Natalie Kusz's *Road Song* faces the uncertainty of the body through mapping the loss of her eye, the death of her mother, and the landscape of Alaska. Taken together these four works (all written in the last five years) point to a significant rethinking of the relationship between words and the body. Each profoundly complicates the American (mis)translation of the notion of writing the body associated with French feminism.

These four texts, however, are dwarfed by the long and careful consideration of the relation between the body and the self most fully articulated in the works of African-American women writers. Beginning with Harriet Jacobs' *Incidents in the Life of a Slavegirl*, through the fiction of Nella Larsen, the "folk tales" of Zora Neale Hurston (best animated in *Spunk*), the autobiographies of Maya Angelou, the fiction of Toni Morrison, especially *The Bluest Eye* and *Beloved*, the biomythography of Audre Lorde, *Zami: A New Spelling of My Name*, one can see a central preoccupation with questions of "ownership" and "maintenance" of a body that is and is not one's own. This preoccupation extends as well to several contemporary African-American women visual artists, especially Renee Green, Lorna Simpson, and Artis Lane. Green has made a multi-media installation directly inspired by Jacobs' narrative. Lane's most recent work is unusual for sculpture because she tries to mold the body as it *is emerging* into matter (and I intend the awkwardness of the present participle). While most sculpture of the body tries to "capture" it, Lane's tries to mirror the moment of the body's transit between conception and form, for both the model and the artist. On a beautiful bronze nude, for example, she may leave the ceramic mold visible. One of her most astonishing pieces, *Birth* (1988), is a "perfect" bronze: it displays a woman knees bent, feet flat, arms open and extended toward the floor, mouth open, neck taut, stomach swollen, with the head of a baby just poking out between her legs. See Lane's essay, "Emergence." It introduces a series of excellent reproductions of the sculptures.

6 See David Wojnarowicz, *Tongues of Flame*.

7 By "the asymmetrical stage" I mean the rules and composition of the Senate confirmation committee. Fourteen white men with histories of plagiarism, drunkenness, and influence peddling (again this is the short list), are prob-

ably not adequate judges of anyone's ability to serve on the Supreme Court, let alone are they able to deal equitably with the particularly difficult issues raised by Thomas' nomination.

Bibliography

Adams, Parveen (guest ed.) (1991) "Rendering the Real A Special Issue," *October* 58 (Fall).

Alcoff, Linda (1980) "Cultural Feminism versus Poststructuralism: The Identity Crisis in Feminist Theory," *Signs* 13(3): 405–36.

Aristotle (1961) *Aristotle's Poetics*, tr. Francis Ferguson, New York: Hill & Wang.

Austin, J. L. (1975) *How To Do Things With Words*, 2nd edn, Cambridge, Mass.: Harvard University Press.

Avedon, Richard (1989) "Borrowed Dogs," in *Performance and Reality: Essays From Grand Street*, ed. Ben Sonnenberg, New Brunswick, NJ and London: Rutgers University Press: 15–26.

Bad Object-Choices (1991) *How Do I Look?: Queer Film and Video*, ed. Bad Object-Choices, Seattle, Wash.: Bay Press.

Bakhtin, Mikhail (1981) *The Dialogic Imagination: Four Essays*, ed. Michael Holquist, tr. Michael Holquist and Caryl Emerson, Austin, Tex.: University of Texas Press.

Barents, Els (1982) *Cindy Sherman*, introduction with interview by Els Barents, Munich: Schimer Mosel.

Barthes, Roland (1975) *The Pleasure of the Text*, tr. Richard Miller, New York: Hill & Wang.

—— (1977) *Roland Barthes by Roland Barthes*, tr. Richard Howard, New York: Hill & Wang.

—— (1981) *Camera Lucida*, tr. Richard Howard, New York: Hill & Wang.

—— (1982) *Empire of Signs*, tr. Richard Howard, New York: Hill & Wang.

Bartlett, Neil (1990) *Ready To Catch Him Should He Fall*, London: Serpent's Tail.

Baudrillard, Jean (1983) *Simulations*, tr. Paul Foss, Paul Patton and Philip Beitchman, New York: Semiotext(e) Inc.

—— (1984) "The Precession of Simulacra," in *Art After Modernism: Rethinking Representation*, ed. Brian Wallis, foreword Marcia Tucker, New York: New Museum of Contemporary Art; Boston, Mass.: D. R. Godine: 253–82.

—— (1988) *Suite Venitienne/Sophie Calle, Please Follow Me*, tr. Danny Barash and Danny Hatfield, Seattle, Wash.: Bay Press.

—— (1990) *Seduction*, tr. Brian Singer, New York: St Martin's Press.

Beale, Lewis (1991) "Paris has Box-office Appeal," *The Philadelphia Inquirer*, August 15: I–C, CTD 5–C.

Bellour, Raymond (1975) "The Unattainable Text," tr. D. Matias, *Screen* 16(3): 19–27.

Benjamin, Jessica (1988) *The Bonds of Love: Psychoanalysis, Feminism, and the Problems of Domination*, New York: Pantheon.

Benveniste, Emile (1971) *Problems in General Linguistics*, tr. Mary Elizabeth Meek, Coral Gables, Fla.: University of Miami Press.

Bersani, Leo (1986) *The Freudian Body*, New York: Columbia University Press.

Bhabha, Homi (1984) "Of Mimicry and Men: The Ambivalence of Colonial Discourse," *October* 28 (Spring): 125–33.

—— (1985) "Signs Taken for Wonders: Questions of Ambivalence and Authority Under a Tree Outside Delhi, May 1817," *Critical Inquiry* 12(1) (Autumn): 144–65.

Bloom, Harold (1981) "Agon: Revisionism and Critical Personality," *Raritan* (Summer): 18–47.

Brodzki, Bella and Schenck, Celeste (eds) (1988) *Life/Lines: Theorizing Women's Autobiography*, Ithaca, NY and London: Cornell University Press.

Brown, Georgia (1991) "Paris is Burning," *The Village Voice*, March 19: 54.

Bryson, Norman (1988) "The Gaze in the Expanded Field," in *Vision and Visuality*, (no. 2), ed. Hal Foster, Seattle, Wash.: Bay Press: 87–113.

Burgin, Victor (1986) *End of Art Theory: Criticism and Postmodernity*, Atlantic Highlands, NJ: Humanities Press.

Butler, Judith (1990) "The Force of Fantasy: Feminism, Mapplethorpe and Discursive Excess," *Differences* 2(2) (Summer): 105–25.

—— (1991) "Imitation and Gender Insubordination," in *Inside/Out: Lesbian Theories, Gay Theories*, ed. Diana Fuss, New York: Routledge: 13–31.

Camera Obscura (1989) "The Spectatrix," special issue, ed. Janet Bergstrom and Mary Ann Doane, *Camera Obscura* 20–1 (May–September).

Canby, Vincent (1991) "Paris Is Burning," *The New York Times*, March 13: C13.

Cary, Lorene (1991) *Black Ice*, New York: Knopf.

Case, Sue-Ellen (1989) "Toward a Butch-Femme Aesthetic," in *Making a Spectacle*, ed. Lynda Hart, Ann Arbor, Mich.: University of Michigan Press: 282–300.

—— (ed.) (1990) "Introduction," in *Performing Feminisms*, Baltimore, Md.: Johns Hopkins University Press.

Cham, Mbye B. and Andrade-Watkins, Claire (eds) (1988) *Black Frames: Critical Perspectives on Black Independent Cinema*, Cambridge, Mass.: Massachusetts Institute of Technology Press.

Cook, David and Kroker, Arthur (1986) *The Postmodern Scene: Excremental Culture and Hyper-Aesthetics*, New York: St Martin's Press.

Copjec, Joan (1989) "The Orthopsychic Subject: Film Theory and the Reception of Lacan," *October* 49 (Summer): 53–71.

—— (1991) "Vampires, Breast-Feeding and Anxiety," in "Rendering the Real a Special Issue," guest ed. Parveen Adams, *October* 58 (Fall): 25–44.

Crary, Jonathan (1988) "Techniques of the Observer," *October* 45 (Summer): 3–35.

Crisp, Quentin (1991) "Paris Is Burning," *The New York Times*, April 7: sec. 2:20.

Davis, Angela (1981) "Racism, Birth Control and Reproductive Rights," in *Women, Race and Class*, New York: Random House.

de Lauretis, Teresa (1984) *Alice Doesn't: Feminism, Semiotics, Cinema*, Bloomington and Indianapolis, Ind.: Indiana University Press.

—— (1987a) "Strategies of Coherence: Narrative Cinema, Feminist Poetics, and Yvonne Rainer," in *Technologies of Gender*, Bloomington and Indianapolis, Ind.: Indiana University Press.

—— (1987b) "The Technology of Gender," in *Technologies of Gender*, Bloomington and Indianapolis, Ind.: Indiana University Press.

—— (1990) "Film and the Primal Fantasy – One More Time: On Sheila

McLaughlin's *She Must Be Seeing Things*," University of Wisconsin-Milwaukee Working Papers 7 (Fall/Winter).

Derrida, Jacques (1977) "Signature, Event, Context," *Glyph* 1–2: 172–97.

—— (1978a) "The Theater of Cruelty and the Closure of Representation," in *Writing and Difference*, tr. Alan Bass, Chicago: University of Chicago Press: 232–50.

—— (1978b) *Writing and Difference*, tr. Alan Bass, Chicago: University of Chicago Press.

—— (1981) "The Double Session," in *Disseminations*, tr. Barbara Johnson, Chicago: University of Chicago Press: 173–226.

—— (1990/1) *Memoires d'aveugle: l'autoportrait et autres ruines* (translated title, *Memories of the Blind: Self-Portrait and Other Ruins*), catalog for exhibit curated at the Louvre, October 1990–January 1991.

De Zayas, Marius (1980) "Photography and Artistic-Photography," in *Classic Essays on Photography*, ed. Alan Trachtenberg, New Haven, Conn.: Leete's Island Books: 125–32.

Diamond, Elin (1989) "Mimesis, Mimicry and the True-Real," *Modern Drama* 32(1): 59–72.

Doane, Mary Ann (1982) "Film and the Masquerade: Theorizing the Female Spectator," *Screen* 23(3–4); reprinted (1991) in *Femmes Fatales: Feminism, Film Theory, Psychoanalysis*, New York and London: Routledge: 17–33.

Faludi, Susan (1989) "Where Did Randy Go Wrong?" *Mother Jones* (November): 25.

—— (1991) *Backlash: The Undeclared War Against American Women*, New York: Crown Press.

Felman, Shoshana (1983) *The Literary Speech Act: Don Juan with J. L. Austin, or Seduction in Two Languages*, tr. Catherine Porter, Ithaca, NY: Cornell University Press.

Ferris, Lesley (ed.) (1989) *Acting Women: Images of Women in Theater*, New York, New York University Press.

Ferry, Anne (1983) *The "Inward" Language: Sonnets of Wyatt, Sidney, Shakespeare, Donne*, Chicago: University of Chicago Press.

Feynman, Richard P. (1990) *QED: The Strange Theory of Light and Matter*, Princeton, NJ: Princeton University Press.

Foucault, Michel (1978) *The History of Sexuality*, tr. Robert Hurley, New York: Pantheon.

Freud, Sigmund (1937–9) *Moses and Monotheism: An Outline of Psychoanalysis*, in *The Standard Edition of the Complete Psychological Works of Sigmund Freud*, ed. and tr. James Strachey in collaboration with Anna Freud, vol. 23, London: Hogarth Press (1953–66); New York: Macmillan (1953–74).

—— (1961) *Beyond the Pleasure Principle*, tr. James Strachey, New York and London: W. W. Norton.

—— (1963a) *Dora: An Analysis of a Case of Hysteria*, ed. Philip Rieff, New York: Collier Books.

—— (1963b) *Three Essays on the Theory of Sexuality*, tr. James Strachey, New York: Basic Books.

—— (1966) *The Interpretation of Dreams*, tr. James Strachey, New York: Avon Books.

Fried, Marlene Gerber, *see* Gerber Fried.

Frye, Marilyn (1983) *The Politics of Reality: Essays in Feminist Theory*, Trumansburg, NY: Crossing Press.

Fusco, Coco (1988) "Fantasies of Oppositionality," *Afterimage* 16(5) (December): 6–9; reprinted in *Screen* 29(4) (Autumn): 80–95.

— (1989) "Reply" to Yvonne Rainer's "More Oppositionality," *Afterimage* 17(2) (September): 3; and *Screen* 30(3) (Summer): 99.

Fuss, Diana (1989) *Essentially Speaking: Feminism, Nature and Difference*, New York: Routledge.

Gaines, Jane (1988) "White Privilege and Looking Relations: Race and Gender in Feminist Film Theory," *Screen* 29(4) (Autumn): 80–93.

— (1989) "Dead Ringer: Jacqueline Onassis and the Look-Alike," *South Atlantic Quarterly* 88(2) (Spring): 461–86.

Gerber Fried, Marlene (ed.) (1990) *From Abortion to Reproductive Freedom: Transforming a Movement*, Boston, Mass.: South End Press.

Ginsburg, Faye (1989) *Contested Lives: The Abortion Debate in an American Community*, Berkeley, Calif.: University of California Press.

— (1992) "Saving America's Souls: Operation Rescue's Crusade Against Abortion," in *Fundamentalisms and the State: Remaking Politics, Economies, and Militants*, ed. Martin Marty and R. Scott Applebee, Chicago: University of Chicago Press.

Goldsby, Jackie (1991) "Queens of Language," *Afterimage* 18(10) (May): 10–11.

Greenblatt, Stephen (1980) *Renaissance Self-Fashioning: From More to Shakespeare*, Chicago: University of Chicago Press.

Grigsby, Darcy Grimaldo (1990) "Dilemmas of Visibility: Contemporary Women Artists' Representations of Female Bodies," *Michigan Quarterly Review* (Fall): 584–619.

Hart, Lynda (forthcoming/1993) "Identity and Seduction: Lesbians in the Mainstream," in *Acting Out: Feminist Performances*, ed. Lynda Hart and Peggy Phelan, Ann Arbor, Mich.: University of Michigan Press.

Hartman, Geoffrey (1981) "Words and Wounds," in *Saving the Text: Literature/ Derrida/Philosophy*, Baltimore, Md.: Johns Hopkins University Press: 118–57.

Heath, Stephen (1981) *Questions of Cinema*, Bloomington, Ind.: Indiana University Press.

Heidegger, Martin (1969) *Identity and Difference*, tr. Joan Stambaugh, New York: Harper & Row.

Hemphill, Essex (1991) "Paris Is Burning," *Guardian*, July 3: 10–11.

Hill, Lynda (forthcoming/1993) "Staging Hurston's Life and Work," in *Acting Out: Feminist Performances*, ed. Lynda Hart and Peggy Phelan, Ann Arbor, Mich.: University of Michigan Press.

Hoberman, J. (1986) "The Purple Rose of Soho," *The Village Voice*, April 8: 64.

Hollander, Elizabeth (1986) "Notes on Being an Artist's Model," *Raritan* 6(1) (Summer): 26–37.

hooks, bell (1991) "Is Paris Burning?" *Z Magazine* (June): 61.

Irigaray, Luce (1985a) *Speculum of the Other Woman*, tr. Gillian C. Gill, Ithaca, NY: Cornell University Press.

— (1985b) "Is the Subject of Science Sexed?" tr. Edith Oberle, in *Cultural Critique* 1: 73–88.

Kierkegaard, Søren (1964) *Repetition: An Essay on Experimental Psychology*, tr. Walter Lawrie, New York: Harper & Row.

Kipnis, Laura (1988) "Feminism: the Political Conscience of Postmodernism?" in *Universal Abandon? The Politics of Postmodernism*, ed. Andrew Ross, Minneapolis, Minn.: University of Minnesota Press: 149–66.

Krauss, Rosalind (1985) *The Originality of the Avant-Garde and Other Modernist Myths*, Cambridge, Mass.: Massachusetts Institute of Technology Press.

Kristeva, Julia (1979) "Ellipsis on Dread and the Specular Seduction," tr. Delores Burdick, *Wide Angle* 3(3): 42–7.

Kusz, Natalie (1990) *Road Song: A Memoir*, New York: Farrar, Straus & Giroux.

Lacan, Jacques (1953/4) *Les Ecrits techniques de Freud*, Paris: Seuil 1975,91; tr. (1987) *Freud's Writings on Technique*, tr. John Forrester, Cambridge: Cambridge University Press.

—— (1968) "The Function of Language in Psychoanalysis," in *The Language of the Self: the Function of Language in Psychoanalysis*, ed. and tr. Anthony Wilden, Baltimore, Md.: Johns Hopkins University Press: 3–8.

—— (1970) *Scilicet* 2–3: 120.

—— (1975) *Encore*, Paris: Edition du Seuil.

—— (1977) *Ecrits: a Selection*, tr. Alan Sheridan, New York: W. W. Norton.

—— (1978) *Four Fundamental Concepts of Psycho-Analysis*, ed. Jacques-Alain Miller, tr. Alan Sheridan, New York: Norton.

—— (1985a) "Intervention in Transference," in *Dora's Case: Freud, Hysteria, Feminism*, ed. Charles Bernheimer and Claire Kahane, New York: Columbia University Press; London: Virago: 92–104.

—— (1985b) "God and the *Jouissance* of The Woman," in *Feminine Sexuality: Jacques Lacan and the "école freudienne,"* ed. Jacqueline Rose and Juliet Mitchell, tr. Jacqueline Rose, New York and London: W. W. Norton: 137–48.

—— (1985c) "A Love Letter," in *Feminine Sexuality: Jacques Lacan and the "Ecole Freudienne,"* ed. Jacqueline Rose and Juliet Mitchell, tr. Jacqueline Rose, New York and London: W. W. Norton.

—— (1987) *Television*, tr. Denis Hollier, Rosalind Krauss and Annette Michelson, New York: Norton, 1990; partial tr. also in "Television," *October* 40 (Spring): 7–49.

Lane, Artis (1991) "Emergence," *The Georgia Review* 45(4) (Winter): 695–704.

Lejeune, Phillip (1989) *On Autobiography*, ed. Paul Eakin, tr. Katherine Leary, foreword Paul Eakin, Minneapolis, Minn.: University of Minnesota Press.

Luker, Kristin (1984) *Abortion and the Politics of Motherhood*, Berkeley, Calif.: University of California Press.

Lynch, Michael (1990) "Last Onsets: Teaching with AIDS," *Profession*, annual publication of the Modern Language Association: 32–6.

MacCannell, Juliet Flower (1986) *Figuring Lacan: Criticism and the Cultural Unconscious*, Lincoln, Nebr.: University of Nebraska Press.

Mapplethorpe, Robert (1987) *Robert Mapplethorpe*, ed. Dimitri Levas, comp. by Gyah Suzuki and Tohru Ide, Tokyo: Parco Company.

Marcus, Ruth (1989) "States Can 'Presume' Husband Is Child's Father," *The Washington Post*, June 16: A22.

Marshall, Richard (1989) *Robert Mapplethorpe*, with essays by Richard Howard and Ingrid Sischy, New York: Whitney Museum of American Art in Association with New York Graphic Society Books.

Marvell, Andrew (1976) *The Complete Poems*, ed. Elizabeth Story Donno, New York: Penguin: esp. p. 52–4.

Mercer, Kobena (1991) "Looking for Trouble," *Transition* 51: 184–97.

Mitchell, Juliet and Rose, Jacqueline (eds) (1985) *Feminine Sexuality: Jacques Lacan and the "école freudienne,"* tr. Jacqueline Rose, New York and London: W. W. Norton.

Modleski, Tania (1989) "Some Functions of Feminist Criticism, or the Scandal of the Mute Body," *October* 49 (Summer): 3–24.

—— (1991) *Feminism Without Women*, London and New York: Routledge.

Moore, Marianne (1961) "He 'Digesth Hard' Yron," *A Marianne Moore Reader*, New York: Viking Press: 24.

Morris, Meaghan (1988) *The Pirate's Fiancée: Feminism, Reading Postmodernism*, London and New York: Verso.

Owens, Craig (1984) "The Allegorical Impulse," in *Art After Modernism: Rethinking Representation*, ed. and intro. Brian Wallis, foreword Marcia Tucker, New York: New Museum of Contemporary Art; Boston, Mass.: D.R. Godine: 203—36.

Petchesky, Rosalind (1987) "Fetal Images: the Power of Visual Culture in the Politics of Reproduction," *Feminist Studies* 13(2): 263—92.

Phelan, Peggy (1988) "Feminist Theory, Poststructuralism, and Performance," *The Drama Review* (Spring): 107–27.

—— (1990a) "Money Talks," *The Drama Review* (Spring): 4–15.

—— (1990b) "Crimes of Passion," *Artforum* 29(9) (May): 173–8.

—— (1991) "Money Talks, Again," *TDR: A Journal of Performance Studies* (Fall): 131–42.

Piper, Adrian (1989) *Cornered*, a video tape available from Visual Data Bank, Chicago, Ill.

—— (1992) "Cornered" (text of video), *Movement Research Performance Journal*, 4 (Winter/Spring): 10.

Poirier, Richard (1981) "Writing Off the Self," *Raritan* (Summer): 107–33.

Price, Debbie (1988) "Prince George's Paternity Court Delivers Results," *The Washington Post*, October 11: AL.

Prigogine, Ilya (1980) *From Being to Becoming: Time and Complexity in the Physical Sciences*, San Francisco, Calif.: W. H. Freeman.

Rainer, Yvonne (1985) *The Man Who Envied Women*, a film distributed by First Run Features, 153 Waverly Place, New York, NY 10014.

—— (1985) "More Kicking and Screaming from the Narrative Front/Back Water," *Wide Angle* 7: 8–13.

—— (1986a) "Some Ruminations Around Cinematic Antidotes to the Oedipal Net(les) While Playing with DeLauraedipeus Mulvey, or He Maybe Off Screen, but . . .," *The Independent*, April: 25.

—— (1986b) "Tell 'Er in the City," *Motion Picture* 1(1) (Spring/Summer): 8.

—— (1989) "More Oppositionality," a "Reply" to Coco Fusco's "Fantasies of Oppositionality," *Afterimage* 17(2) (September): 2–3; and *Screen* 30(3) (Summer): 91–8.

—— (1990) *The Films of Yvonne Rainer*, Bloomington, Ind.: Indiana University Press: esp. 173–218.

Reynaud, Berenice (1989) "Response" to Coco Fusco's "Fantasies of Oppositionality," *Screen* 30(3) (Summer): 79–91.

—— (1990) "Impossible Projections," in *The Films of Yvonne Ranier*, Bloomington, Ind.: University of Indiana Press: 24–35.

Rilke, Rainer Maria (1982) "Aus einer Sturmnacht," *Das Buch der Biler*, in *Rainer Maria Rilke: Werke, Band One*, 2nd edn, vol. 1, Frankfurt am Main: Insel Verlag, zweite Autlage: 220.

Riviere, Joan (1929) "Womanliness as a Masquerade," *The International Journal of Psychoanalysis* 9: 303–13; reprinted (1991) in *The Inner World and Joan Riviere: Collected Papers, 1920–1958*, ed. Athol Hughes, London and New York: Karnac Books: 90–101.

Rose, Jacqueline (1986) *Sexuality in the Field of Vision*, London and New York: Verso.

Rubinstein, Meyer (1991) "Sight Unseen," *Art in America* 79(4) (April): 47(5).

Sachdev, Paul (ed.) (1988) *International Handbook on Abortion*, New York: Greenwood Press.

Said, Edward (1978) *Orientalism*, New York: Pantheon Books.

Scarry, Elaine (1985) *The Body in Pain: The Making and Unmaking of the World*, New York: Oxford University Press.

Schafer, Roy (1981) "Narration in the Psychoanalytic Dialogue," in *On Narrative*, ed. W. T. J. Mitchell, Chicago, Ill.: University of Chicago Press: 25–49.

Schechner, Richard (1985) *Between Theater and Anthropology*, foreword Victor Turner, Philadelphia, Pa.: University of Pennsylvania Press.

Schor, Mira (1988) "Representations of the Penis," *M/E/A/N/I/N/G* 4 (November): 3–17.

—— (1989) "Figure/Ground," *M/E/A/N/I/N/G* 6 (November): 18–27.

Schor, Naomi (1989) "This Essentialism Which is Not One: Coming to Grips with Irigaray," *Differences* 1(2) (Summer): 38–58.

Sedgwick, Eve Kosofsky (1987) "A Poem is Being Written," *Representations* 17 (Winter): 110–43.

Silverman, Kaja (1988) *The Acoustic Mirror: The Female Voice in Psychoanalysis*, Bloomington, Ind.: Indiana University Press.

Solomon, Alisa (1991) "Oppression Theology," *The Village Voice*, August 27: 35.

Solomon-Godeau, Abigail (1991) "Living with Contradictions: Critical Practices in the Age of Supply-side Aesthetics," in *Universal Abandon? The Politics of Postmodernism*, ed. Andrew Ross, Minneapolis, Minn.: University of Minnesota Press: 191–213.

Spillers, Hortense (1984) "Interstices: A Small Drama of Words," in *Pleasure and Danger: Exploring Female Sexuality*, ed. Carole Vance, Boston, Mass.: Routledge & Kegan Paul: 73–100.

Stern, Gerald (1981) "Little White Sister," in *The Red Coal*, Boston, Mass.: Houghton Mifflin.

Stevens, Wallace (1972) "Stars at Tallapoosa," in *The Palm at the End of the Mind: Selected Poems and a Play*, ed. Holly Stevens, New York: Vintage Books: 81.

Stoppard, Tom (1967) *Rosencrantz and Guildenstern Are Dead*, New York: Grove Press.

—— (1982) *The Real Thing*, London: Faber & Faber.

—— (1988) *Hapgood*, London and Boston, Mass.: Faber & Faber.

Strand, Mark (1980) "Keeping Things Whole," in *Selected Poems*, New York: Atheneum: 10.

Stryon, William (1990) *Darkness Visible: A Memoir of Madness*, New York: Random House.

Taussig, Michael (1991) *The Nervous System*, New York and London: Routledge.

Trachtenberg, Alan (ed.) (1980) *Classic Essays on Photography*, New Haven, Conn.: Leete's Island Books.

Tribe, Laurence (1990) *Abortion: The Clash of Absolutes*, New York: W. W. Norton.

Trinh, Minh-Ha (1989) *Woman, Native, Other: Writing Postcoloniality and Feminism*, Bloomington, Ind.: Indiana University Press.

Tyler, Carole-Anne (1991) "Boys Will Be Girls: the Politics of Gay Drag," in *Inside/Out: Lesbian Theories, Gay Theories*, ed. Diana Fuss, New York: Routledge: 32–70.

Wallace, Michele (1990) *Invisibility Blues*, London and New York: Verso.

White, Allon (1989) "Too Close to the Bone: Fragments of an Autobiography," *Raritan* 8(4) (Spring): 34–69.

Whitman, Walt (1980) "There Was a Child Went Forth," in *Poems 1855–1856*, vol. 1, *Leaves of Grass, A Textual Variorum of the Printed Poems*, ed. Sculley Bradley, Blodgett, Golden, White, New York: New York University Press: 149–52.

Wiehl, Lis (1989) "DNA Test Dooms Paternity Trials, Lawyers Say," *The New York Times*, July 21: B9.

Wilczek, Frank and Devine, Betsy (1987) *Longing for the Harmonies: Themes and Variations from Modern Physics*, New York and London: W. W. Norton.

Wilkinson, Frances (1989) "The Gospel According to Randall Terry," *Rolling*

Stone, October 5: 85–9.

Willensky, Elliott and White, Norval (1988) *American Institute of Architecture Guide to New York*, 3rd edn, San Diego, New York and London: Harcourt Brace.

Williams, Patricia (1991) *The Alchemy of Race and Rights*, Cambridge, Mass.: Harvard University Press.

Williamson, Judith (1983) "Images of Women," *Screen* 24(6) (November – December): 102–16.

Wojnarowicz, David (1990) *Tongues of Flame*, Normal, Ill.: University Galleries of Illinois State University.

Woolf, Virginia (1975) *The Letters of Virginia Woolf*, vol. 4, ed. Nigel Nicholson and Joanne Trautmann, New York: Harcourt, Brace, Jovanovich.

Žižek, Slavoj (1989) *The Sublime Object of Ideology*, London and New York: Verso.

INDEX

abortion 29–31, 130–45, 169–70
African-Americans 7–8, 10, 28–9, 45, 51, 64, 97–8, 158, 184 n40, 191 n12, 193 n5 *see also* Piper; Simpson; Mapplethorpe; *Paris Is Burning*; racism
AIDS 38–40, 94, 135, 182 n14, 185 n9, 190 n9, 193 n5
Ajitto [Mapplethorpe] 1981 47
Alice Neel [Mapplethorpe] 1984 40, 43
Audition [Schor] 1988 55
Austin, J.L. 149, 164; *see also* speech act
autobiography 3, 11–13, 181 n6
avant-garde film 29, 73, 81, 88; *see also* Rainer, Yvonne
Avedon, Richard 35, 37
aversion (of gaze) 47, 64, 151, 156, 158, 161, 163–4; *see also* blind spot

Baby M. 184 n41, 190 n19
Barthes, Roland 34–6, 79, 108, 148, 187 n6
Baudrillard, Jean 10, 66, 69, 112, 123, 125, 186 n28, 191 n1
Beckett, Samuel 114–15
Benjamin, Walter 36
Bhabha, Homi 187 n3
blindness, blind spot 1, 3, 13, 15, 18, 19, 21, 25, 32–3, 69; *see also* aversion
Bloom, Harold 183 n19
Bourgeois, Louise 21–2
Bowers v. Hardwick 106, 136–7
Brian Ridley and Lyle Heeter [Mapplethorpe] 1979 42, 44
Bryson, Norman 24, 25
Butler, Judith 2, 94, 172, 187 n1, 188 n7, 192 n3

Calle, Sophie 146–7, 165
Camera Lucida [Barthes] 34–5, 148
capitalism 11, 47, 64, 80, 74, 79, 87, 94–5, 102, 105, 135, 173
Cary, Lorene 10, 30
Case, Sue-Ellen 69, 165, 186 n30, 187 n10, 192 n17
castration 1, 17–8, 25–6, 125, 135, 151–2
Caul of Self [Schor] 1987 51–3
Chicago, Judy 52
Chodorow, Nancy 77
Copjec, Joan 6, 15, 18, 24–5, 90, 181 n2, 183 n25, 183 n29
Cornered [Piper] 1989 8, 23
Cronenberg, David 30

Davis, Angela 190 n9
death 5, 11–13, 26–8, 30, 38, 40–2, 108–11, 152, 162, 177
Dead Ringers [Cronenberg] 30
de Lauretis, Teresa 71, 87–8, 183 n21, 187 n4, n10
Derrida, Jacques 5, 6, 13, 15–16, 68, 75, 86, 113, 115, 124–5, 149, 183 n24, 189 n7
Diamond, Elin 49, 69, 124, 126, 181 n4, 186 n30, 189 n6
Dinner Party, The [Chicago] 52
disappearance 19, 25, 27, 31, 35, 68–9, 91, 115, 118–19, 123, 146–9, 151–3, 158, 165–6, 173, 177
Doane, Mary Ann 69, 186 n30
Don't Forget Me [Schor] 1989 55
doubt 115, 171, 174, 181 n2; *see also* paternity
drag performance 17, 29, 93–111, 183 n27, 188 n7

essentialist/ism 30, 35, 58, 145
ethnographic film 93–4, 102, 104, 106;
   see also Paris Is Burning

Faludi, Susan 138, 190 n6
failure 4, 6, 15, 16, 19–21, 26, 30, 32,
   89, 152, 170–2
Felman, Shoshana 32, 165
feminist film theory 6, 18, 26, 28,
   71–92; *see also* male gaze
Festa, Angelika 31, 152–8, 160–4
fetal imagery 132–4, 144
fetishism, fetishization 6, 10, 19, 25,
   51, 76, 91, 94, 101, 106–7
film 28, 29, 71–92, 93–111
Film Stills [Sherman] 60–2
fort/da 21, 69, 167, 171, 177, 180, 184
   n34; *see also* Freud
Foucault, Michel 81–3, 90, 112, 139,
   163, 192–3 n4
Freud, Freudian Theory 2–6, 11, 14,
   18–19, 25, 30–1, 45, 49, 52, 75–7, 96,
   107, 112, 124, 126, 132, 138–9,
   167–72, 182 n8, 183 n28, n30, 184
   n34, 188 n10, 189 n4
Fuss, Diana 182 n10, n13, 183 n26

Gaines, Jane 181 n3, 187 n10
gaze: symmetrical/reciprocal 4, 16–18,
   20, 21–7, 30, 32–40, 45, 47, 73, 145,
   150, 156, 158, 161–2; impotency of
   inward 15, 18, 22, 23, 27–33, 66,
   90–1; male 71, 87–91
gender identity 4–6, 17, 28, 87–9,
   93–7, 99, 102–6, 123–4, 131–7, 172;
   see also identity
Ghosts [Calle] 147
Ginsburg, Faye 133, 189 n1
given to be seen, the 3 15, 19, 20,
   64–6, 91; *see also* visible real
Guarded Conditions [Simpson] 158
Guerrilla Girls 19, 178

Hapgood [Stoppard] 29, 112–29
Hart, Lynda 182 n13
Heath, Stephen 183 n21
heterosexual narratives,
   heterosexuality 17–1, 47, 51, 57, 64,
   72, 75, 96, 89, 99, 103–4, 106, 136
Hill, Anita 178–80
Hill, Lynda 181 n4
Hoberman, J. 75, 81

Hollander, Elizabeth 185 n5
Hollywood film 28–9, 60–1, 66, 75, 83,
   84, 88, 183 n32
hommo-sexual 5–6, 17–18, 30, 42, 51,
   58–60, 64, 75, 163–4, 170, 172,
   179–80; *see also* self-same
homoerotic desire 47, 51, 91–111; *see
   also* Mapplethorpe
homophobia 101, 104, 105, 135, 188
   n8
homosexuality 29, 37–51, 91–114, 135,
   136, 187 n11; *see also* lesbianism
hooks, bell 102–3, 108
hope 4, 18, 170, 172, 174–8

identification: filmic 71, 73, 87–92,
   104; Symbolic 18, 29, 94–5, 182 n13,
   187 n2
identity 4, 5, 11–13, 15–16, 25, 34, 64,
   69, 93, 98, 102, 104–5; *see also*
   gender identity
identity politics *see* visibility politics
Imaginary, the Lacanian 21, 23, 30,
   184 n35; *see also* mirror stage
Imperfect Transmission [Schor] 1989
   55–8
Impregnation of M, The [Schor] 1987 52
invisibility 6, 11–13, 19, 26, 28–9, 31,
   71–4, 86–91, 93–6, 98, 114–15, 121,
   124–5, 130, 133, 137, 139–40, 145,
   153, 156, 164
Irigaray, Luce 5, 6, 45, 69–70, 111,
   124, 126, 128, 181 n4, 182 n11, 185
   n14, 186 nn30–1, 188 n4

Judd, Donald 72–3, 80, 87

Ken and Tyler [Mapplethorpe] 1985
   49–50
Ken Moody and Robert Sherman
   [Mapplethorpe] 1984 49
Krauss, Rosalind 36, 49, 185 n4
Kristeva, Juila 1, 181 n1
Kusz, Natalie 193 n5

Lacan, Jacques 1, 3, 5–6, 11, 13–20,
   24–6, 45, 75, 81, 86, 124–5, 151–2,
   164, 167, 181 n2, n5, 183 n28, n33,
   184 nn34–6, n39, n41, 188 n10, 189
   n4, 192 n3; *see also* Imaginary;
   Symbolic; Real

Lane, Artis 193 n5
language 2, 6, 15–17, 21, 23–4, 32, 55,
    149–50, 164–5, 168; *see also* speech
    act; metaphor
law 2, 3, 6, 30, 42, 107, 111, 119, 135,
    137, 139–40, 144, 170–1, 190 n20; *see
    also* Baby FM.; *Bowers v. Hardwick*;
    Michael H. v. Gerald D.; *Planned
    Parenthood v. Danforth*; *Roe v. Wade*
Left, the 2, 6, 7, 28–9, 134, 140 and
    passim
Leland Richard [Mapplethorpe] 1980
    45–6, 158
lesbianism 182 n13, 186 n10, 187
    nn10–11; *see also* homosexuality;
    National Endowment for the Arts
Livingston, Jennie 29, 93–111, 177
loss 11, 13–15, 17, 18, 23, 25–6, 35, 74,
    79–80, 152, 163, 174–7, 192 n3
love 1, 5, 6, 32, 112, 114, 117,
    119–121, 123, 149, 167, 174–7; *see
    also Hapgood*
lure 34, 37, 58, 64, 66, 68
Lynch, Michael 193 n5

MacCannell, Juliet Flower 6, 151, 184
    n36, 191 n9
Man in Polyester Suit [Mapplethorpe]
    1980 42, 47
Man Who Envied Women, The [Rainer]
    28, 71–92, 161
Mapplethorpe, Robert 28, 37–51, 52,
    158, 185 nn6–7
masculinity 38, 40, 42, 45, 47, 51, 81F;
    see also paternity
masochism 42, 94, 101–2, 107, 184
    n34; *see also* ordeal art
memory 1, 5, 6, 32, 112, 114, 127, 146,
    148, 149
metaphor 5, 23–4, 108, 150–2, 168,
    172, 184 n36; *see also* value
metonomy 150–2
Michael H. v. Gerald D. 141–2
mimicry 55, 64, 69, 95–6, 107, 126, 187
    n3
mimesis 4, 5, 7, 11, 36, 45, 49, 55, 60,
    64, 76, 95, 126, 184 n1; *see also*
    Diamond, Elin
mirror stage 15, 21–2, 192 n3
Modleski, Tania 97, 149–50
Morris, Meaghan 82–3
Mother *see* Symbolic Mother

National Endowment for the Arts
    135, 148, 185 n12, n17, 190 n8
Nature Study, Velvet Eyes [Bourgeois]
    1984 21
negative, the 5, 6, 11, 17, 19, 27–8, 36,
    40, 42, 45, 51, 64, 66, 70, 122,
    151–3, 163–5, 178
nonreproductive, the 18, 27, 30, 31,
    38, 135, 148; *see also* disappearance;
    performance art
not-all, the 17, 18, 24–5, 27, 32; *see
    also* phallic function

Oedipal narrative, Oedipus 84, 86,
    125, 151, 182 n8
Operation Rescue 29–30, 130–145,
    169–70
ordeal art 31, 152–7, 162–3

painting 4, 15, 24, 25, 30, 51–60, 66–8
Paris Is Burning [Livingston] 29, 60,
    93–111, 177
passing performances 96–8, 102, 109
paternity 130–145, 169–70, 182 n8; *see
    also* doubt
pedagogy 173–7
performance, performance art 3–6,
    8–9, 27, 30–3, 40, 60–1, 96–102,
    104–5, 107, 112–29, 131–2, 144–5,
    146–66, 167, 169, 172–80
performative exchange 27, 30, 35, 37,
    42, 60, 68, 147, 163, 165
performative writing 108–9, 148–150,
    165, 174–8
Petchesky, Rosemary 133–4, 169
phallic function 17–18, 58, 183 n27; *see
    also* not-all
phallus 18, 23, 38, 42, 58, 60, 64, 99, 151
Phelan, Peggy 185 n12, n17, 186 n22,
    191 n8
photography 4, 14, 17, 27, 28, 34–51,
    60–70, 158, 160, 185n3
physics 167, 171; *see also* quantum
    theory
Piper, Adrian 7–9, 23, 97–8, 183 n15,
    188 n6
Planned Parenthood v. Danforth 142
poststructuralism 3, 79, 86; *see also*
    Barthes; Derrida
presence 115, 117, 121, 162–3, 180
Prigogine, Ilya 29, 127–9
psychic desire 3, 20, 34, 94, 107 and
    passim

psychoanalysis 2–5, 30, 77, 145, 167–9, 171–3, 178, 180; *see also* Freudian theory; Lacanian Theory

quantum theory 2–3, 20, 29, 112–129, 148, 167–9, 171, 174, 188 nn2–3; *see also* uncertainty

racial difference 7–10, 45–7, 49, 51, 93–8, 105–6; *see also* African-Americans; whiteness
racism, racist ideology 7–8, 19, 29, 45, 47, 89, 97–9, 104–5, 135–6, 158, 173, 187 n11, 190 n9; *see also Paris Is Burning*
Rainer, Yvonne 28, 71–92, 161, 178
Real: the visible 1–3, 6–8, 10, 14, 18, 28, 36, 68, 69, 72, 91; and the representational 1, 2, 6, 66, 171, 180, 182 n13; Lacanian 30, 31, 68, 87, 167, 171–3, 178, 180, 181 n5, 184 n35; Real-ness 93–111 and *passim*
reproduction: human 21, 29–30, 122–3, 130–145; cultural 5–7, 11, 27, 33, 36, 45, 47, 49, 55, 58, 64, 68, 70, 91, 111, 122–3 and *passim*
representation, theories of 1–8, 15–18, 24–7, 91–2, 126, 130, 140, 163–5, 172, 177, 180
Reynaud, Berenice 6, 73
Right, the New 2, 27–9, 40, 42, 58, 130–145
Rilke, Rainer Maria 31–2, 184 n42
Roe v. Wade 136, 169
Rose, Jacqueline 6, 151, 183 n29, n31
Rubinstein, Meyer Raphael 183 n24

sadomasochism 42; *see also* masochism
Said, Edward 184 n38
Schafer, Roy 182 n19
Schechner, Richard 192 n2
Schor, Mira 28, 37, 51–60, 185 n11, 186 n23, n25
Schor, Naomi 189 n8
secrets 38, 40, 92, 118, 125, 182 n8; *see also Hapgood*
self-image 3–5, 11–13, 15–17, 20, 27, 40, 60–1, 64, 71
self-portraits 15, 16, 35, 37, 40, 52, 64; *see also* Mapplethorpe; Sherman

self-same 33, 49, 62, 68–9, 91–2, 164; *see also hommo-sexual*
sexual difference 4, 5, 16–18, 24, 28, 37, 51, 58, 79, 81, 93, 172 and *passim*
Shakespeare, William 114, 119
Sherman, Cindy 28, 37, 60–70, 107, 150
sight 1, 5, 6, 13, 15, 20, 32, 113, 114, 149; *see also* blindness; gaze
signification 6, 16–19, 21–4, 95, 107–8, 125, 149–50
Silverman, Kaja 187 n1
Simpson, Lorna 158–60
skin 8, 10, 51, 93; *see also* racial difference
Small Ear [Schor] 1989 52, 55, 57
spatial dimension 71–92
speech act 32, 146, 149, 164–5
Spillers, Hortense 186 n21
stereotyping 36, 47, 60–1, 81, 95, 138, 160
Stern, Gerald 185 n20
Stoppard, Tom 29, 112–129
surveillance 6, 10, 30, 42, 95, 106, 107, 111, 139–40, 145, 166
Symbolic, the Lacanian 15–18, 22–4, 30, 36, 55, 58, 60, 69, 95–6, 101–4, 108, 113–14, 151–2, 184 n35; *see also* identification
Symbolic Mother 23, 29–30, 45, 52, 69, 95, 96, 101, 114, 117–18, 126, 128–9, 137–8, 144–5, 151–2, 191 n10

Taussig, Michael 192 n1
Terry, Randall 130–45, 169
theatre 29, 112–29
Thomas, Clarence 8, 178–80
Thomas in a Circle [Mapplethorpe] 1987 47
Tracings of Caul of Self [Schor] 1987 51–2
transference/counter-transference 24, 125, 168, 171–2, 174
Tribe, Laurence 142, 169, 190 n4

uncertainty 3, 20, 113, 116, 167, 169, 171; *see also* quantum theory
unconscious, the 4–6, 14, 19, 24, 52, 64, 114 and *passim*
Unmarked 1, 3–5, 19, 26, 27, 30, 32, 66, 68, 171

Untitled Dance (with fish and others)
 [Festa] 1987 152–8, 160–4

value 5, 17, 24, 29, 51, 135, 149,
 150–2, 164, 166, 169–70; *see also*
 metaphor
visibility 3–7, 28–30, 71, 91, 93, 96–8,
 130, 132–3, 139–40, 145, 153, 156,
 169–70
visibility politics 1–3, 6–11, 19, 26–30,
 64, 74, 79, 86–7, 93–111, 130–45,
 148, 169–70, 182 n14
visual field 1, 6, 14, 24, 25, 32, 76 and
 passim

voyeurism 10, 76, 77, 183 n30, n32;
 see also feminist film theory

Wallace, Michele 184 n40, 191 n12
War Frieze [Schor] 1991 58
Wilkinson, Frances 189 nn2–3
Williams, Patricia 170, 181 n3, 184
 n41, 191 n22
White, Allon 193 n5
whiteness 45, 47, 62, 89, 94–5, 102,
 103
Wojnarowicz, David 177, 193 n5

Žižek, Slavoj 181 n5, n7, 183 n16, 187
 n2